Samuel Rutherford Crockett

Cleg Kelly

Arab of the City

Samuel Rutherford Crockett

Cleg Kelly
Arab of the City

ISBN/EAN: 9783744752947

Printed in Europe, USA, Canada, Australia, Japan

Cover: Foto ©ninafisch / pixelio.de

More available books at **www.hansebooks.com**

CLEG KELLY

ARAB OF THE CITY

BY

S. R. CROCKETT

LONDON
SMITH, ELDER, AND CO.
15 WATERLOO PLACE
MDCCCXCVI

To

J. M. BARRIE

with the hand of a comrade
and the heart of a friend

CONTENTS

ADVENTURE	PAGE
I. THE OUTCASTING OF CLEG KELLY	1
II. THE BURNING OF THE WHINNY KNOWES	6
III. WHY CLEG KELLY HATED HIS FATHER	15
IV. HOW ISBEL KELLY HEARD SWEET MUSIC	24
V. THE BRIGANDS OF THE CITY	34
VI. CLEG TURNS BURGLAR	44
VII. THE ADVENTURE OF THE COCKROACHES	52
VIII. THE FLIGHT OF SHEEMUS	58
IX. THE WARMING OF THE DRABBLE	65
X. THE SQUARING OF THE POLICE	71
XI. THE BOY IN THE WOODEN HUT	78
XII. VARA KAVANNAH OF THE TINKLERS' LANDS	83
XIII. CLEG'S SECOND BURGLARY	92
XIV. CLEG TURNS DIPLOMATIST	99
XV. THE FIRE IN CALLENDAR'S YARD	107
XVI. IN THE KEY OF BOY NATURAL	115
XVII. THE KNUCKLE DUSTERS	126
XVIII. BIG SMITH SUBDUES THE KNUCKLE DUSTERS	132
XIX. THE PILGRIMS OF THE PENNY GAFF	140
XX. THE DIFFICULTIES OF ADONIS BETWIXT TWO VENUSES	147
XXI. AN IDYLL OF BOGIE ROLL	158

ADVENTURE	PAGE
XXII. THE SEDUCTION OF A BAILIE . . .	163
XXIII. THE AMOROUS ADVENTURES OF A NIGHT-SHIFT MAN	168
XXIV. THE CROOK IN THE LOT OF CLEAVER'S BOY	175
XXV. A COMELY PROVIDENCE IN A NEW FROCK.	180
XXVI. R.S.V.P.	186
XXVII. JANET OF INVERNESS TASTES THE HERB BITTER-SWEET	191
XXVIII. THE ENGINE-DRIVER WITH THE BEARD .	197
XXIX. MUCKLE ALICK'S BANNOCKBURN. . .	204
XXX. HOW GEORDIE GRIERSON'S ENGINE BROKE ITS BUFFER	209
XXXI. THE 'AWFU' WOMAN'	213
XXXII. MAID GREATHEART AND HER PILGRIMS .	219
XXXIII. THE BABES IN THE HAYSTACK . . .	224
XXXIV. MARY BELL, BYRE LASS . . .	228
XXXV. THE KNIGHT IN THE SOFT HAT. . .	233
XXXVI. THE MADNESS OF HUGH BOY . . .	239
XXXVII. BOY HUGH FINDS OUT THE NATURE OF A KISS	245
XXXVIII. MISS BRIGGS AND HER TEN CATS . .	249
XXXIX. THE ADVENTURE OF SNAP'S PORRIDGE .	256
XL. A NEW KIND OF HERO	262
XLI. 'TWA LADDIES—AND A LASSIE'. . .	269
XLII. MUCKLE ALICK CONSIDERS. . .	279
XLIII. TOWN KNIGHT AND COUNTRY KNIGHT .	284
XLIV. CLEG RELAPSES INTO PAGANISM. . .	290
XLV. THE CABIN ON THE SUMMIT . .	301
XLVI. A CHILD OF THE DEVIL	308
XLVII. THE SLEEP OF JAMES CANNON, SIGNAL-MAN	316

CONTENTS

ADVENTURE	PAGE
XLVIII. MUCKLE ALICK SEES THE DISTANT SIGNAL STAND AT 'CLEAR'	326
XLIX. CLEG COLLECTS TICKETS	334
L. GENERAL THEOPHILUS RUFF	344
LI. THE GENERAL'S ESTABLISHMENT	354
LII. THE THREE COFFINS IN THE STRONG ROOM	364
LIII. A STORMY MORNING AT LOCH SPELLANDERIE	373
LIV. KIT KENNEDY'S FAREWELL	382
LV. A YOUNG MAN'S FANCY	389
LVI. THE VOICES IN THE MARSH	398
LVII. FIGHTING THE BEASTS	410
LVIII. WITHIN THE RED DOOR	419
LIX. THE BEECH HEDGE	430
LX. CLEG'S TREASURE-TROVE COMES TO HIM	437

CLEG KELLY

ARAB OF THE CITY

ADVENTURE I

THE OUTCASTING OF CLEG KELLY

'IT's all a dumb lie !—God's dead !'

Such a silence had never fallen upon the Sunday-school, since the fatal day when the grate was blown into the middle of the floor by Mickey McGranaghan, a recent convert (and a temporary one) to the peculiar orthodoxy of Hunker Court. But the new explosion far outstripped the old in its effects. For it contained a denial of all the principles upon which the school was founded, and especially it confounded and blas- phemed the cheerful optimism of Mr. James Lugton, its superintendent, otherwise and more intimately known as 'Pund o' Cannles.'

The statement which contained so emphatic a denial of the eternity of the Trinity was made by Cleg Kelly, a bare-legged loon of twelve, who stood lone and unfriended on the floor before the superin- tendent's desk in the gloomy cellar known as Hunker Court Mission School. Cleg Kelly had at last been reported by his teacher for incorrigible persistence in misconduct. He had introduced pins point upwards through the cracks in the forms. He had been caught with an instrument of wire cunningly plaited about his fingers, by means of which he could nip unsuspecting boys sitting as many as three or four from him—which is a great advantage to a boy in a Sunday-school. Lastly, he had fallen backwards over a seat when asked a question. He had stood upon his hands and head while answering it, resuming his first position as if nothing had happened so soon as the examination passed on to the next boy. In fact, he had filled the cup of his iniquities to the brim.

His teacher did not so much object to the pranks of Cleg Kelly himself. He objected mainly because, being ragged, barelegged, with garments picturesquely ventilated, and a hat without a crown, he was as irresistible in charm and fascination to all the other members of his class as if he had been arrayed in silver armour starry clear. For though Hunker Court was a mission school, it was quite a superior mission. And (with the exception of one division, which was much looked down upon) the lowest class of children were not encouraged to attend. Now Cleg Kelly, by parentage and character, was almost, if not quite, as the mothers of the next social grade said, 'the lowest of the low.'

So when Cleg's teacher, a respectable young journeyman plumber, could stand no more pranks and had grown tired of cuffing and pulling, he led Cleg up to the awful desk of the superintendent from which the rebukes and prizes were delivered.

Thereupon ' Pund o' Cannles,' excellent but closefisted tallow chandler and general dealer, proceeded to rebuke Cleg. Now the rebukes of ' Pund o' Cannles ' smelt of the counter, and were delivered in the tone in which he addressed his apprentice boys when there were no customers in the shop—a tone which was entirely different from the bland suavity he used when he joined his hands and asked, ' And what is the next article, madam ?'

'Do you know, boy,' said the superintendent, ' that by such sinful conduct you are wilfully going on the downward road ? You are a wicked boy, and instead of becoming better under your kind teacher, and taking advantage of the many advantages of this institution devoted to religious instruction, you stick pins—brass pins—into better conducted boys than yourself. And so, if you do not repent, God will take you in your iniquity and cast you into hell. For, remember, God sees everything and punishes the bad people and rewards the good.'

The superintendent uttered, though he knew it not, the most ancient of heresies—that which Job refuted.

It was at this point in the oration of ' Pund o' Cannles' that Cleg Kelly's startling interruption occurred. The culprit suddenly stopped making O's on the dusty floor with his toe, amongst the moist paper pellets which were the favourite distraction of the inattentive at Hunker Court ; and, in a clear voice, which thrilled through the heart of every teacher and scholar within hearing, he uttered his denial of the eternity of the Trinity.

' It's all a dumb lie—God's dead ! ' he said.

There was a long moment's silence, and small wonder, as the school waited for the shivering trump of doom to split the firmament. The patient and self-sacrificing teachers who gave their unthanked care to the youth of the court every Sunday, felt their breaths come quick and short, and experienced a feeling as if they were falling over a precipice in a dream. At last Mr. James Lugton found his voice.

'Young and wicked blasphemer!' he said sternly, 'your presence must no longer, like that of the serpent in Paradise, poison the instruction given at this Sabbath school—I shall expel you from our midst——'

Here Cleg's teacher interposed. He was far from disliking his scholar, and had anticipated no such result arising from his most unfortunate reference of his difficulty to the superintendent. For he liked Cleg's ready tongue, and was amused by the mongrel dialect of Scots and Irish into which, in moments of excitement, he lapsed.

'I beg pardon, sir,' he said, 'but I am quite willing to give Kelly another chance—he is not such a bad boy as you might think.'

The superintendent waved his hand in a dignified way. He rather fancied himself in such scenes, and considered that his manner was quite as distinguished as that of his minister, when the latter was preaching his last memorable course of sermons upon the imprecatory psalms, and making solemn applications of them to the fate of members of a sister denomination which worshipped just over the way.

'The boy is a bold blasphemer and atheist!' he said; 'he shall be cast out from among our innocent lambs. Charles Kelly, I solemnly expel you upon this Christian Sabbath day, as a wicked and incorrigible boy, and a disgrace to any respectable mission school.'

The attitude of the superintendent was considered especially fine at this point. And he went home personally convinced that the excellent and fitting manner in which he vindicated the good name of Hunker Court upon this occasion, was quite sufficient to balance an extensive practice of the use of light weights in the chandler's shop at the corner of Hunker's Row. He further entirely believed that judicious severity of this kind was acceptable in the highest quarters.

So as the resisting felon is taken to prison, Cleg Kelly, heathen of twelve years, was haled to the outer door and cast forth of Hunker Court. But as the culprit went he explained his position.

'It's all gammon, that about prayin',' he cried; 'I've tried it heaps of times—never fetched it once! An' look at my mother. She just prays lashings, and all the time. An' me father, he's never a bit the better —no, nor her neither. For he thrashes us black and blue when he comes hame just the same. Ye canna gammon me, Pund o' Cannles, with your lang pray-prayin' and your short weight. I tell you God's dead, and it's all a dumb lie!'

The last accents of the terrible renunciation lingered upon the tainted air even after the door had closed, and Cleg Kelly was an outcast. But the awed silence was sharply broken by a whiz and jingle which occurred close to the superintendent's ear, as Cleg Kelly, Iconoclast, punctuated his thesis of defiance by sending a rock of offence clear through the fanlight over the door of Hunker Court Mission School.

ADVENTURE II

THE BURNING OF THE WHINNY KNOWES

CLEG KELLY was now outcast and alien from the commonwealth. He had denied the faith, cast aside every known creed, and defied the Deity Himself. Soon he would defy the policeman and break the laws of man—which is the natural course of such progression in iniquity, as every one knows.

So leaving Hunker Court he struck across the most unfrequented streets, where only an occasional stray urchin (probably a benighted Episcopalian) was spending the Sabbath chivying cats, to the mountainous regions of Craigside, where the tall 'lands' of St. Leonards look out upon the quarried craigs and steep hill ridges of Arthur's Seat. For Cleg was fortunate enough to be a town boy who had the country at his command just over the wall—and a wall, too, which he could climb at as many as twenty points. Only bare stubby feet, however, could overpass these perilous clefts. Cleg's great toes, horny as if shod with iron, fitted exactly into the stone crevices from which the mortar had been loosened. His grimy little fingers found a purchase in the slightest nicks. And once on the other side, there was no policeman, park-keeper, or other person in authority, who could make the pace with Cleg's bare brown legs, at least up the loose clatter of the shingle between the lower greensward and the Radical Road.

So, after being expelled from Hunker Court, Cleg made straight for a nook of his own among the crags. Here, like a prudent outlaw, he took account of his possessions with a view to arranging his future career of crime. He turned out his pockets into his hat. This was, indeed, a curious thing to do. For the article which he wore upon his shaggy locks was now little more than the rim of what had once been a covering for the head, proof against wind and water. But though Cleg's treasures rested upon the ground, the fact that they were within his hat-rim focussed them, as it were, and their relative worth was the more easily determined.

The first article which Cleg deposited upon the ground inside his hat was a box of matches, which had been given him to light the gas with in the outlying corners of Hunker Court School, for that dank cellar was gloomy enough even on a summer's afternoon. Then came some string, the aforesaid long-pronged nipping-wires which he had taken from his father's stores, a pair of pincers, a knife with one whole and one broken blade, a pipe, some brown-paper tobacco of a good brand, a half-written exercise-book from the day-school at which Cleg occasionally looked in, five marbles of the variety known as 'commonies,' one noble knuckler of alabaster which Cleg would not have parted with for his life, a piece of dry bread, and, lastly, half an apple with encroaching bays and projecting promontories, indicating in every case but one, the gap in Cleg's dental formation on the left side of his upper jaw, which dated from his great fight with Hole in the Wa' in the police yard. The exception was a clean, crisp semicircle, bitten right in to the apple-core. This was the tidemark of a friendly bite Cleg had given to a friend, in whose shining double row were no gaps. The perfect crescent had been made by the teeth of a lassie—one Vara Kavannah.

The box of matches was to its owner the most attractive article in all this array of wealth. Cleg looked into his hat-rim with manifest pleasure. He slapped his knee. He felt that he was indeed well equipped for the profession of outlaw. If he had to be a Cain, he could at least make it exceedingly lively in the Land of Nod.

It was a chilly day on the craigs, the wind blowing bask from the East, and everything underfoot as dry as tinder. The wild thought of a yet untried ploy surged up in Cleg's mind. He grasped the matchbox quickly, with thoughts of arson crystallising in his mind. He almost wished that he had set Hunker Court itself on fire. Just in time he remembered Vara Kavannah and her little brother Hugh.

'I'll get them to gang to anither school first,' he said.

But in the meantime, with the thought of setting fire to something in his heart and the matchbox in his hand, it was necessary to find the materials for a blaze. He had no powder with him or he would have made a 'peeoye'—the simple and inexpensive firework of metropolitan youth.

He glanced up at the heather and whin which covered the Nether Hill. His heart bounded within him at the thought. He looked again at his matchbox, which was one of the old oval shape, containing matches so exceedingly and gratuitously sulphurous, that the very smell of one of them was well worth the halfpenny charged for the lot. So, without any further pause for reflection, Cleg stowed away all the possessions, inventoried with such accuracy above, into various outlying nooks and crevices among the seams and pockets of his flapping attire.

Having collected the last one of these, Cleg climbed up a crumbling cliff at the eastern end of the craigs, where the fallen stones lie about in slats. Upon each of them, for all the world like green post-office wax dripped upon grey paper, was to be found some curious mineral—which Cleg, in his hours of decent citizenship, collected and sold at easy rates to the boys of the Pleasance as a charm. This mysterious green stuff had even been made a seal of initiation into one of the most select, aristocratic, and bloody secret societies of which Cleg was a member. Indeed, if the truth must be told, Cleg had formed the association chiefly that he might be able profitably to supply these badges of membership, for he had a corner in green mineral wax—at least so long as the mine at the east angle of the craigs remained undiscovered by the other adventurous loons of the south side.

Cleg soon reached the tawny, thin-pastured, thick-furzed slopes which constitute the haunch of Arthur's lion hill. In the days of Cleg's youth these were still clad thick with whins and broom, among which the birds built in the spring, and where in the evenings lovers sat in long converse on little swarded oases.

' I'll juist set fire to this wee bit knowe,' said Cleg, his heart beating within him at the enormity of the offence. ' There's no a " keelie " in the toon that wad dare to do as muckle ! '

For the ranger of that particular part of the hill was an old soldier of great size and surprising swiftness in a race. And many had been the Arthur Street urchins who had suffered a sore skin and a night in the cells after being taken in dire offence. So 'the Warrior' they called him, for an all-sufficient name.

In a sheltered spot, and with the wind behind him, Cleg opened his matchbox. He struck a match upon the rough oval bottom. It spurted faintly blue, burned briskly, and then flickered out within Cleg's hollowed hands. Cleg grunted.

'A fizz an' a stink,' said he, summing up the case in a popular phrase.

The next went somewhat better. The flame reached the wood, dipped as if to expire, took hold again, and finally burned up in a broad-based yellow triangle. Cleg let it drop among the crisp, dry, rustling grasses at the roots of the whin bushes. Instantly a little black line ran forward and crossways, with hardly any flame showing. Cleg was interested, and laid the palm of his hand upon the ground. He lifted it instantly with a cry of pain. What had seemed a black line with an edge of flickering blue was really a considerable fire, which, springing from the dry couch grass and bent, was briskly licking up the tindery prickles of the gorse.

The next moment, with an upward bound and a noise like the flapping of a banner, the flame sprang clear of the whin bushes, and the blue smoke streamed heavenwards. Cleg watched the progress, chained to the spot. He well knew that it was time for him to be off. But with the unhallowed fascination of the murderer for the scene of his crime, he watched bush after bush being swallowed up, and shouted and leaped with glee. But the progress of the flame was further and swifter than he had intended. One little knoll would have satisfied him. But in a minute, driven forward by a level-blowing, following wind, the flame overleaped the little strait of short turf, and grasped at the next and far larger continent of whin.

Cleg, surprised, began to shrink from the consequences of his act. He had looked to revenge himself upon society for his expulsion from Hunker Court by making a little private fire, and lo! he had started a world conflagration. He ran round to the edge of the gorse covert. Two hedge-sparrows were fluttering and dashing hither and thither, peeping and crying beseechingly. Cleg looked for the objective point of their anxiety, and there, between two whin branches, was the edge of a nest, and a little compact yellow bundle of three gaping mouths, without the vestige of a body to be seen.

'Guid life,' cried Cleg, who kept kindness to birds and beasts as the softest spot of his outlaw heart, 'guid life, I never thocht the birds wad be biggin' already!'

And with that he took off his coat, and seizing it in both hands he charged boldly into the front of the flame, disdainful of prickles and scorchings. He dashed the coat down upon a bush which was just beginning to crackle underneath; and by dint of hard fighting and reckless bravery he succeeded in keeping the fire from the little island, in the central bush of which was situated the hedge-sparrows' nest. Here he stood, with his coat threshing every way, keeping the pass with his life—brave as Horatius at the bridge (or any other man) —while the flames crackled and roared past him.

Suddenly there burst forth a great fizzing and spitting from the ragged coat which Cleg wielded as a quenching weapon. The fatal matchbox, cause of all the turmoil, had exploded. The fumes were stifling, but the flames still threatened to spread, and Cleg laid about him manfully. The tails of the coat disappeared. There was soon little left but the collar. Cleg stood like a warrior whose sword has broken in his hand in the face of the triumphant enemy. But the boy had a resource which is not usually open to the soldier. He cast the useless coat-collar from him, stripped a sleeved waistcoat, which had been given him by the wife of a mason's labourer, and, taking the garment by the two arms, he made an exceedingly efficient beater of the moleskin, which had the dried lime yet crumbly upon it at the cuffs.

When at last 'the Warrior' came speeding up the hill, warned out of his Sabbath afternoon's sleep by the cry that the whins were on fire, he was in no pleasant temper. He found, however, that the fire had been warded from the greater expanses by a black imp of a boy, burned and smutted, who held the remains of a moleskin garment clasped in a pair of badly singed hands.

When the inevitable crowd of wanderers had gathered from all parts of the hill, and the fire had been completely trampled out, the ranger began his inquiries. Cleg was the chief suspect, because no one had seen any other person near the fire except himself. On the other hand no one had seen him light the whins, while all had seen him single-handed fighting the flames.

'It's Tim Kelly's loon, the housebreaker, him that leeves in the Sooth Back!' said the usual officious stranger with the gratuitous local knowledge. At his father's ill-omened name there was an obvious hardening in the faces of the men who stood about.

'At ony rate, the loon is better in the lock-up,' said the ranger sententiously.

At this Cleg's heart beat faster than ever. Many

had been his perilous ploys, but never yet had he seen the inside of the prison. He acknowledged that he deserved it, but it was hard thus to begin his prison experience after having stayed to fight the fire, when he could so easily have run away. There was unfairness somewhere, Cleg felt.

So, with the burnt relics of his sleeved waistcoat still in his hands, Cleg was dragged along down the edge of the Hunter's Bog. The ranger grasped him roughly by a handful of dirty shirt collar, and his strides were so long that Cleg's short legs were not more than half the time upon the ground.

But at a certain spring of clear, crystal water, which gushes out of the hillside from beneath a large round stone, the ranger paused.

He too had fought the flames, and he had cause to thirst. For it was Sunday afternoon, and he had arisen from his usual lethargic after-dinner sleep upon the settle opposite the kitchen fire.

So at the well he stooped to drink, one hand still on Cleg's collar, and the palm of the other set flat on the side of the boulder. It was Cleg's opportunity. He twisted himself suddenly round, just after the ranger's lips had touched the water. The rotten cloth of his shirt tore, and Cleg sprang free. The ranger, jerked from the support of the stone, and at the same moment detached from his prisoner, fell forward with his head in the spring, while Cleg sped downhill like the wind. He was ready stripped for the race. So, leaving the panting chase far behind, he made for a portion of the encompassing wall, which none but he had ever scaled. Having clambered upon the top, he crossed his legs and calmly awaited the approach of the ranger.

'It's a warm day, Warrior,' said Cleg; 'ye seem to be sweatin'!'

'Ye limb o' Sawtan,' panted the ranger, 'gin ever I get ye this side o' the dyke, I'll break every bane in your body.'

'Faith,' answered Cleg, 'ye should be braw an' thankfu', Warrior, for ye hae gotten what ye haena had for years, and had muckle need o'!'

'And what was that, ye de'il's buckie?' cried the angry ranger.

'A wash!' said Cleg Kelly, as he dropped down the city side of the wall, and sped home to his fortress.

ADVENTURE III

WHY CLEG KELLY HATED HIS FATHER

THIS is a bad, black tale; yet, for the sake of what comes after, it must be set down.

Cleg Kelly had a father. He was a deeply pock-marked man who hated his son; but not so bitterly as his son hated him. Once on a time Cleg Kelly had also a mother, and it is the story of his mother which remains to be told. The story of most men is the story of their mother. They drank love or hatred, scorn or sympathy, at her breasts.

Thus it was with Cleg Kelly. So let the story of Isbel Kelly be told. How a woman may be murdered in this land and none swing for it! How a woman may be put to the torture every day and every night for years, and the voice of her crying mount (we must believe it) into the ears of the God of Sabaoth, yet no murmur reach her nearest neighbour upon the earth! Gladly would I tell a merrier tale, save that it is ever best to get the worst first over, as bitter medicine goes before barley-sugar.

Isbel Kelly had not always been Isbel Kelly. That is to say, she had not always been unhappy. There was a time when Timothy Kelly had not come into her life. Isbel Beattie was once a country girl. She had sung in the morn as she went afield to call the dappled kine, as glad a milkmaid as any in song or story. Her foot was the lightest in the dance at the 'kirn,' her hand the deftest at the spinning-wheel, her cheerful presence the most desired when the butter would not come. For the butter ever comes fastest for a good-tempered woman. A vixenish disposition only sours and curdles the milk. That is why young men, landward but wise, so eagerly offer to help the maids at the butter-making. And no sweeter maiden than Isbel Beattie ever wore print gowns and lilted 'O whistle and I'll come to ye, my lad,' in all the parish of Ormiland—that is, till Timothy Kelly came, and Isbel sang no more.

Isbel Beattie was 'fey,'[1] they said, and would take no advice. Lads tight and trig stood in rows to wait for her as she came out of the kirk, on fine Sabbath days when the lilac blossoms, white and purple, were out, and there was a drooping sprig in every spruce bachelor's coat. But Isbel passed them all by with a toss of her head. She could have married a rather stupid young farmer of the best intentions and unquestioned solvency, had she so chosen. But Isbel was 'fey,' and would take counsel neither from maid nor matron.

Now the reason was that Timothy Kelly, the weasel-faced Irish harvest-man, had wormed himself into the girl's affections by ways of his own, as before and after he had undone many a trebly fastened door with his steel picklock.

From that day until the hour of her death Isbel Beattie saw no good day. A week after they were married, Timothy Kelly was drinking Isbel's last half-year's wages in a public-house, and Isbel was crying at home with a bruised cheek. She sang no more late or

[1] Bewitched.

early ; but learned to endure hardness and to pray that the kind Lord of whom she had heard in the kirk, might send her a swift and easy death as the best thing left to wish for.

Timothy Kelly was not long in Ormiland before he removed to Edinburgh in the interests of business. He needed the metropolis for the exercise of his talents. So Isbel packed what he had left her, and followed him, faithful and weary-foot, to the squalid city lane, and Timothy Kelly cursed her over his shoulder all the way. But she did not hear him, and so his words did not hurt her. God had stopped her ears. For the sound of a dearer voice was in them, and the promise of the Eden joy answered Isbel, as though the Lord Almighty himself walked with her through the streets of the city in the cool of the day.

A week after an infant lay on the breast of Isbel Kelly, in a garret up Meggat's Close, off the Pleasance. A kindly neighbour looked in now and then when Tim Kelly was out, and comforted the young mother. When Tim came in he cursed them all impartially. His foul words sent the neighbours forth again, full of pity and indignation ; and so he cast himself down to sleep off drink and temper on the couch of rags in the corner.

Towered fair-faced Edinburgh and its seething underworld held no man like Timothy Kelly. A sieve-net might have been drawn through it and no worse rascal caught than he. Cruel only where he dared with impunity be cruel, plausible and fawning where it was to his interest so to be, Timothy Kelly was a type of the criminal who lives to profit by the strange infatuations of the weakest women. From silly servant girls at kitchen doors who thought him 'a most civil-spoken young man,' he obtained the professional information which enabled him to make unrecognised but accurate lists of the family silver upon some stormy midnight, when the policemen stood in doorways, or stolidly perambulated the city with their helmets pulled down upon their brows.

Isbel Kelly wore thin and white, and the bruises on her face became chronic, only occasionally changing the side. For in this matter Timothy Kelly had no weak partiality. Yet, in the midst of all, Cleg Kelly gained in years and strength, his mother many a time shielding him from blows with her own frail body. There was a soft light on her face when she looked at him. When her husband was out, Isbel watched Cleg all day long as he lay on the bed and kicked with sturdy limbs, or sprawled restlessly about the house. The dwelling was not extensive. It consisted of one room, and Tim Kelly's 'hidie holes,' where he kept the weapons of his craft—curious utensils, with iron crab fingers set at various angles upon the end of steel stalks.

Now, it is the strangest, yet one of the commonest, things in this world that Isbel Kelly loved her husband, and at the worst times said no word against him. It was a mistake. She ought to have outfaced him, insulted him, defied him, given him blow for blow. Then he might have been a reasonably decent husband, according to the standard of Meggat's Close.

But Cleg Kelly made no such mistake. From the time that he was a toddling little fellow till the parish buried his mother, Cleg Kelly looked at his father with level brows of hate and scorn. No one had taught him; but the perception of youth gauged the matter unerringly.

There are but two beings in the universe whom a really bad-hearted man cannot deceive: his Maker and a young child. Cleg Kelly never quailed before his father. Neither words nor blows daunted him. Whenever his father went out, he said:

'Bad mannie gone away, minnie!'

'Na, Cleg,' said his mother, 'ye mauna speak that way o' yer faither!'

'Bad mannie, minnie!' Cleg repeated, determinedly; 'bad mannie gone away.'

And from this she could not move him.

Then as soon as his father began to beat the lad, and his mother was no longer able to protect him, Cleg developed a marvellous litheness and speed. At five years of age he could climb roofs like a cat, and watch his father from the ledge of an outlying wall or the side of a reeking chimney-can, where even the foot of the practised burglar dared not venture.

Then came a year black and bitter. It was the unforgotten year of the small-pox. That part of Edinburgh where the Kellys lived became a walled city. There was one death in every three or four attacked. And Tim Kelly went to the seaside for his health.

But Isbel and her boy battled it out alone. She had seven shillings a week for cleaning a day-school. But soon the schools were closed, and her pay ceased. Nevertheless, she earned money somehow, and the minister of the McGill-Gillespie church visited her. It would take a whole treatise on Church History, and a professor thereof, to tell why that church was called the McGill-Gillespie. However, the unlearned may be assured that these excellent gentlemen were not canonised Scottish saints, nor were their effigies worshipped inside. But at this time the minister of the church came very near to being worshipped outside.

The children knew his step, and ran—*to*, not *from*,

him. He was the only man, except the doctor, at whom the urchins of Meggat's did not fling dirt. One of these had even been known to touch his hat to the minister of McGill-Gillespie. But this was a great risk, and of course he could not do it when any one was looking.

One day Cleg Kelly sickened, and though at the time he was a great boy of six, his mother carried him about in her arms all day, soothing him. But the hot dry spots burned ever brighter on his cheeks, and his eyes shone like flame. The minister brought the doctor, for in famine time and fever time they hunted in couples—these two. Some of the ministers had gone to the seaside with Timothy Kelly, and along with them a few great professional men from the West-End. But the Pleasance doctor, a little fair man, and the minister of McGill-Gillespie, a tall dark man, remained with the small-pox. Also God was there—not very evidently or obtrusively, perhaps; but so that the minister of McGill-Gillespie knew where to find Him when He was wanted.

And He was needed badly enough in the sick-room of Cleg Kelly. No doubt Cleg ought to have gone to the hospital. But, for one thing, the hospitals were overcrowded. And, for another, if they had taken Cleg, they might have taken his mother also. At all events Cleg was nursed in his home, while his father remained at the seaside for his health.

One night, when the trouble was at its height, Cleg ran deliriously on about 'the bad mannie.' His mother stilled and tended him. The doctor ordered a little warm wine to be given to Cleg occasionally, and the minister of McGill-Gillespie had brought it. But Cleg wavered between life and death in spite of the wine—and much nearer death than life. Isbel had seen the doctor earlier in the day, and she was to go for him again if a certain anticipated change did not come within six hours. The change did not come, though the mother never took her eyes off her boy. Cleg lay back on his pallet bed, inert and flaccid, his eyes glassy and fixed in his head. His mother softly closed the door, took her shawl over her head, and fled through the midnight streets to the doctor's house.

A sudden summer storm had arisen off the sea. The wind swirled about the old many-gabled closes of Edinburgh. It roared over the broken fortress line of the Salisbury Crags. The streets were deserted. The serried ash-backets were driven this way and that by the gale. Random cats scudded from doorstep to cellar, dipped, and disappeared. *Clash!* fell a great shutter on the pavement before her. Isbel Kelly was at the doctor's door. He was not in. Would she leave a message? She would, and the message was that a little boy was sinking, and that unless the doctor came quickly a mother's only son would die. She cried out in agony as she said it, but the wind swirled the cry away.

So through the turmoil of the storm she came back, and ran up the evil-smelling dark stairs, where the banister was broken, and only the wind-blown fleer of the gas-lamp outside, flickering through the glassless windows of the stairway, lighted her upwards. She had once been a milkmaid, but she had long forgotten how the cowslips smelled. And only in her dreams did she recall the scent of beehives over the wall on a still summer night.

She opened the door with a great yearning, but with no presentiment of evil.

'Tim!' she said, her face whitening.

A man, weasel-faced and hateful to look upon, stood by the little cupboard. He had a purse in his hand, and a bottle stood on the mantelshelf beside him.

'Oh, Tim!' she cried, 'for the Lord's sake dinna tak' my last shillin'—no frae me an' the boy. He's deein', Tim!'

She ran forward as if to beseech him to give the money back to her; but Tim Kelly, reckless with drink, snatched up the minister's wine-bottle and it met his wife's temple with a dull sound. The woman fell in a heap. She lay loosely on the floor by the wall, and did not even moan. Tim Kelly set the bottle to his lips to drain the last dregs with an empty laugh. But suddenly from the bed something small and white flew at his throat.

'Bad mannie, bad mannie, bad mannie!' a shrill voice cried. And before Tim Kelly could set down the bottle, the little figure in flying swathings had dashed itself again and again upon him, biting and gnashing on him like a wolf's cub. For the blood of Tim Kelly was in the lad, as well as the blood of the milkmaid who lay athwart the floor as one dead.

And this was what the doctor found, when he stumbled up the stair and opened the door. He had seen many strange things in his day, but none so terrible as this. He does not care to speak about it, though he told the minister that either Providence or the excitement had saved the child's life. Yet for all that he tended Timothy Kelly, when his turn came, as well as the best of paying patients. For Tim's was an interesting case, with many complications.

So this adventure tells the reason of three things very important to be known in this history—why, six months after, Isbel Kelly was glad to die ; why Cleg Kelly hated his father ; and why smooth-faced Tim, who had once deceived the servant girls, was ever after a deeply pock-marked man.

What it does not tell is, why God permitted it all.

ADVENTURE IV

HOW ISBEL KELLY HEARD SWEET MUSIC

CLEG KELLY did not die just then, which was in some ways a good thing. But neither did his mother Isbel, which, for herself, was a pity. It was also a mistake for society. For then Tim Kelly might also have died for the want of a nurse, and Providence and the city authorities would have been saved a vast deal of trouble.

But in spite of all boasts to the contrary, this is so little a free country that people cannot always die when they want—some not even when they ought to. And not a few have got themselves into trouble only for assisting manifest destiny. But no one, not even the chief constable, would have been sorry had Isbel Beattie forgotten to help Tim Kelly, her husband, at some crisis of his disease. Then he might have gone betimes to his own place, and thus have been compelled to leave alone a great number of other places and things, with which he had no proper concern.

But Isbel Kelly did not think of that. Moreover, Tim Kelly behaved himself better as an invalid than he had ever done as a whole man. And as for little Cleg, he got better rapidly in order to get out of his father's way.

But there came a day when both her invalids were out of her hands, and Isbel had time to clean her house and give her attention to dying on her own account. She did not wish to put any one to an inconvenience. But, indeed, there was little else left for her to do. Tim Kelly was again able to attend to business—which, strictly speaking, consisted in the porterage of other people's goods out of their houses, without previous arrangement with the owners, and in a manner as unobtrusive as possible.

Cleg was as yet too young for this profession, but according to his father's friends his time was coming. In the meanwhile he spent most of the day in a brickyard at the back. For Tim Kelly, owing to a little difficulty as to rent, had moved his household goods from Meggat's Close to the outskirts of the city. Now they do not use many bricks about Edinburgh; but there are exceptions, especially in the direction of Leith, and this was the place where they made the exceptions.

The brickyard was a paradise to Cleg Kelly in the warm days of summer. The burning bricks made a strange misty fume of smoke in the air, which was said to be healthy. People who could not afford to go to Portobello for convalescence, brought their children to the brickyard. They made drain-pipes and other sanitary things there; and on that account also the brickyard was accounted healthy for people in the position of the Kellys.

At any rate Cleg Kelly was well content, and he played there from morn to night. His mother generally watched him from a window. There was but one window in the little 'rickle of brick' which their pawnbroking Jew landlord called a 'commodious cottage.' He might call it what he liked. He never got any rent for it from Tim Kelly.

Yet Isbel was happier here than in the city. At least she could see the trees, and she had neighbours who came in to visit her when her husband was known to be from home.

'Eh, Mistress Kelly, I wonder ye can pit up wi' sic a man,' said the wife of Joe Turner, a decent labourer steadily employed on the brickfields, who only drank half his wages.

Isbel signed frantically towards the bed with her hand. But without noticing her signals of distress, the innocent Mrs. Turner went on with the burden of her tale.

'Gin *I* had sic a man, I wad tak' him to bits like a clock, an' set him up again anew—the black-hearted scoondrel o' a red-headed Irishman!'

Tim Kelly rose from the bed where he had been resting himself. They do not set a bed in a room in that country. They put it down outside a room and build it round on three sides. Then they cover the remaining side in with as many cloths as possible, for the purpose of keeping out the air. From such a death-trap Tim Kelly rose slowly, and confronted Mistress Turner.

'Get out av me house, Misthress Turner, afore I break the thick skull av yer ill-conditioned face,' said Tim, whose abuse was always of the linked and logical kind.

''Deed an' I'll gang oot o' yer hoose wi' pleesure, Timothy Kelly; gin I had kenned that the likes o' you was in it, Mary Turner wad never hae crossed yer doorstep.'

'Well, now that ye are here, be afther takin'

yoursilf acrost the durestip, as suddent an' comprehensive-like as ye can—wid yer brazen face afore ye an' yer turned-up nose in the air. When ye are wanted bad in this house, ye'll get an invite wid a queen's pictur' on it—an' me kyard!' said Tim Kelly, sarcastically.

Mary Turner betook herself to the door, in a manner as dignified as it is possible to retain when retreating with one's face to the foe. But when she got there, she put her arms akimbo and opened the vials of her wrath on Tim Kelly. The neighbours came to the doors to listen. It was a noble effort, and the wives remembered some of Mistress Turner's phrases long after, and reproduced them every fortnight upon pay-nights, for the benefit of their husbands when they came home with only eleven intact shillings out of twenty-three.

But Tim Kelly hardly troubled to reply. He only said that Mary Turner was a 'brass-faced ould Jezebel,' a statement which he repeated several times, because he observed that it provoked on each occasion a fresh burst of the Turnerian vocabulary.

Tim Kelly never wasted animosity. After all, Mistress Turner was not his wife, and there were other means of getting even with her. He could win money at cards from her husband, or he could teach her son, Jamie, who had just left school, a fine new game with the lock of a door and one of his curious pronged hooks. There are more ways of killing a cat than drowning it in cream—also many deaths less agreeable to the cat. So Tim Kelly bided his time.

But for some reason Tim Kelly grew less unkind to his wife than he had ever been, since those terrible days when in Ormiland parish bonny Isbel Beattie grew 'fey.'

It was said that Tim was afraid of his son Cleg. At any rate, certain it is that he beat his wife no more, and very occasionally he even gave her a little money. So in her heart Isbel Kelly counted these good days, and sometimes she could almost have wished to live a little longer.

It was not often that Cleg stayed in the house with her. That she did not expect. But at all times of the day she could see him, rushing about the brickfield, sometimes piling bricks into castles; at other times helping Joe Turner; then again playing at marbles for 'keeps' in the red dust of the yard, with the sun pouring down upon his head. It was a constant marvel to Isbel that he was never tired. She was always tired.

Sometimes Cleg Kelly fought, and then his mother called him in. He always came—after the fight was over. He wore a hat of straw with a hole in it, or rather he wore, as usual, a hole with a little rim of hat round it. He loved his mother, and, on the whole, attended to what she told him. He did not steal anything of value, nor would he go near Hare's public. He did not tell more lies than were just and necessary. He minded his mother's wants, and was in the main a fairly good boy, as boys go down by the Easter Beach brickyard. The standard is not an exacting one.

'Mind, now, Cleg,' she used to say, 'when I gang awa', ye are to bide wi' your faither, an' no cross him ower sair. He is your faither, mind, an' I leave him to you.'

Cleg promised—to please his mother, but he loved his other parent none the better. The next time he saw him come home drunk, he clouted him with a paving-stone from behind the yard wall. He excused himself by saying that his mother was not gone away yet.

This was the lesson Isbel taught Cleg every day when he came in to his scanty meals, many of which good Mistress Turner slipped into the house under her apron, when the 'brute beast and red-headed gorilla' of her anathema was known to be out of the way.

After a while there came an afternoon when Isbel Kelly felt strangely quiet. It was a drowsy day, and the customary sounds of the brickfield were hushed in the doze of the afternoon sun. Outside it was hot with an intense heat, and a kind of pale bluish smother rose off the burning bricks. The filmy reek of the kilns drifted across the fields, too lazy to rise through the slumberous sunshine. The whole yard radiated blistering heat like an oven.

Isbel sat by the window in a chair which Tim had made during his convalescence; for he was exceedingly handy with tools, and during those days he had nothing worse to do.

She made the house as tidy as she could compass during the morning hours, steadying herself with one hand on the walls as she went about. Cleg, of course, was playing outside. He had come racing in for his dinner with a wisp of hair sticking out of the hole in his hat. Isbel smoothed it down, and because her hand touched him like a caress Cleg put it from him, saying, 'Dinna, mother; somebody micht see ye!'

It was hot, and the boy was a little irritable; but his mother understood.

Then, as he took the plate of broth, he told his mother all that had happened in the brickfield that day. He had carried clay for Joe, and Joe had given him a penny. Then he had been at a rat-hunt with the best terrier in the world. He had also chased Michael Hennessy twice round the yard after a smart bout of fisticuffs. Thereupon, the men had cheered him, and called him a 'perfect wull-cat'—which Cleg took to be a term of praise, and cherished as a soldier does the 'penn'orth o' bronze' which constitutes the Victoria Cross.

Isbel only sat and rested and listened. Tim was away for the day, she knew not wher , and the minutes Cleg remained indoors and talked to her were her sole and sufficient pleasure. She thanked the Lord for each one of them. But she never called the boy in against his will, nor yet held him longer than he cared to stay.

Yet, somehow, on this day Isbel was more eager than usual to detain her son. She clung to him with a strange kind of yearning. But as soon as Cleg had finished his bread and soup he snatched up his white straw hat-brim and raced out, crying, as he ran, 'I'm awa', mither—Tam Gillivray has stealed my auld basin withoot the bottom.'

This was a serious offence, and Cleg went down in haste to avenge the insult. Soon there was the noise of battle below—chiefly, however, the noise of them that shout for the mastery. And then, in a little, when the bottomless basin had been recovered by its rightful owner, the noise of them that cry for being overcome.

From the window Isbel watched. Her thin hair fell over her wasted temples, and she pressed her hand on her breast, searching as though something were missing there. And so there was. It was about a lung and a half which she missed. Nevertheless there had fallen a peace upon Isbel to which she had long been unaccustomed. Faint tremors ran through her body, and though the window was wide open, she often gasped for breath. A blissful, painless weariness stole dreamily over her.

Cleg was playing below. He had achieved a victory, complete, yet not quite bloodless, for Tam Gillivray was staunching his nose at the smith's cauldron with a lump of cold iron at the back of his neck. Cleg, prancing in haughty state and followed by a little train of admirers, was now dragging the basin in triumph round the yard. He was pretending that it was a railway train, drawn by an engine of extremely refractory disposition, which curvetted and reared in a most unenginely manner.

Isbel watched him from her window.

'He is happy, puir laddie—maybe happier than he'll ever be again. Let him bide a wee. I'll gie him a cry, in time.'

Then she looked again. She prayed a little while with her eyes shut. Beneath, Cleg was holding his court. He had crowned himself with the basin, and pulled his hair through it in the shape of a plume. As an appropriate finish for the whole, he had stuck the mop of protruding locks full of feathers, and now he was presiding over a court of justice at which Michael Hennessy was being tried for his life on the charge of murdering a 'yellow yoit.' In due course the verdict of justifiable homicide was returned, and the culprit sentenced to kill another, or be belted round the brickyard.

Then, wearying for a fresher ploy, the boys decided to build a fortress, and instantly, as soon as they had thought of it, they set to work with a mountain of refuse bricks, Cleg Kelly putting no hand to the manual labour, but being easily first in the direction of affairs. This 'gaffership' suited Cleg so well that he turned three excellent wheels in the greatness of his content, and then immediately knocked over several boys for presuming to imitate him, when they ought to have been fulfilling orders and building bricks into a fortress.

From the window his mother still watched him. She smiled faintly to see his light-heart joy, and said again, as if to herself, 'In a while I shall cry to him —I dinna need him yet!'

All about there seemed to rise to her ears a sound of sweet music, as of the many singers in the kirk on still, warm Sabbath days, singing the psalms which she remembered long ago in Ormiland. Only now they sounded very far away. And at times the brickyard reeled and dazzled, the arid trodden ground and steaming bricks fell back, the cracked walls opened out, and she saw the sun shining upon golden hills, the like of which she had never seen before.

'What is this? Oh, what's this?' she asked herself aloud, and the sound of her own voice was in her ears as the roaring of many waters.

It seemed to her to be almost time now. She leaned forward wearily to call her son to help her. But he was sitting on a brick throne in the midst of his castle, dressed as Robin Hood, with all his merry men about him. He looked so happy, and he laughed so loud, that Isbel said again to herself—

'I can manage yet for half an hour, and then I shall cry to him.'

But her son caught sight of her at the window. He was so elated that he did not mind noticing his mother, as a common boy would have done. He waved his hand to her, calling out loud—

'Mither, mither, I'm biggin' a bonny hoose for you to leeve in!'

Isbel smiled, and it was as if the sun which shone on the hills of her dream, had touched her thin face and made it almost beautiful for the last time before sundown.

'My guid boy—my nice boy,' she said, 'the Lord will look till him! He said he was biggin' a hoose for his mither. Let him big his hoose. In a while I shall cry to him—my ain laddie!'

Yet in a while she did not cry, and it was the only time she had ever broken her word to her son.

But that was because Isbel Kelly had journeyed where no crying is. Neither shall there be any more pain.

ADVENTURE V

THE BRIGANDS OF THE CITY

CLEG KELLY's mother lay still in her resting grave, and had no more need of pity. Cleg abode with his father in the tumble-down shanty by the brickfield at Easter Beach, and asked for no pity either. Cleg had promised his mother, Isbel, that he would not forsake Tim Kelly.

'Na, I'll no rin awa' frae ye,' so he told his father, frankly, 'for I promised my mither; but gin ye lick me, I'll pit my wee knife intil ye when ye are sleepin'! Mind ye that!'

And his father minded, which was fortunate for both.

Cleg was now twelve, and much respected by his father, who fully believed that he was speaking the truth. Tim Kelly, snow-shoveller, feared his son Cleg with his sudden wild-cat fierceness, much more than he feared God—more, even, than he feared Father Donnelly, to whom he went twice a year to ease his soul of a portion of his more specially heinous sins.

Yet Tim Kelly was distinctly a better man, because of the respect in which he held his son. He even boasted of Cleg's cleverness when he was safe among his old cronies in Mother Flannigan's kitchen, or in the bar-parlour at Hare's public.

'Shure, there's not the like av him in this kingdom av ignorant blockheads. My Cleg's the natest and the illigantest gossoon that stips in his own boot-leather. Shure, he can lick anything at all near his own weight. Sorra's in him, he can make his ould man stand about. Faith, 'tis him that's goin' to be the great man intoirely, is our little Cleg.'

These were the opinions of his proud father.

But Jim Carnochan, better known as the 'Devil's Lickpot,' demurred. If Cleg were so clever a boy, why was he not set to work? A boy so smart ought long ere this to have been learning the profession. To this Mother Flannigan agreed, for she shared in the profits.

'My Peether, rest his sowl for a good lad—him as was hanged be token of false evidence—and the bobbies findin' the gintleman's goold watch in Peether's pocket, was at wurrk whin he was six years av his age. Take my wurrd for it, Timothy Kelly, there never yet was a thruely great man that didn't begin his education young.'

'Maybe,' said Tim, 'and that's the raison, Misthress Flannigan, that so few av them grew up to be ould men.'

'Gin he was my boy,' said Sandy Telfer, whose occupation was breaking into houses during the summer holidays (one of the safest 'lays' in the profession, but looked down upon as mean-spirited), 'I wad be hacin' him through the windows and openin' the front doors every dark nicht.'

'Ah, you wud, wud ye?' replied Tim Kelly contemptuously; 'you're the great boy to talk, you that has no more manhud in ye than a draff-sack wid a hole in it. Yuss, ye can do yer dirthy way wid your own mane-spirited spalpeens, wid no more spunk in them than a dure-mat. But I'd have ye know that my Clig cud make hares av you an' ivvery Telfer av the lot o' ye—hear to me now!'

And Tim Kelly shook his fist within an inch of the nose of Sandy Telfer, who, not being a man of war, showed by the curl of his nostril and the whitening of his lip, that he did not find the bouquet of Tim Kelly's bunch-of-fives an agreeable perfume. Tim Kelly waited to see if on any pretext he could bring his fist into closer contact with Sandy Telfer's face, but he found no cause.

'My Clig,' he said emphatically, 'is goin' to be a great characther. He is jist the boy that is to climb the top laddher av the profession. It's his father that must be out at night, an' run the risk av the dirthy bobby wid his lanthern, an' the gintleman av the house in his night-shirt wid a cruel poker. But Clig shall sit safe and aisy in his chair, an' make his thousands a year with the scrap av his pen. He'll promothe companies, an' be out av the way when they burst. He'll write so illegant that he cud turn ye off another gintleman's signathure as fast as his own, an' worth a deal more on a bit av paper——'

'Come away hame, faither, sittin' bletherin' there. Ye hae been here lang enough.'

It was the face of Cleg Kelly, dirty, sharp, and good-natured, which appeared at the door of the boozing ken.

Mistress Flannigan caught up a pound weight and threw it at Cleg with a woman's aim. It flew wide, and would surely have smashed some of the unclean vessels standing ready for the wash on the dresser, had Cleg not stepped briskly within, and, catching the

missile deftly, made a low bow as he laid it on the
table. Then he said, with his rare disarming smile—

'Your obedient servant, Cleg Kelly!'

'Hear to him now, the young bliggard!' cried his
delighted and well-intoxicated father. 'He has come
to arm the ould man home, an' the ould man'll have
to be stippin' too when Clig gives the wurrd.'

Isbel Kelly had indeed been a happy woman if, ten
years ago, she had learned Cleg's method.

'Come on, faither,' reiterated Cleg, who had again
retreated to the door, for he had no liking for the company or the place.

Tim Kelly got himself on his feet unsteadily, and
lurched towards the door. His son caught him deftly
on the descending swoop.

'Steady, faither, mind the stair. Gie us yer han'.'

And so Cleg got Timothy, his father, who deserved
no such care, tenderly up the filthy exit of Mistress
Flannigan's cellar.

'Tim's not the man he was,' Sandy Telfer said, as
the pair went out.

'It's fair undecent doin' as the boy bids him, an'
never so much as puttin' the laddie to an honest bit o'
wark. Ah, he'll suffer for that, or a' be dune! There'll
be raisons annexed to that,' continued the summer
housebreaker—who had been respectably brought up on
the Shorter Catechism, but who, owing to a disappointment in love, had first of all joined another denomination, and then, the change not answering its purpose,
had finally taken to housebreaking and drink.

'Ye may say so, indeed,' said Bridget Flannigan.

So Cleg took his father home to the rickety house
by the brickyard. Cleg kept the room clean as well
as he could. But the sympathetic neighbour, who

remembered his mother, occasionally took a turn round the place with a scrubbing-brush when it was absolutely certain that the 'red-headed gorilla' was absent, attending, as usual, to other people's business.

Whenever Cleg saw his father refrain from Hare's public and the evening sessions of Mistress Flannigan's interesting circle, he knew that Tim had a project on hand. Generally he took no particular heed to these. For it was his custom, as soon as he saw his father off on any of his raids, to go and report himself casually at the nearest police-station, where the sergeant's wife knew him. She often gave him a 'piece' with sugar on it, having known his mother before ever she left the parish of Ormiland.

The sergeant's wife remembered her own happy escape from being Mrs. Timothy Kelly. And though her heart had been sore against Isbel at the time, she had long forgotten the feeling in thankfulness that her lines had fallen on the right side of the law. But she had never confided to the sergeant that she had once known Tim Kelly somewhat intimately.

Cleg did not mean to be mixed up in any of his father's ill-doings if he could help it, so upon these occasions he frequented the precincts of the police-station as much as the sergeant's wife would let him.

It was his custom to take his 'piece'—an excellent thick slice of bread with brown sugar on it—and seat himself on a luxurious paling opposite to eat it. The fact that a great many message boys passed that way may have had something to do with Cleg's choice of locality. Cleg liked to be envied. And, seeing the 'piece,' more than one boy was sure to give chase. This introduced a healthy variety into Cleg's life. He

liked to fool with these young men of the message
basket. Exercise sharpens the appetite, and when this
morning the butcher's boy chivied him over the
parched-up grass field that lay between the station and
the brickyard, Cleg fairly whooped in his joy.

At first he ran slowly, and apparently with great
alarm, so that the butcher's boy had not the least
doubt he could catch him easily. Cleg held the
sergeant's wife's 'piece' in his hand as he ran, so that
the butcher's boy could see the thick sugar on the top
of the yellow butter. This stirred up the pursuer's
desires, and he made a spurt to seize Cleg. Had the
assailant been the grocer's boy, to whom sugar and
butter were vain things, Cleg would have had to try
another plan. Now, when the butcher's boy spurted,
Cleg almost let himself be caught. He heard close
behind him the labouring of the pursuer. With a
sudden rush he sped thirty yards in front; then he
turned and ran backwards, eating the sergeant's wife's
'piece' as he ran. This aggravated the butcher's boy
to such an extent that he had to stop with his hand on
his panting side, and curse Cleg's parentage—which,
sad to relate, pleased Cleg more than anything. He
said it was prime. By which he meant, not the sergeant's wife's 'piece,' but the whole situation, and
especially the disgust of the butcher's boy.

Then Cleg, being happy and contented, offered
honourable terms, for he and the butcher's boy were
in reality very good friends. He gave his late pursuer
a fair half of the bread and sugar, but reserved the crust
for himself. So, munching amicably, Cleg and the
butcher's boy returned together to the paling on which
Cleg had been sitting.

But alas! during his temporary absence from his

care, Tam Luke, the baker's boy, had come along. And in pursuit of the eternal feud between butchers' boys and bakers' boys, he had overturned the basket and rolled the meat on the road. Luke was now sitting on the rail a little way along, smoking a pipe loaded with brown paper, and lifting his chin up at every draw with a kind of ostentatious calmness.

When half-way across the field the butcher's boy observed the insult to his basket. Yet he said nothing till he came quite near. Then, in the most friendly manner possible, he seized the defiled leg of mutton, destined for the dinner of an eminent Doctor in Divinity, and hit Tam Luke a swingeing blow over the head with it, which not only broke that youth's pipe, but for a season spoiled the shape of his mouth, and tumbled him incontinently over the fence.

The baker's boy rose, shedding freely bits of clay pipe and exceedingly evil words. A battle royal seemed imminent to any one who did not know the commonplaces of friendly intercourse among these worthies. But the baker's boy contented himself with stating over and over in varied and ornamental language, highly metaphorical in parts, what he would do to the butcher's boy if he hit him again. However, the butcher's boy had too great an advantage in handling Professor Hinderland's leg of mutton, and the tempest gradually blew itself out.

Whereupon all parties betook themselves to a street pump, to wash the various articles which had been strewed in the mire, and to dry them on the butcher's boy's bluestriped apron, which he wore girt about him like a rope. It was a highly instructive sight. And had the cooks of various respectable families seen the process, they would have had sufficient answer to their frequent in-

THE BRIGANDS OF THE CITY   41

dignant question that morning, 'What can be keeping Cleaver's young vaigabond?'

Also, had they happened to pass by, a number of the good ladies who sat down so comfortably to enjoy their dinners (which they called 'lunch' if anybody happened to call) would certainly have gone without the principal course.

But the butcher's boy and the baker's boy were not in the least distressed. Such things happened every day. It was all in the way of business. And as for our hero, he, as we have indicated before, merely remarked in his vulgar way, that it was prime.

So far he had had a good, interesting day, and was exceedingly pleased with himself.

Presently all three went and calmly smoked on the side of the road, roosting contentedly on the paling; while Tam Luke, who had got a prize for good reading at the school, drew out of his pocket 'The Bully Boys' Budget'—an international journal of immense circulation, which described the adventures of associated bands of desperate ruffians (aged, on an average, nine) chiefly in New York, a city which Cleaver's loon looked upon as a boys' Paradise. Boys were discouraged in Edinburgh. They got no chance of distinguishing themselves.

'It's a most michty queer thing,' said Cleg, 'that the story says, if Tam Luke reads it richt——'

'I'll smash yer tawtie heid!' remarked that gentleman, mightily offended at the insinuation.

'If Tam Luke reads it richt,' continued Cleg, 'that in New York the bobbies rin frae the boys; but here the boys rin frae the bobbies like fun.'

'*Me?*' said Cleaver's boy. 'I wadna rin for ony bobby in the hale toon.'

'An' *me*,' cried Tam Luke, with mighty contempt, 'I lickit a big bobby the nicht afore yestreen. I could fecht a bobby wi' yae hand tied ahint my back.'

'Bobbies are nane sic bad folks. The sergeant's wife over there gied me a "piece,"' said Cleg gratefully.

'Ye are a reid-heided Irish traitor!' said the butcher's boy with emphasis.

'It's my faither that's reid-heided,' said Cleg promptly; 'but tak' that ony way for speaking ill o' the family!'

And with the back of his hand he knocked the libeller of his forbears over into the field.

'I'm gaun to be captain o' a band o' robbers—will ye baith join?' said Tam Luke.

Cleaver's boy was about to wreak his vengeance on Cleg from the other side of the fence, but he paused with his arm suspended to think over the proposal.

'I'm gaun to be captain o' a band mysel'! Will *ye* join?' cried the butcher's boy eagerly to Cleg, instead of assaulting him as he had first intended.

'What to do?' asked practical Cleg.

'To fecht the poliss, of course!' cried the butcher's boy and the baker's boy together. Their unanimity was wonderful.

'*There's the sergeant the noo!*' said Cleg quietly, pointing across the road.

And it was indeed the sergeant, who, having been on night duty, had just risen and strolled out to see what kind of weather it was.

Whereupon the valiant captains of the decimating bands which were to terrorise the police of the city descended from their several roosts as with one mind, seized their baskets, and sped round opposite corners with amazing speed.

Cleg Kelly was left alone, sitting on the paling. He pulled out what remained of his crust, and, as he ate it with relish, he laughed aloud and kicked his heels with glee, so that the sergeant, stretching himself after his day sleep, called across to the boy—

'What's up wi' ye, Cleg? Ye seem to be enjoyin' yoursel'!'

But all the answer he could get out of Cleg was just, 'O man, sergeant, it's prime!'

But whether he meant the crust or only things in general, the sergeant was none the wiser.

ADVENTURE VI

CLEG TURNS BURGLAR

CLEG had watched his father furtively all day. Little conversation passed between these two. Cleg devoted much of his time to a consideration of the best means of legitimate gain in his new profession of capitalist. He possessed the large sum of one shilling and a penny. It was banked upon sound old principles in the hollow end of a brick, which was buried under a flag in the backyard of a brewery. Cleg had hidden it with mystic incantations, and now carried a red worsted thread twisted round his finger to remind him of its whereabouts.

But there was another reason besides his large capital, why Cleg was unusually watchful of his father that day. First of all, Tim Kelly had come home sober from Hare's public the night before. That was a suspicious circumstance in itself. It showed not only that his ready cash had all been liquefied, but that Mistress Hare had drawn a line under the big chalk score behind her door. This line was the intimation that the single file of figures must be wiped off before another dram was served.

'Ye've had Larry on your back long enough, sure, Tim!' said Mistress Hare, who regulated these matters in person. 'Idleness is a most deadly sin, Father Malony says!' continued the landlady devoutly.

'Shure, an' it's not the divil's sin, thin, Mistress Hare,' said Tim acutely, 'for he's busy enough!'

Tim was the only burglar with a brogue in the city, and as such was dear to the heart of Mistress Hare. For the Scot, when he takes to the investigation of other people's houses, does so grimly and without romance. But Tim had always a hint of Celtic imagination and even poetry in his creations.

For instance, all that day on which Cleg kept his eye on his father, Tim was meditating a raid on the house of Mr. Robert Greg Tennant, a comfortable burgess of the burgh, who for the ease of his later life had built himself—not a lordly pleasure house indeed, but a comfortable mansion of Craigleith stone, exactly like three hundred and sixty-five other mansions on the south side of the city.

There was at the back of Aurelia Villa a little bordering of flowers and strawberries. These, however, never came to much, for the cats broke the flowers and extraneous small boys stole the strawberries. There was also a little green plot, big enough for parlour-croquet, but not big enough for lawn-tennis. Yet this did not prevent the serious-minded and inventive young woman of the house, Miss Cecilia Tennant, from frequently playing what she called 'pocket-handkerchief tennis' on this scraplet of lawn. And it was indeed a lively game, when two or three of her admirers arrived with racquets and rubber shoes to engage in the silk-striped summer strife.

When a couple of champions of the Blackhouse Club met on the same side of the net, they winked at each other, and amusement struggled with politeness within them. But when each one of their services came near to annihilating an opponent's nose, and as they sent their returns out of court and over boundary walls turn about with monotonous regularity, they changed their minds. Especially was this so, when Miss Cecilia Tennant and a certain Junior Partner in a mercantile concern in the town, put in with equal certainty next services and returns, dropping the ball unexpectedly into odd corners as if playing with egg spoons. They asked the Junior Partner how he did it. The Junior Partner said it was native genius. But perhaps the undisclosed fact that Cecilia Tennant and he played together three nights out of six on that lawn, had rather more to do with it. Pocket-handkerchief tennis is certainly convenient for some things. It keeps the players very close to one another, except when they fall out—an advantage which it shares with ballooning.

But Tim Kelly was not interested in this house because of the desirable young men who played tennis there, nor yet because of any love of the young woman for whose sweet sake they bought new scarves and frequented the neighbourhood on the chance of a casual meeting. On the contrary, to put it plainly, Timothy was after the spoons. Hall-marked silver was his favourite form of sport. And for this he had all the connoisseur's eagerness and appreciation.

His son was, on the contrary, exceedingly interested in the house itself. He was the most fervent of Miss Cecilia Tennant's admirers, though he had never told her so. This peculiarity he shared with a great many other young gentlemen, including every male teacher except two (already attached) in Hunker Court school.

Yet in spite of all this devotion, before midnight of that autumn night, Cleg Kelly, future Christian, became a burglar, and that upon the premises of his benefactress, Miss Cecilia Tennant. It happened in this wise.

Tim sat all day on the floor of his house at home. He did so from necessity, not from choice. For his apartment was airily furnished in the Japanese fashion, with little except a couple of old mattresses and as many rugs. There were no chairs. They had been removed by the landlord during Tim's last absence in the 'Calton,' in lieu of rent. So Tim sat on the floor and worked with a file among a bundle of keys and curiously constructed tools. There was, for instance, a great lever with a fine thin edge set sideways to slip beneath windows on stormy nights, when the wrench of the hasp from its fastening would not be heard.

There were delicate little keys with spidery legs which Tim looked at with great admiration, and loved more than he had ever loved his wife and all his relations. There were also complicated wrenching implements, with horror latent about them, as though they had come from some big, arm-chaired, red-glassed dental surgery. Tim Kelly was putting his tools to rights, and Cleg watched him intently, for he also was a conspirator.

At midday the boy vanished and reported himself at the police-sergeant's. He asked for a 'piece,' and the sergeant's wife told him to be off. She was busy and he might come back when the weans came in for their dinners. She had not time to be always giving the likes of him 'pieces' in the middle of the day.

Cleg did not care. He was not particularly hungry. But he hung about all afternoon in the neighbourhood of the police-station, and so pestered the good-natured policemen off duty, that one of them threatened him with a 'rare belting' if he did not quit.

Whereupon Cleg buttoned up his jacket, made to himself a paper helmet, and with a truncheon in his hand stalked about in front of the station, taking up stray dogs in the name of the law. One of these he had previously taught to walk upon its hind legs. This animal he arrested, handcuffed with a twist of wire, and paraded over against the station in a manner killingly comic—to the infinite amusement of the passers-by, as well as most detrimental to the sobriety and discipline of the younger officers themselves. But Cleg was seldom meddled with by the police. He was under the protection of the sergeant's wife, who so often gave him a 'piece.' She also gave 'pieces' sometimes to the officers at the station-house. For according as a policeman is fed, so is he. And it was the sergeant's wife who stirred the porridge pot. Therefore Cleg was let alone.

In this manner Cleg amused himself till dark, when he stole home. His father was already coming down the stairs. Cleg rapidly withdrew. His father passed out and took the narrowest lanes southward till he entered the Queen's Park under the immanent gloom of the Salisbury Crags. Cleg followed like his shadow. Tim Kelly often looked behind. He boasted that he could hear the tramp of the regulation police boot at least half a mile, and tell it from the tread of a circus elephant, and even from the one o'clock gun at the Castle. But he saw no silent boy tracking him noiselessly after the fashion of the Indian scout, so vividly described in the 'Bully Boys' Journal.'

Tim Kelly bored his way into the eye of a rousing south wind that 'reesled' among the bare bones of

Samson's Ribs, and hurled itself upon Edinburgh as if fully determined to drive the city off its long, irregular ridge into the North Sea. Bending sharply to the right, the burglar came among buildings again. He crossed the marshy end of Duddingstone Loch. It was tinderdry with the drought. At the end of a long avenue was to be seen the loom of houses, and the gleam of lights, as burgess's wife and burgess moved in this order to their bedrooms and disarrayed themselves for the night.

Tim Kelly hid behind a wall. Cleg crouched behind his father, but sufficiently far back not to attract his attention. Cleg was taking his first lessons in the great craft of speculation—which is the obtaining of your neighbour's goods without providing him with an equivalent in exchange. The trifling matter of your neighbour's connivance, requisite in betting and various stock transactions, escaped the notice of the Kellys. But perhaps after all that did not matter.

Aurelia Villa, the home of Miss Cecilia Tennant (incidentally also of her father, Mr. Robert Greg Tennant), darkened down early; for Mr. Robert Tennant was an early riser, and early rising means early bedding (and a very good thing too).

Tim Kelly knew all that, for his local knowledge was as astonishing as his methods of obtaining it were mysterious. It was not twelve of the clock when Tim drew himself over the wall out of the avenue, and dropped lightly as a cat upon the pocket-handkerchief lawn, which all the summer had been worn at the corners by the egg-spoon tennis of Cecilia and the Junior Partner.

Tim Kelly was at the back door in a minute. It was down three steps. He laid a bag of tools, which clinked a little as he took them out of his pocket, on the stone ledge of the step. It might be safer, he thought, to take a look round the house and listen for the hippopotamus tread of the regulation bull-hide. In a moment after Tim was round at the gable end flat among the strawberries. There it came! Clear and solemnising fell upon the pavement the tread of the law in all its majesty—a bull's-eye lantern swinging midships a sturdy girth, which could hardly, even by courtesy, be called a waist. Flash! Like a searchlight ran the rays of the lantern over the front of the property of Mr. Robert Greg Tennant.

But the regulation boots were upon the feet of a man of probity. The wearer opened the front gate, tramped up the steps, conscientiously tried the front door and dining-room window of the end house in the row. They were fast. All was well. Duty done. The owners might sleep sound. They paid heavy police rates to a beneficent local authority. Why should they not sleep well? But, alas! the regulation boots did not take any cognisance of Tim Kelly with his nose among the strawberries, nor of a small boy who, at that moment, was speeding over the waste fields and back yards into the Park. The small boy carried a parcel. He was a thief. This small boy was Cleg Kelly, the hero of this tale.

Timothy Kelly rose from among the strawberries with laughter and scorn in his heart. If the bobby had only gone to the back door instead of the front, there was a parcel there, which it would have made him a proud policeman to take to the head office. Tim Kelly stooped at the steps to take up his precious satchel of tools. His hand met the bare stone. His bag was gone! His heart dinned suddenly in his ears. This was not less than witchcraft. He had never been ten yards from them all the time. Yet the tools were gone without sound or sight of human being. Then there was an interval.

.   .   .   .

During this interval Tim Kelly expressed his opinions upon things in general. The details are quite unfit for publication.

But at that very moment, over at the end of Duddingstone Loch, a boy was whirling a small but heavy bag round his head.

'Once! Twice! Thrice—and away!' he cried with glee. Something hurtled through the air, and fell with a splash far in the black deeps of the loch. Generations after this the antiquary of the thirtieth century may find this bundle, and on the strength of it he will take away the honest character of our ancestors of the Iron Age, proving that burglary was commonly and scientifically practised among them. But the memory of Cleg Kelly will be clear.

Indeed, he was sound asleep when his father came in, breathing out threatenings and slaughter. Tim listened intently with his ear at his son's mouth, for it is well to be suspicious of every one. But Cleg's breathing was as natural and regular as that of an infant.

Yet there is no doubt whatever, that Cleg and not his father had been guilty of both burglary and theft that night; and that Duddingstone Loch was indictable for the reset of the stolen property.

Then Cleg Kelly, burglar, winked an eye at his father's back, and settled himself to sleep the genuine sleep of the just.

ADVENTURE VII

THE ADVENTURE OF THE COCKROACHES

One day Cleg Kelly became paper-boy at the shop of Mistress Roy at the top corner of Meggat's Close. And he wanted you to know this. He was no longer as the paper-boys who lag about the Waverley, waiting for stray luggage left on the platforms, nor even as this match-boy. He was in a situation.

His hours were from half-past six in the morning to half-past six in the morning, when he began again. His wages were three shillings a week—and his chance. But he was quite contented, for he could contrive his own amenities by the way. His father had been in a bad temper ever since he lost his tools, and so Cleg did not go home very often.

This was the way in which he got his situation and became a member of the established order of things, indeed, the next thing to a voter. There had been a cheap prepaid advertisement in the 'Evening Scrapbook' which ran as follows:—

'WANTED, *an active and intelligent message-boy, able to read and write. Must be well recommended as a Christian boy of good and willing disposition. Wages not large, but will be treated as one of the family.—Apply No. 2,301, "Scrapbook" Office.*'

THE COCKROACHES

Now Miss Cecilia Tennant thought this a most interesting and encouraging advertisement. She had been for a long time on the look-out for a situation to suit Cleg. The Junior Partner indeed could have been induced to find a place for Cleg in 'The Works,' but it was judged better that the transition from the freedom of the streets to the lettered ease of an office desk should be made gradually. So Celie Tennant went after this situation for Cleg in person.

The arrangement with Mistress Roy in the Pleasance was a little difficult to make, but Celie made it. She went down one clammy evening, when the streets were covered with a greasy slime, and the pavements reflected the gloomy sky. In the grey lamp-sprinkled twilight she reached the paper-shop. There were sheafs of papers and journals hung up on the cheeks of the door. Coarsely coloured valentines hung in the window, chiefly rude portraitures of enormously fat women with frying-pans, and of red-nosed policemen with batons to correspond.

Celie Tennant entered. There was a heavy smell of moist tobacco all about. The floor of the little shop was strewn with newspapers, apparently of ancient date, certainly of ancient dirt. These rustled and moved of themselves in a curious way, as though they had all untimely come alive. As indeed they had done, for the stir was caused by the cockroaches arranging their domestic affairs underneath. Celie lifted her nose a little and her skirts a good deal. It took more courage to stand still and hear that faint rustling than to face the worst bully of Brannigan's gang in the Sooth Back. She rapped briskly on the counter.

A man came shuffling out of the room in the rear. He was clad in rusty black, and had a short clay pipe in his mouth. His eyes were narrow and foxy, and he looked unwholesomely scaly—as if he had been soaked in strong brine for half a year, but had forgotten either to finish the process or to remove the traces of the incomplete pickling.

'Servant, m'am!' said he, putting his pipe behind him as he came into the shop.

'I was referred here—to this address—from the office of the " Evening Scrapbook,"' said Celie, with great dignity, standing on her tiptoes among the papers. 'I called about the situation of message-boy you advertised for.'

'Ye wasna thinkin' o' applyin' yersel'?' said the man, with a weak jocularity. 'For my ain part I hae nae objections to a snod bit lass, but the mistress michtna like it.'

Miss Cecilia Tennant looked at him in a way that would have frozen a younger man, but the frowsy object from the back shop only smirked and laughed. With care, the jest would serve him a week. He made up his mind to whom he would tell it when the lady was gone.

'I wish to recommend one of the boys from my class for the position. His name is Charles Kelly. He is a smart boy of about thirteen, and he is anxious to get good and steady work. What are the wages you offer?'

The man looked cunningly all about the shop. He craned his neck over the counter and looked up the street. He had a long-jointed body, and a neck that shut up and pulled out like a three-draw telescope. Celie Tennant shrank instinctively when the man protruded his head past her in this curious manner, as she might have shrunk from some loathly animal.

Then, having resumed his normal slouch behind

the counter, he looked at his visitant and said, 'The wage is half a croon a week, and his chance o' the drawer—the same as mysel'.'

'His chance of the drawer!' said Celie, not understanding.

'When *she's* oot,' the man continued, laying his finger against the side of his nose and winking with meaning and expression at his visitor. The expression of disgust at the corner of Miss Tennant's nose threatened to result in a permanent tilt, which might have been unbecoming, and which certainly would have frightened the Junior Partner.

'When she's oot,' repeated the frowsy one, confidentially, 'your friend is welcome to his chance o' the drawer—if,' he added, with infinite caution, 'she was to leave it unlocked, which she seldom does. It's lock'd the noo! See!' And he shook a greasy knob under the counter till the drawer rattled against the bolt of the lock. 'Oh, it's just like her! She aye does that when she gangs oot. She's an awsome near woman! She has nae confidence, nae open-hearted leeberality, sic' as a wife ought to hae wi' the husband of her bosom.'

'Do you want a message-boy, or do you not?' said Celie, who felt that in the interests of Cleg she would face a battery of artillery, but who really could not stand the rustling among the papers on the floor very much longer.

'Certain she do that!' said the man, 'an active boy, an intelligent boy, a Christian boy—half a croon a week—and his chance o' the drawer.'

Once more he protruded his head in that monstrously serpentine manner round the corner of the low shop-door. But this time he retracted it quick as lightning, and shuffled back into the room behind. Celie heard him throw himself on a chair, which groaned under him.

'I'm sleepin' noo,' he said, 'sleepin' soond. Dinna say that I ever spoke till ye, for I'll deny it if ye do!' he said.

Cecilia Tennant stood her ground bravely, though the newspapers on the floor rustled continuously. She wondered why the path of duty was such a cockroachy one. A moment afterwards a grim-looking, hard-faced woman entered. She was a tall woman, with a hooked nose and a broad masculine face. The eyes were at once fierce and suspicious. She marched straight round the counter, lifting the little flap at the back and letting it fall with a bang. The cat was sitting on the end of the counter nearest the door of the inner room. The woman took her hand and swept it from the board, as though she had merely knocked off a little dust. The cat went into the inner room like a projectile.

Then, having entrenched herself at the back of the counter, the fierce-eyed woman turned sharp round and faced Celie Tennant.

'Well?' she said, with a certain defiance in her tone such as women only use to one another, which was at once depreciatory and pitiful. The Junior Partner would have turned and fled, but Celie Tennant was afraid of no woman that walked.

'I came,' she said, clearly and coldly, 'to ask about the situation of message-boy for one of my Mission lads. I was sent here from the office of the newspaper. Has the situation been filled?'

'What is the boy's name?' asked the woman, twitching the level broad line of her black brows at her visitor.

'His name is Charles Kelly.'

'Son o' Tim Kelly that lives in the brickfield?' asked the woman quickly.

'I believe that is his father's name,' said Celie, giving back glance for glance.

'Then we dinna want the likes o' him here!' said the woman, half turning on her heel with a certain dark contempt.

'But my name is Cecilia Tennant of Glenleven Road, and I am quite willing to give security for the boy—to a reasonable amount, that is——' continued Celie, who had a practical mind and much miniature dignity.

'Will ye leave the money?' asked the woman, as if a thought struck her.

'Certainly not,' replied Celie, 'but I will write you a line stating that I hold myself responsible for anything he is proved guilty of stealing, to the extent of ten pounds.'

It was thus that Cleg Kelly became newsboy and general assistant to Mistress Roy and her husband at Roy's corner.

As Celie went out, she heard Mr. Roy stretching himself and yawning, as though awakening out of a deep sleep.

'Wha's that ye hae had in?' he inquired pleasantly.

'What business is that o' yours, ye muckle slabber?' returned his wife with instant aggression.

And the cockroaches continued to rustle all the time beneath the carpet of old newspapers.

ADVENTURE VIII

THE FLIGHT OF SHEEMUS

NEXT morning Cleg Kelly entered upon his duties. He carried orders to the various publishing offices for about two hundred papers in all. He had often been there before upon his own account, so that the crowd and the rough jocularity were not new to him. But now he practised a kind of austere, aristocratic *hauteur*. He was not any longer a mere prowler on the streets, with only a stance for which he might have to fight. He was a newsvendor's assistant. He would not even accept wager of battle upon provocation offered. He could, however, still kick; and as he had an admirable pair of boots with tackety soles an inch thick to do it with, he soon made himself the most generally respected boy in the crowd.

On returning to the Pleasance, he was admitted through the chink of the door by Mistress Roy, who was comprehensively dressed in a vast yellow flannel bed-gown, which grew murkier and murkier towards her feet. Her hair was tumbling about her eyes. That, too, was of a yellowish grey, as though part of the bed-gown had been ravelled out and attached loosely to her head. Feathers and woolly dust were stuck impartially over hair and bed-gown.

'Write the names on the papers as I cry them,' she said to Cleg, 'and look slippy.'

Cleg was quick to obey. He had, in fact, his pencil ready.

'Cready, number seventeen—three stairs back. Dinna write a' that. Write the name, an' mind the rest,' said Mistress Roy.

'MacVane, twenty-wan, shop,' and so on went the list interminably.

Mistress Roy kept no books, but in her memory she had the various counts and reckonings of all grades of her customers. She retained there, for instance, the exact amounts of the intricate scores of the boys who took in the 'Boys of the City.' She knew who had not paid for the last chapter of 'Ned Kelly ; or, the Iron-clad Australian Bushranger.' She had a mental gauge on the great roll of black twist tobacco which lay on the counter among old 'Evening Scraps.' She knew exactly how much there was in the casks of strong waters under the stairs, from which, every Sunday, her numerous friends and callers were largely entertained.

When Cleg went out to deliver his papers he had nearly a hundred calls to make. But such was his sense of locality and his knowledge of the district that, with the help of a butcher's boy of his acquaintance (to whom he promised a reading of the 'Desperadoes of New Orleans ; or, the Good Ku Klux'), he managed to deliver all—except a single 'Scotsman' to one Mackimmon, who lived in a big 'land' at the corner of Rankeillor Street. Him he was utterly unable to discover.

Upon his return Mistress Roy was waiting for him.

'Did ye deliver them a'?' she asked, bending forward her head in a threatening manner as if expecting a negative reply.

'A' but yin!' said Cleg, who was in good spirits and pleased with himself.

His mistress took up a brush. Cleg's hand dropped lightly upon a pound weight. He did not mean to play the abused little message-boy if he knew it.

'And what yin might that be?' said Mistress Roy.

'Mackimmon,' said the boy briefly. 'He's no in Rankeillor Street ava'.'

The hand that held the brush went back in act to throw. Now this was, from the point of view of psychological dynamics, a mistake in tactics. A woman should never attempt to throw anything in controversy, least of all a brush. Her stronghold is to advance to the charge with all her natural weapons and vigour. But to throw a brush is to abdicate her providential advantages. And so Mistress Roy found.

A straight line is the shortest distance between two points, and that was the course described by the pound weight on which Cleg Kelly dropped his hand. It sped fair and level from his fingers, flung low as many a time he had skimmed stones on Saint Margaret's Loch in the hollow under the Crags.

'*Ouch!*' said suddenly Mistress Roy, taken, as she herself said, 'in the short of the wind.' The hearth-brush with which she had been wont to correct her former message-boys fell helplessly to the ground.

'Fetch me a toothfu' frae the back o' the door. Oh, ye villain, Cleg Kelly! I'm a' overcome like,' she said.

Cleg went to the back of the door, where there was

a keg with a spigot. He brought his mistress a drink in a little tinnikin.

She seemed to have forgotten to be angry, and bent her brows upon him more pleasantly than she had yet done.

'I thocht that ye were a religious boy,' she said.

Cleg stood back a little with Mackimmon's paper still in his hand.

'Pund wecht for besom shank is good religion,' said the imperfect Christian but excellent message-boy.

'Gang and deliver that paper!' Mistress Roy commanded, again looking up.

'I want my breakfast,' said Cleg, with an air of sullen determination.

His mistress looked at him a moment, still sitting with the tinnikin of undutied whisky in her hand, and occasionally taking a sip. Cleg eyed her levelfronted.

She gave in all at once.

'Tak' the knife and help yoursel',' she grumbled, pointing to a loaf and a piece of yellow cheese.

She went into a back room.

'Get up, Jock,' she said, giving the clothes a jerk over the foot of the bed, and seizing a water-can. Her husband rose to his feet on the floor without a word. Thus was business begun in Mistress Roy's paper-shop on the Pleasance.

And so that day went on, the first of many. When Celie Tennant asked Cleg how he was getting on, he said, as the manner of his kind is, 'Fine!' And no word more could she get out of him. For Cleg was not a boy to complain. His father, Timothy Kelly, was safely in gaol, and that of itself was enough to give Cleg an interest in life. Moreover, he could save part of his three shillings a week to give to Vara Kavannah to help her with the children.

He had not as yet taken advantage of the 'chance of the drawer' offered by Mr. Roy. But, on the other hand, he had stuck out for three silver shillings and his keep.

Also, as the advertisements which he read every day in the papers said, he meant to see that he got it.

Vara Kavannah was a friend of Cleg's. She lived with her mother in a poor room in the Tinklers' Lands, and she tried to do her duty by her little baby brother Gavin and her younger brother Hugh. Her mother was a friend of Mr. Timothy Kelly's, and there is no more to be said. The only happy time for all of them was when both Mr. Kelly, senior, and Sal Kavannah were provided for in the gaol on the Calton. But this did not happen often at one time. When it did, Cleg went up the long stairs and told Vara. Then they started out and took the baby and Hugh for a long walk in the Queen's Park. Cleg carried the baby. The boys of his own age did not mock him to his face for doing this. The Drabble had done it once, and severely regretted it for several days, during which time his features conveyed a moral lesson to all beholders.

It was also a happy time for Vara Kavannah when her mother was safely locked up on a long sentence, or when for some weeks she disappeared from the city. Her father, a kindly, weak man, stood the dog's life his wife led him as long as possible.

Sheemus Kavannah was a poet. The heart was in him which tells men that the world is wide and fair. He had endured his shame in the bitterness of his heart, till late one evening he rose, and with his wife lying on the floor, a log, he awaked his little lass. There were tears streaming down his cheeks. His daughter started from her bed with all her hair floating about her shoulders. She was used to sudden and painful wakenings.

'Vara,' he said, speaking in Irish, 'daughter of Sheemus, Vara Kavannah, hark to me. Mavourneen, my heart is broke with your mother. It's no good at all to stay. I am going to Liverpool for work, and when I get it I shall come back and take you away—you Vara, and Hugh and little Gavin. Lonely shall my road be and far. But I shall return, I shall return!'

Now Vara, being bred where they spoke not the tongue of the old country, understood nothing but the last words, 'I shall return, I shall return!'

So it was in this way that Cleg Kelly became father and mother to the little company of three in the Tinklers' Lands.

As he went on the way of his duty, he found out some things about the business capacity of Mistress Roy that would have astonished the police. He had, in the impetuous ardour of youth, cleared away the accumulated papers on the floor, and raided the swarming cockroaches.

'Hullo, mother, what's the matter here?' cried one of the customers of the place, coming to Mistress Roy, who sat in the little den at the back.

'Naething,' said that lady. 'It's only that daft laddie. He disna think I gie him aneuch to do, so he's ta'en to finding wark for himsel'.'

The customer, a burly, clean-shaven man, took a long look at Cleg.

'Tim Kelly's kid,' said the woman by way of explanation.

The man whistled—a long mellow whistle—with an odd turn at the end.

'No,' said Mistress Roy, shaking her head, 'the lad's square. And what's mair, I'm no gaun to hae him meddled. He's the first boy that ever took oot the papers without cheatin'.' A good character is a valuable asset, even in a shebeen.

ADVENTURE IX

THE WARMING OF THE DRABBLE

THE Kavannahs lived in the Tinklers' Lands at the foot of Davie Dean's Street. That was where Sheemus Kavannah left them when he went to Liverpool to seek work. Originally they had lived on the second floor of this great rabbit warren of a land, but now they had sunk till they occupied one room of the cellar. Their sole light came from an iron grating let into the pavement.

The Kavannahs had no furniture. It was just possible for Vara to get some little things together during the periods when her mother was under the care of the authorities. But as soon as Sal Kavannah came out, everything that would sell or pawn was instantly dissolved into whisky.

At all times it was a sore battle in the Tinklers' Lands, for these were the days before city improvements. In his wildest days Cleg Kelly had always befriended the Kavannahs, and he had been as much Vara's friend on the sly, as a boy could be who valued the good opinion of his companions. But when Cleg grew stronger in his muscles and less amenable to public opinion, he openly announced that he would 'warm' any boy who said a word to him about the Kavannahs.

One day he heard that Archie Drabble had kicked over the Kavannahs' family bed, and left it lying, when Vara was out getting some things for the children. Cleg started out to look up the Drabble. He had formerly had an interview with that gentleman, which has been chronicled elsewhere.[1] Cleg Kelly was on the way to reformation now, so would not kick the Drabble. But as a faithful friend he would 'warm' him for his soul's good. Cleg did not mind doing this. It was an entirely congenial sphere of Christian work.

The Drabble was found trying to steal collars off a clothes-line at the back of Arthur Street. Cleg Kelly had no objections to this feat. He was not a policeman, and if the Drabble wished to get into the lock-up, it was not his business. But first of all he must settle the matter of the Kavannahs' bed. After that the Drabble, an it liked him, might steal all the collars in the Pleasance.

'Drabble!' cried Cleg, 'come here, I want ye!'

'Want away,' cried the Drabble. 'Gang and say yer prayers!'

This was intended for an insult, and so Cleg took it.

'Ye had better say yours!' he retorted. 'Certes, when I catch you, it'll no be ordinar' prayers that will help you!'

Cleg had a disbelief in the efficacy of the prayers of the wicked which was thoroughly orthodox. The Drabble was of the wicked. Once he had thrown mud at a Sunday School teacher. Cleg only threw snow, as soft as he could get it.

There was a wall between Cleg and the Drabble, a wall with a place for your toes. With his boots off Cleg could have shinned up like a cat. But three-

---

[1] *The Stickit Minister*, 11th edition, p. 153.

shilling boots with toe caps are tender things and need to be treated with respect. Whereupon Cleg had resort to guile.

'Hae ye seen the last number o' "Gory Dick, the Desprader of the Prairies," Drabble?' cried Cleg over the wall.

'Gae 'way, man, an' eat sawdust, you paper-boy!' cried the Drabble over the wall.

The Drabble was of the more noble caste of the sneak thief. He had still his eye on the collars. Cleg raged impotently. All his Irishry boiled within him.

'Be the powers, Archie Drabble, wait till I catch ye. I'll not leave a leevin' creature on ye from head to fut!'

The completeness of this threat might have intimidated the Drabble, but he was on the safe side of the wall, and only laughed. He had a vast contempt for Cleg, inasmuch as he had forsaken the good and distinguished ways of Timothy Kelly, his father, and taken to Missions and Sunday Schools. Cleg foamed in helpless fury at the foot of the wall. He grew to hate his boots and his mended clothes, in his great desire to get at the Drabble. To his original sin with regard to the bed of the Kavannahs, the Drabble had now added many actual transgressions. Cleg was the vindicator of justice, and he mentally arranged to a nicety where and how he would punch the Drabble.

But just then the Drabble came over the wall at a run. He had been spotted from a distance by an active young officer, Constable Gilchrist, who was noted for his zeal in providing for the youth of the south side. The Drabble dropped to the ground like a cat, with the drawn pale face and furtive eyes which told Cleg that the 'poliss' were after him.

Without doubt Cleg ought to have given the offender up to justice, as a matter of private duty. He might thus also have settled his own matters with the pursued. But the traditional instincts of the outlaw held. And, seeing the double look which the Drabble turned up and down the street, he said softly,

'Here, Drabble; help me to deliver thae papers.'

The Drabble glanced at Cleg to make out if he meant to sell him to justice. That was indeed almost an impossibility. But the Drabble did not know how far the evil communications of Sunday Schools might have corrupted the original good manners of the Ex-Captain of the Sooth-Back Gang.

However, there was that in Cleg's face which gave him confidence. The Drabble grabbed the papers and was found busily delivering them up one side of the street while Cleg Kelly took the other, when Constable Gilchrist, reinforced by a friend, came in sight over the wall by the aid of a clothes-prop and the nicks in the stones.

Now, the peaceful occupation of delivering evening newspapers is not a breach of the peace nor yet a contravention of the city bylaws. Constable Gilchrist was disappointed. He was certain that he had seen that boy 'loitering with intent'; but here he was peacefully pursuing a lawful avocation. The Drabble had a reason, or at least an excuse, for being on the spot. So the chase was in vain, and Constable Gilchrist knew it. But his companion was not so easily put off the scent.

'Cleg Kelly,' he cried, 'I see you; hae you a care, my son, or you'll end up alongside of your father.'

'Thank ye, sir,' said Cleg Kelly. 'Buy a *News*, sir.'

'Be off, you impudent young shaver!' cried the sergeant, laughing.

And Cleg went off.

'That's a smart boy, and doing well,' said Constable Gilchrist.

'Decent enough,' returned the sergeant, 'but he's in a bad shop at Roy's, and he'll get no good from that Drabble loon!'

And this was the truth. But at that very moment, at the back of the Tinklers' Lands, the Drabble was getting much good from Cleg Kelly. Cleg had off his coat and the Drabble was being 'warmed.'

'That'll learn ye to touch the Kavannahs' bed!' cried Cleg.

And the Drabble sat down.

'That's for miscaain' my faither!'

The Drabble sat down again at full length.

'That's for tellin' me to say my prayers! I'll learn you to meddle wi' my prayers!'

Thus Cleg upheld the Conscience Clause.

But the Drabble soon had enough. He warded Cleg off with a knee and elbow, and stated what he would do when he met him again on a future unnamed occasion.

He would tell his big brother, so he would, and his big brother would smash the face of all the Kellys that ever breathed.

Cleg was not to be outdone.

'I'll tell *my* big brother on you, Drabble. He can fecht ten polissmen, and he could dicht the street wi' your brither, and throw him ower a lamp-post to dry.'

Cleg and the Drabble felt that they must do something to uphold the honour of their respective houses, for this sort of family pride is a noble thing and much practised in genealogies.

So, pausing every ten yards to state what their several big brothers would do, and with the fellest intentions as to future breaches of the peace, the combatants parted. The afternoon air bore to the Drabble from the next street—

'*You—let—the Kavannahs—alane frae this oot—or it'll be the waur for you!*'

The Drabble rubbed his nose on his sleeve, and thought that on the whole it might be so.

Then he took out the three papers which he had secreted up his sleeve, and went joyfully and sold them. The Drabble was a boy of resource. Cleg had to come good for these papers to Mistress Roy, and also to bear her tongue for having lost them. She stopped them out of his wages. Then Cleg's language became as bad as that of an angry Sunday School superintendent. The wise men say that the Scots dialect is only Early English. Cleg's was that kind, but much debased by an admixture of Later Decorated.

He merely stated what he meant to do to the Drabble when he met him again. But the statement entered so much into unnecessary detail that there is no need to record it fully

ADVENTURE X

THE SQUARING OF THE POLICE

CLEG was free and barefoot. His father was 'in' for twelve months. Also it was the summer season, and soft was the sun. The schools were shut—not that it mattered greatly as to that, for secular education was not much in Cleg's way, compulsory attendance being not as yet great in the land. Cleg had been spending the morning roosting on railings and 'laying for softies'—by which he meant conversing with boys in nice clean jackets, with nice clean manners, whose methods of war and whose habit of speech were not Cleg's.

Cleg had recently entered upon a new contract with the mistress of Roy's paper shop. He was now 'outdoor boy' instead of 'indoor boy,' and he was glad of it. He had also taken new lodgings. For when the police took his father to prison, to the son's great relief and delight, the landlord of the little room by the brickfield had cast the few sticks of furniture and the mattress into the street, and, as he said, 'made a complete clearance of the rubbish.' He included Cleg.

But it was not so easy to get rid of Cleg, for the boy had his private hoards in every crevice and behind every rafter. So that very night, with the root of a candle which he borrowed from a cellar window to which he had access (owing to his size and agility), he went back and ransacked his late home. He prised up the boards of the floor. He tore aside the laths where the plaster had given way. He removed the plaster itself with a tenpenny nail where it had been recently mended. He tore down the entire series of accumulated papers from the ceiling, disturbing myriads of insects both active and sluggish, which do not need to be further particularised.

'I'll learn old Skinflint to turn my faither's property oot on the street,' said Cleg, his national instinct against eviction coming strongly upon him. 'I'll wager I can make this place so that the man what built it winna ken it the morn's morning!'

And he kept his word. When Nathan, the Jew pawnbroker and cheap jeweller, came with his men to do a little cleaning up, the scene which struck them on entering as a stone strikes the face, was, as the reporters say, simply appalling. The first step Mr. Nathan took brought down the ceiling-dust and its inhabitants in showers. The next took him, so far as his legs were concerned, into the floor beneath, for he had stepped through a hole, in which Cleg had discovered a rich deposit of silver spoons marked with an entire alphabet of initials.

The police inspector was summoned, and he, in his turn, stood in amaze at the destruction.

'It's that gaol-bird, young Kelly!' cried Nathan, dancing and chirruping in his inarticulate wrath. 'I'll have him lagged for it—sure as I live.'

'Aye?' said the inspector, gravely. He had his own reasons for believing that Mr. Nathan would do nothing of the sort. 'Meantime, I have a friend who will be interested in this place.'

And straightway he went down and brought him. The friend was the Chief Sanitary Inspector, a medical man of much emphasis of manner and abruptness of utterance.

'What's this? What's this? Clear out the whole damnable pig-hole! What d'ye mean, Jackson, by having such a sty as this in your district? Clean it out! Tear it down! It's like having seven bulls of Bashan in one stable. Never saw such a hog's mess in my life. Clear it out! Clear it out!'

The miserable Nathan wrung his hands, and hopped about like a hen.

'Oh, Doctor Christopher, I shall have it put in beautiful order—beautiful order. Everything shall be done in the besht style, I do assure you——'

'Best style, stuff and nonsense! Tear it down—gut it out—take it all away and bury it. I'll send men to-morrow morning!' cried the doctor decidedly.

And Dr. Christopher departed at a dog-trot to investigate a misbehaving trap in a drain at Coltbridge.

The police inspector laughed.

'Are you still in a mind to prosecute young Kelly, Mr. Nathan?' he said.

But the grief and terror of the pawnbroker were beyond words. He sat down on the narrow stair, and laid his head between his hands.

'I shall be ruined—ruined! I took the place for a debt. I never got a penny of rent for it, and now to be made to spend money upon it——'

The police inspector touched him on the shoulder.

'If I were you, Nathan,' he said, 'I should get

this put in order. If it is true that you got no rent for this place, the melting-pot in your back cellar got plenty.'

'It's a lie—a lie!' cried the little man, getting up as if stung. 'It was never proved. I got off!'

'Aye,' said the inspector, 'ye got off? But though "Not proven" clears a man of the Calton Gaol, it keeps him on our books.'

'Yes, yes,' said the little Jew, clapping his hands as if he were summoning slaves in the Arabian Nights, 'it shall be done. I will attend to it at once.'

And the inspector went out into the street, laughing so heartily within himself, that more than once something like the shadow of a grin crossed the stern official face which covered so much kindliness from the ken of the world.

The truth of the matter was that Cleg Kelly had squared the police. It is a strange thing to say, for the force of the city is composed of men staunchly incorruptible. I have tried it myself and know. The Edinburgh police has been honourably distinguished first by an ambition to prevent crime, next, to catch the criminal, and, lastly, to care for the miserable women and children whom nearly every criminal drags to infamy in his wake.

Yet with all these honourable titles to distinction, upon this occasion the police had certainly been squared, and that by Cleg Kelly. And in this wise.

When Cleg had finished his search through the receptacles of his father and his own hidie-holes, he found himself in possession of as curious a collection of miscellaneous curiosities as might stock a country museum or set a dealer in old junk up in business. There were many spoons of silver, and a few of Britannia metal which his father had brought away in mistake, or because he was pressed for time and hated to give trouble. There were forks whole, and forks broken at the handle where the initials ought to have come, teapots with the leaves still within them, the toddy bowl of a city magnate—with an inscription setting forth that it had been presented to Baillie Porter for twenty years of efficient service in the department of cleaning and lighting, and also in recognition of his uniform courtesy and abundant hospitality. There were also delicate ormolu clocks and nearly a score of watches, portly verge, slim Geneva, and bluff serviceable English lever.

Cleg brought one of his mother's wicker clothes-baskets which had been tossed out on the street by Mr. Nathan's men the day before, and, putting a rich Indian shawl in the bottom to stop the crevices, he put into it all the spoil, except only such items as belonged strictly to himself, and with which the nimble fingers of his father had had no connection.

Such were the top half of a brass candlestick, which he had himself found in an ash-backet on the street. He remembered the exact ' backet.' It was in front of old Kermack, the baker's, and he had had to fight a big dog to get possession, because, the brass at the top being covered with grease, the dog considered the candlestick a desirable article of *vertu*. There was a soap-box, for which he had once fought a battle ; the basin he used for dragging about by a string on the pavement, with hideous outcries, whenever the devil within made it necessary for him to produce the most penetrating and objectionable noise he could think of. There was also (his most valuable possession) a bright brass harness rein-holder, for which the keeper of a livery stable had offered him five shillings if he would bring the pair, or sixpence for a single one—an offer which Cleg had declined, but which had made him ever after cherish the rein-holder as certainly worth more than all the jewellers' shops on Princes Street.

These and other possessions to which his title was incontrovertible he laid aside for conveyance to his new home, an old construction hut which now lay neglected in a builder's yard near the St. Leonards Station.

All the other things Cleg took straight over to the police-office near the brickfield, where his friend, the sergeant's wife, held up her hands at sight of them. And she delayed to call her husband till she had been assured that Cleg had personally had nothing to do with the collection of them.

When the sergeant came in his face changed and his eyes glittered, for here was stolen property in abundance, of which the Chief—that admirable gentleman of the quiet manners and the remorseless memory —had long ago given up all hope.

'Ah! if only the young rascal had brought us these things before Tim's trial, I could have got him twenty years!' said the Chief.

But though Cleg Kelly hated and despised his father, his hatred did not quite go that length. He did not love the police for their own sake, though he was friendly enough with many of the individual officers—in especial, with the sergeant's wife, who gave him 'pieces' in memory of his mother, and, being a woman, also perhaps a little in memory of what his father had once seemed to her.

Cleg did not stay to be asked questions as to how he came into possession of so many valuables. He

THE SQUARING OF THE POLICE

had found them, he said ; but he could not be induced to condescend upon the particulars of the discovery.

The sergeant was forced to be content. But ever after this affair it was quite evident that Cleg was a privileged person, and did not come within Mr. Nathan's power of accusation. So it was manifest that Cleg Kelly had corrupted the incorruptible, and crowned his exploits by squaring the metropolitan police.

ADVENTURE XI

THE BOY IN THE WOODEN HUT

THE wooden hut where Cleg had taken up his abode was on the property of a former landlord, who in his time had tired of Tim Kelly as a tenant, and had insisted upon his removal, getting his office safe broken into in consequence. But Mr. Callendar had never been unkind to Isbel and Cleg. So the boy had kindly memories of the builder, and especially he remembered the smell of the pine shavings as Callendar's men planed deal boards to grain them for mahogany. The scent struck Cleg as the cleanest thing he had ever smelled in his life.

So, with the help of an apprentice joiner, he set up the old construction hut, which, having been used many years ago in the making of the new coal sidings at the St. Leonards Station, had been thrown aside at the end of the job, and never broken up.

The builder saw Cleg flitting hither and thither about the yard, but, being accustomed to such visitors, he took no great notice of the boy till one day, poking about among some loose rubbish and boards at the back of his premises, he happened to glance at the old hut. Great was his astonishment to see it set on its end, a window frame too large for the aperture secured on the outside by large nails driven in at the corners, a little fringe of soil scraped roughly about it as if a brood of chickens had worked their way round the hut, and a few solitary daisies dibbled into the loose earth, lying over on their sides, in spite of the small ration of water which had been carefully served out to each.

Thomas Callendar stood a moment gathering his senses. He had a callant of his own who might conceivably have been at the pains to establish a summer-house in his yard. But then James was at present at the seaside with his mother. The builder went round the little hut, and at the further side he came upon Cleg Kelly dribbling water upon the drooping daisies from a broken brown teapot, and holding on the lid with his other hand.

'Mercy on us! what are ye doing here, callant?' cried the astonished builder.

Cleg Kelly stood up with the teapot in his hand, taking care to keep the lid on as he did so. His life was so constant a succession of surprises provided against by watchfulness, that hardly even an earthquake would have taken him unprepared.

He balanced the teapot in one hand, and with the other he pulled at his hat-brim to make his manners.

'If ye please, sir,' he said, 'they turned me oot at the brickyaird, and I brocht the bits o' things here. I kenned ye wadna send me away, Maister Callendar.'

'How kenned ye that I wadna turn ye away, boy?' said the builder.

'Oh, I juist preferred to come back here, at ony rate,' said Cleg.

'But why?' persisted Mr. Callendar.

Cleg scratched the turned-up earth of his garden thoughtfully with his toe.

'Weel,' he said, 'if ye maun ken, it was because I

had raither lippen [1] to the deil I ken, than to the deil I dinna ken!'

The builder laughed good-naturedly.

'So ye think me a deil?' he asked, making believe to cut at the boy with the bit of planed moulding he was carrying in his hand, with black pencil marks at intervals upon it like a measuring-rod.

'Ow, it's juist a mainner o' speaking!' said Cleg, glancing up at Mr. Callendar with twinkling eyes. He knew that permission to bide was as good as granted. The builder came and looked within. The hut was whitewashed inside, and the black edges of the boards made transverse lines across the staring white.

Cleg explained.

'I didna steal the whitewash,' he said; 'I got it frae Andrew Heslop for helpin' him wi' his lime-mixing.'

'It's a fine, healthsome, heartsome smell,' the boy went on, noticing that the builder was sniffing. 'Oh, man, it's the tar that ye smell,' he again broke in. 'I'm gaun to tar it on the ootside. It keeps the weather off famous. I gat the tar frae a watchman at the end o' the Lothian Road, where they are laying a new kind o' pavement wi' an awesome smell.'

The interior of the hut was shelved, and upon a pair of old trestles lay a good new mattress. The builder looked curiously at it.'

'It was the Pleasance student missionary got it in, for my mither to lie on afore she died,' said Cleg in explanation.

'Aye, and your mither is awa,' said the builder; 'it's a release.'

'Aye, it is that,' said Cleg, from whose young

[1] Trust.

heart sorrow of his mother's death had wholly passed away. He was not callous, but he was old-fashioned and world-experienced enough to recognise facts frankly. It was a release indeed for Isbel Kelly.

'Weel,' said the builder, 'mind ye behave yoursel'. Bring nae wild gilravage o' loons here, or oot ye gang.'

'Hearken ye, Maister,' said Cleg. 'There's no a boy atween Henry Place an' the Sooth Back that wull daur to show the ill-favoured face o' him within your muckle yett. I'll be the best watch that ever ye had, Maister Callendar. See if I'm no!'

The builder smiled as he went away. He took the measuring-rod of white moulding in his hand, and looked at the marks to recall what particular business he had been employed upon. But even as he did so a thought struck him. He turned back.

'Mind you,' he said to Cleg, 'the first time that ye bring the faither o' ye aboot my yaird, to the curbstane ye gang wi' a' your traps and trantlums!'

Cleg peeped elvishly out of his citadel.

'My faither,' he said, 'is snug in a far grander hoose than yours or mine, Maister Callendar. He has ta'en the accommodation for a year, and gotten close wark frae the Government a' the time!'

'What mean ye?' said the builder; 'your faither has never reformed?'

'Na, no that,' answered Cleg; 'but he got a year for ganging intil anither man's hoose without specring his leave. And I was there and saw the judge gie him a tongue-dressing afore he spoke oot the sentence. "One year!" says he. "Make it three, my Lord!" says I frae the back of the coort. So they ran me oot; but my faither kenned wha it was, for he cried, "May hunger, sickness, and trouble suck the life from ye, ye bloodsucking son of my sorrow! Wait till I get hoult o' ye! I'll make ye melt off the earth like the snow off a dyke, son o' mine though ye are!"'

The respectable builder stood aghast.

'And your ain faither said the like o' that till ye?' he exclaimed, with a look of awe in his face as if he had been listening to blasphemy. 'And what did you say to him?'

'Faith! I only said, "I hope ye'll like the oakum, faither!"'

ADVENTURE XII

VARA KAVANNAH OF THE TINKLERS' LANDS

CLEG, having finished his dispositions, shut to his door, and barred it with a cunning bolt shot with string, which he had constructed temporarily, till he should be able to find an old lock to manipulate with the craft inherited from his father. Then he set forth for the Tinklers' Lands, to visit his friends the Kavannahs. He had delivered his papers in the early morning, and now he was free till the evening. For since a threatened descent of the police, Mistress Roy, that honest merchant, had discouraged Cleg from 'hanging round' after his work was finished. In fact, she attempted to do the discouraging with a broomstick or anything else that came handy. But Cleg was far too active to be struck by a woman. For, turning upon his mistress with a sudden flash of teeth like the grin of a wild cat, he sent that lady back upon the second line of her defences—into the little back shop where that peculiar company assembled which gave to Roy's paper-shop its other quality of shebeen.

Cleg had just reached the arched gateway which led into the builder's yard, when he saw, pottering along the side-walk twenty yards before him, the squat, bandy-legged figure of his late landlord, Mr. Nathan. He had been going the round of the builders, endeavouring to discover which of them would effect the repairs upon Tim Kelly's mansion at the least expense, and at the same time be prepared to do it so as to satisfy the fiery Inspector of Sanitation.

Without a moment's hesitation, and as a mere matter of duty, Cleg bent his head, and, running full-tilt between his late landlord's legs, he overset him on the pavement and shot ahead on his way to make his morning call on the Kavannahs. The mere fulfilment of healthy natural function required that a well-conducted boy of good principles should cheek a policeman and overset a Jew landlord whenever met with. In such a holy war there could be no truce or parley.

Tinklers' Lands was in one of the worst parts of the city. Davie Dean's Street goes steeply down-hill, and has apparently carried all its inhabitants with it. Tinklers' Lands is quite at the foot, and the people there have come so low that they can fear no further fall. The Kavannahs, as has been said, dwelt in the deepest cellar of the worst house in Tinklers' Lands.

Cleg ran down into the area and bent over the grating.

'Vara!' he cried, making a trumpet of the bars and his hands.

'Aye, Cleg, is that you?' said Vara. '*She's* oot; ye can come in.'

So Cleg trotted briskly down the slimy black steps, from which the top hand-rail had long since vanished. The stumpy palings themselves would also have disappeared, if they had been anything else than cast metal, a material which can neither be burned nor profitably disposed of to the old junk man.

Vara met him at the foot. She was a pleasant round-faced, merry-eyed girl of ten—or, rather, she would have been round-faced but for the pitiful drawing about the mouth, and the frightened furtive look with which she seemed to shrink back at any sudden movement near her. As Cleg arrived at the door of the cellar a foul, dank smell rose from the depths to meet him; and he, fresh from the air and cleanliness of his own new abode among the shavings and the chips, noticed it as he would not have done had he come directly from the house by the brickfield.

'She gaed awa' last nicht wi' an ill man,' said Vara, 'and I hae seen nocht o' her since.'

Vara Kavannah spoke of Sheemus Kavannah as 'faither,' but always of her mother as 'she.' To-day the girl had her fair hair done up in a womanly net and stowed away on the top of her head. When one has the cares of a house and family, it is necessary to dress in a grown-up fashion. Indeed, in some of her moods, when the trouble of Hugh and the baby lay heavy on her, Vara looked like a little old woman, or as if she had been her own fairy godmother fallen upon evil times.

But to-day she had her head also tied up in a napkin, rolled white and smooth about her brows. Cleg glanced at the bandage with the quick comprehension which comes from a kindred bitterness.

'Her?' he queried, as much with his thumb and eyebrow as with his voice.

'Aye,' said Vara, looking down at the floor (for in the Lands such occurrences were not spoken of outside the family), 'yestreen.'

Hearing the voices at the door, little Hugh, Vara's brother, came toddling unevenly upon legs which ought to have been chubby, but which were only feeble and uncertain. He had one hand wrapped in a piece of white rag; and, whenever he remembered, he carried it in his other hand and wept over it with a sad, wearying whimper.

Cleg again looked his query at Vara.

'Aye,' said the girl, her eyes lighting this time with a glint of anger; 'the bairn toddled to her when she cam' hame, and he asked for a bit piece. And wi' that she took him and gied him a fling across the floor, and he hurt his airm on the corner of the bed.'

And Cleg, though he had given up swearing, swore.

'The wean's asleep!' said Vara; 'speak quietly.'

And upon tiptoe she led the way. The dusk of the cellar was so dense and the oppression of the foul air so terrible that had not Cleg been to the manner born, he could hardly have reached the little crib where the baby lay huddled among swathings of old petticoats and bits of flannel, while underneath was a layer of hay for a bed.

Vara stood gazing with inexpressible rapture at the babe.

'Isna he bonny—bonny?'

She clasped her hands as she spoke, and looked for the answering admiration in Cleg's face.

'Aye,' said Cleg, who knew what was demanded of him, if he expected to remain any longer Vara Kavannah's friend; 'he's juist terrible bonny—as neat as a pictur'!'

He had heard his father say that of a new 'jemmy.'

In good truth, the babe was but skin and bone, with the drawn face of a mummy of five thousand years—and tiny wrinkled hands, prehensile like those of a monkey.

'Vara,' said Cleg, 'ye canna bide here. I maun get ye awa'. This is no to be tholed. What hae ye had to eat the day?'

'We had some broth that a neighbour brocht in

yesterday and some fish. But the fish was bad,' said Vara, flushing and hesitating to say these things even to Cleg.

The badness of the fish, indeed, sufficiently advertised itself.

At the mention of something to eat little Hugh sharpened his croon of pain into a yell.

' Hugh's awsome hungry ! Hugh boy wants his dinner ! '

Vara went to him and knelt beside him.

' Hush thee, Hugh boy ! ' she said, speaking with a fragrance of motherliness which must have come to her from some remote ancestor, for certainly never in her life had she experienced anything like it. ' Hush ! Hugh boy shall have his dinner if he is a good boy. Poor handie ! Poor, poor handie ! '

And the girl took the swollen wrist and torn hand into hers and rocked to and fro with the boy on her knee.

' Hugh is gaun to be a man,' she said. ' He wadna greet. Na, he will wait till faither comes hame. And then he will get ham, nice ham, singing in the pan ; aye, and red herring brandering on the fire, and salmon in tins, an' aipples, an' oranges, and cancellaries.'

' Losh, aye, but that wull be guid ! ' said Hugh, stopping his crying to listen to the enthralling catalogue.

' Aye,' said Vara, ' and when faither comes hame, he will tak' us away to a bonny hoose to leeve, where the ships sail by. For dadda has gane to the seaside to look for wark. It will be a bonny hoose wi' swings at every door, and blacky men that dance in braw, striped claes, and shows. And Hugh boy shall gang to them a'. We'll howk holes in the sand, and fill the dirt into buckets, and row our girds, Hughie. And we shall paidle in the tide, and splash the bonny water high aboon oor heids!'

'Oh, oh,' cried the child, 'Hugh boy wants to gang there noo. He wants to paidle in the bonny water and eat the oranges!'

'Bide ye, bonny man,' said Vara, fondling him, 'that's a' to be when dadda comes hame.'

'Hugh boy is gangin' to the door to look for dadda!' said the boy as he moved off with his bandaged hand clutched to his side.

The baby in the bunk among the old clouts set up a faint, elvish crying, and Cleg went to it, for he was touched to the heart by the voice of dumb things in pain, whether babes or beasts.

But little Gavin (called after a Scottish comrade of Sheemus Kavannah's who had been kind to him) was wrinkling all his face into a myriad crinkles. Then, lifting up the tiniest shrill pipe, he wept with the cry of underfed and ill-used childhood—a cry that breaks off sharp in the middle and never attains to the lusty roar of the healthy and well-nourished malcontent.

Vara flew to Gavin and, taking the babe in her arms, she hushed him back again to sleep, making a swift gesture of command for silence. She kept her eyes fondly fixed upon the peaked little face, till the wailing ceased, the tiny clenched hand fell back from the puckered face, and the infant dropped again to sleep, clasping the frill of Vara's pinafore with fingers like bird claws.

'I was feared he wad waken an' I had no meat to gie him!' she explained, simply.

'God!' said Cleg; 'I canna stand this.'

And without a word he skimmed up the cellar

steps and out. He went straight to his mistress of the paper-shop, and with her he had a loud-voiced and surprisingly maledictory interview, in which he endeavoured to uplift his week's wage before it was due. There were threats and recriminations on both sides before a compromise was effected. It ended in the half, which had already been worked for, being paid over in view of the boy's instant necessities—which, it is to be regretted, Cleg did not quite truthfully represent to Mistress Roy.

Then, with two intact silver shillings in his hand, Cleg went and bought twopence worth of meat from the neck and a penny bone for boiling, a pennyworth of carrots, a halfpenny cabbage, a large four-pound loaf, and twopence worth of the best milk. To this he added two apples and an orange for Hugh, so that he might have a foretaste of the golden time when dadda should come home.

It was as good as a circus procession when Cleg went back laden like a bee, and no humble bee either, to the cellar in Tinklers' Lands. He walked with his head in the air and his chest out, just as he used to march when he heard the regiments coming down the High Street from the Castle, and caught the first glimpse of their swinging tartans and towering plumes.

Vara met him at the door. She raised her hands in amaze, but mechanically she checked the cry of gladness and admiration on her lips as Cleg came scrambling down, without ever minding his feet on the slippery stairs.

'Cleg Kelly!' said she, speaking under her breath, 'what are ye doin' wi' a' that meat?'

'Oh, it's naething ava,' said Cleg, lightly; 'it's juist some things that I had nae use for this week. Ye ken I'm watchman noo at Callendar's as weel as working at the paper-shop!'

'Save us!' said Vara, 'this is never a' for us. I canna tak' it. 'Deed I canna!'

'Aye, is it!' said Cleg, 'an' you tak' it for the bairns' sake. Sheemus will pay me when he comes back, gin ye like!'

Vara's heart broke out in a cry, 'O Cleg, I canna thank ye!' And her tears fairly rained down while she sobbed quickly and freely.

'Dinna, Vara, dinna, lassie!' said Cleg, edging for the door; 'ye maun stop that or I declare I'll hae to rin!'

From within came the babe's cry. But it had no terrors for Vara now.

'Greet, Gavin, greet,' she cried; 'aye, that is richt. Let us hear something like a noise, for I hae gotten something to gie ye at last.'

So she hasted and ran for the baby's bottle—which, as in all poor folks' houses, was one of Maw's best. She mixed rapidly the due proportions of milk and water, and tested the drawing of the tube with her mouth as she ran to the cot. At first the babe could not be brought to believe in the genuineness of the nourishment offered, so often had the cold comfort of the empty tube been palmed off upon him. It was a moment or two before he tasted the milk; but, as soon as he did so, his outcry ceased as if by magic, the puckers smoothed out, and the big solemn baby eyes fixed themselves on the ceiling of the cellar with a stare of grave ineffable rapture.

Then Cleg took himself off, with a hop and a skip up the steps, having seen Hugh settled to his bread and butter, eating eagerly and jealously, but never for a moment letting the orange, earnest of the Promised Land of his father's return, out of the firm clutch of his other hand. Vara was putting away the great store of provision in the empty cupboard, when Cleg looked his last down the grating which admitted the scanty light to the Kavannahs' home.

There had been few happier days in Cleg Kelly's life, than this on which he spent half of his week's wage for the benefit of the Kavannahs.

So altogether happy did he feel that as soon as he found himself in a respectable street, he went and cuffed the ears of two well-dressed boys only for looking at him. Then he threw their new bonnets in the gutter and departed in a perfect glow of happiness and philanthropy.

ADVENTURE XIII

CLEG'S SECOND BURGLARY

CLEG slept soundly on his bed within the whitewashed hut. The last thing he did the night before was to go to the bench where the men had been working, and bring an armful of the fragrant pine shavings for a bouquet to scent his chamber. And never did boy sleep better. It must be confessed, however, that the position of night-watchman at Callendar's, of which he had so confidently boasted to Vara Kavannah, was entirely a sinecure. For it was not till he heard the voices of the men clicking their tools and answering one another in gruff pre-breakfast monosyllables, that he realised he had changed his abode. Then he stirred so sharply that the mattress fell off the trestles, and Cleg was brought up all standing against the side of the hut.

All that day he went about his duties as usual. He trotted to the newspaper office and distributed his roll of papers mechanically; but his mind was with the Kavannahs, and he longed for the time to come when he could, with some self-respect, go and gloat over the results of his generosity. Doubtless there was a touch of self-glorification in this, which, however, he kept strictly to himself. But who will grudge it to a boy, who for the sake of a lassie has spent nearly half of his week's wage, and who knows that he will have to live on bread and water for ten days in consequence ?

Cleg judged that it would not be advisable for him to go to Tinklers' Lands before noon. So in the meanwhile he betook himself to Simon Square to 'lag for' Humpy Joe, who had called him 'Irishman' the previous evening, at a time when, with his papers under his arm, Cleg was incapacitated for warfare, being, like Martha, much cumbered with serving.

But Humpy Joe proved unattainable. For he had seen his enemy's approach, and as soon as Cleg set foot within the square, he saluted him with a rotten egg, carefully selected and laid aside for such an emergency. And had it not been for the habitual watchfulness of Cleg, Joe's missile would have 'got him.' But as it was, a sudden leap into the air like that of a jack-in-the-box just cleared the danger, and the egg, passing between Cleg's bare feet, made a long yolky mark of exclamation on the ground.

Being defeated in this, Humpy Joe looked forth from a gable window, and entertained the neighbourhood with a gratuitous and wholly untrustworthy account of Cleg's ancestors. And Cleg, in reply, devised ingenious tortures, which he declared at the shrillest pitch of his voice would be the portion of Humpy Joe, when next he caught him 'out.'

Then, after tiring of this, the embattled belligerents separated in high delight and with much mutual respect and good feeling, vowing the most sanguinary vengeances when next they should meet at Sunday-school.

At last the time came for Cleg the millionaire to feast his happy eyes upon the table which had been spread by his means for his friends the Kavannahs. But first he lingered awhile about the end of Davie Dean's Street, ostentatiously looking for a boy to lick, and throwing stones over the wall at the baker's fat watch-dog to make it bark. In reality he was making sure that none of his companions were in the neighbourhood, lest, with some colour of truth, they should cast up at him the capital offence of 'speaking to a lassie.'

At last the coast was clear. The only boy within half a mile had been chased under the protection of the great guns of his own fortress, being the vicinity of his mother's wash-tubs. Then Cleg dived quickly down to the cellar beneath Tinklers' Lands.

For the first time in his experience, the door was shut. Cleg had set his ear to the keyhole and listened. Then he put his eye there. But neither sense told him anything.

'Vara!' he cried softly, and set his ear against the floor. Cleg knew that the place to hear behind a door (if there is no danger of its being hastily opened) is not at the keyhole, but close to the floor. He listened, holding his breath. At first he could hear nothing; but in a little, a low choking sob detached itself at stated intervals from the cursory noises made by the other tenants of Tinklers' Lands and from the steady growl of the streets above.

'Vara!' he cried, a little louder; 'Vara Kavannah, are ye in? What's wrang?'

Still nothing came back to him but the faint mechanical sob, which wore his patience suddenly to the breaking point.

'They're a' killed,' said Cleg, who had once been at the opening of just such a door, and had seen that which was waiting within. 'I'll break open the lock.' And with that he dashed himself against it. But the strength of the bolt resisted his utmost endeavours.

'Cleg,' said a voice from within, very weak and feeble, 'gang awa' like a guid lad. Dinna come here ony mair——'

It was Vara's voice, speaking through pain and tears.

'Vara,' said Cleg, 'what's wrang? What for will ye no open the door?'

'I canna, Cleg; she's here, lyin' on the floor in the corner. I canna turn the key, for she has tied me to the bed-foot.'

Cleg instantly understood the circumstances. They were none so unprecedented in the neighbourhood of Tinklers' Lands. Sal Kavannah had come home drunk, singly or in company. She had abused the children, and ended by tying up Vara, lest she should go out and leave her while she lay in her drunken sleep. Such things had been done within Cleg's knowledge—aye, things infinitely worse than these. And with his sad unchildish wisdom Cleg feared the worst.

But he was not Tim Kelly's son for nothing. And it did not cost him a moment to search in his pockets for a fine strong piece of twine, such as all shoemakers use. He always carried at least ten sorts of cord about with him. This cobbler's string was a special brand, so wonderful that Cleg had made friends with the shoemaker's boy (whom he loathed as a sneak) solely in order to obtain it.

Cleg knew that the key was in the lock, but that the wards were turned clear, for his eyes, growing accustomed to the gloom, could now look into the cellar. He also knew that nine doorkeys out of ten have a little groove at the end of the shank just below the wards. So he made a noose of the fine, hard cobbler's twine, and slipped it into the keyhole just as if he had been 'girning' sticklebacks and 'bairdies' in the shallow burns about the Loch of Lochend.

After a failure or two the loop caught and tightened. Then Cleg shook the string about with a cunning see-saw motion, learned from his father, till he felt the wards of the key drop down perpendicularly. Whereupon he took a long piece of stick, and, thrusting it into the keyhole, he had the satisfaction of feeling the key drop out inside the door, and hang by the cobbler's twine. He eased it down to the floor, and found that, as is the case with most doors, the bottom of that of the cellar of Tinklers' Lands did not come quite close to the floor. It was therefore easy for Cleg to dangle the key a little till he could bring the end of it to the place where the arch was worn widest. Then he took his hooked wire and pulled the key towards him. It was in itself a pretty trick, and was executed by Cleg in far less time than it takes to tell about it.

With the key in his hand, and in the other an open clasp-knife, Cleg turned the bolt back and stepped within. A terrible enough sight met his eyes, though not that which he dreaded. In the corner lay Sal Kavannah, with a pair of empty bottles tossed at her side, her heavy black hair over her face. She lay all drawn together in a heap. Tied to the bed was Vara, bleeding from a cut on the head, and trying to cover her arms and hands from his sight. But Hugh and the baby remained in the bunk together, sleeping peacefully. It was upon poor Vara that the brunt of the woman's maniac fury had fallen.

Cleg stood stricken; but the sight of Vara bleeding and bound with cords aroused him. He had the knife in his hand, and it did not take a moment to free her. But she was so stiff and exhausted that she fell forward on her face so soon as the straps were removed. Then, after Cleg had lifted her, he turned upon the sodden heap in the corner, and, with his knife glittering in his hand and the wild-cat grin on his face, he said, with a deep indrawing of his breath, 'Oh, if ye had only been my ain faither!'

And it was as well that it was Sal Kavannah and not Tim Kelly that had done this thing.

Now, in an emergency Cleg always acted first and asked leave afterwards.

'Come awa' oot o' this, Vara, and I'll bring the bairn and Hugh,' said he to the girl, when she was somewhat recovered.

'But, Cleg, where are we to gang?' said Vara, starting back.

'Never you heed, Vara; there maun be nae mair o' this frae this time oot.'

His manner was so positive that the girl gave way. Anything rather than abide with the fiendish thing which lay there in the corner.

'Hae ye ocht that ye wad like to bring wi' ye?' Cleg asked of Vara, as he shouldered Hugh and took up the baby on his other arm.

'Aye,' said Vara, 'wee Gavin's feedin' bottle.'

And she had to step over the sodden face of her mother to get it.

So the four went out of the grim murkiness of the cellar in Tinklers' Lands into the blinding noonday streets, and Cleg marched along like the pipe-major of the Black Watch—than whom no king on earth walks with more dignity and pomp, when there is a big parade and the full band of pipers leads the regiment.

Cleg almost wished that Humpy Joe might see and taunt him, so that on Sunday he could beat him to a jelly. But, as it chanced, the streets were deserted, for it was the very middle of the workmen's dinner-hour. So that the streams that went and came a quarter of an hour sooner and a quarter of an hour later were for the moment all safely housed; while those who had brought their dinners with them sat or reclined on benches in the shade, and took no notice of the small forlorn company passing along the causeway.

There was another way to the old construction hut at the back of Callendar's yard, one which did not lead through the main gateway, but entered from some waste ground where only broken bottles and old tin cans perennially dwelt.

The children passed in safe and unobserved by this way, and in a little while Cleg had them safely housed in his own city of refuge. But Vara was in great fear lest some of the men should find them and turn them out upon the street. So Cleg shut the door upon them with the lock of his own devising, and started at a run to find Mr. Callendar himself.

ADVENTURE XIV

CLEG TURNS DIPLOMATIST

JAMES CALLENDAR, honest man and pillar of the Seceder Kirk, was sitting down to his dinner when Cleg rapped at his door. The one servant lass whom the Callendars kept was 'tidying' herself for the afternoon, and very much resented having to answer the door for a ragged boy with bare legs.

'Gae 'way, we hae nocht for the likes o' you here!' said she, and would have shut the door upon him.

'No even ceevil mainners,' said Cleg, stepping lightly past her into the little side room, where he knew that Mr. Callendar ordinarily took his meals. The builder was just putting a potato into his mouth. He was so surprised to see Cleg enter unannounced that the fork with the round, well-buttered, new potato upon it remained poised in mid-air.

Cleg plunged into his affairs without preamble, lest he should be captured from behind and ignominiously expelled. But the trim servant merely listened a moment at the back of the door, to make sure that the intruder had some genuine business with her master, and then returned to the graver duties of her own toilet. It was her evening out, and her 'young man' had hinted at a sail to Aberdour on the pleasure-boat, if they could get to the West Pier in time.

'Oh, Maister Callendar,' Cleg began, eager and breathless, 'ye hae been a kind man to me, and I want ye to help me noo——'

'What's this, Cleg?' said the builder; 'surely the police are not after you?'

Cleg shook his head.

'Nor your faither gotten off?'

Again and more vigorously Cleg shook his head, smiling a little as he did so.

'Oh, then,' said the builder, much relieved, carrying the suspended potato to his mouth, 'it can be naething very dreadfu'. But when ye came jumpin' in like that on me, I declare that I thocht the woodyaird was on fire!'

Then Cleg proceeded with his tale. He told how the Kavannahs had been deserted by their father, who had gone to look for work in Liverpool. He sketched with the direct inevitable realism of the street-boy the career of Sal Kavannah. He stated in plain language the fate which threatened Vara. He described Sal's treatment of Hugh.

'And she battered her ain bairn till the blood ran on the floor. She tossed the bairn against the wall till its arm was near broke. She never hears her wee bit wean greetin' for the milk without cursing it. Will ye turn them away to gang back to a' that?'

This was Cleg's climax, and very artfully he had worked up to it. The builder, good man, was troubled. The tale spoiled the relish of his new potatoes, and it was the first time he had had them that year. He turned with some little asperity upon Cleg.

'But I dinna see what I can do,' he said; 'I canna' tak' them here into my house. The mistress wadna alloo it.'

It was the first time he had referred to the ruler of his fortunes, who at that moment was declaring to an acquaintance at the seaside that she paid two shillings a week less for her rooms than her friend in the next pew at church. 'And how she can afford it is mair than I can tell.' It was no wonder that honest Mr. Callendar said that his wife would not allow him to bring the Kavannahs within his door.

'But,' said Cleg, 'if you will let them bide in the auld hut at the back o' the yaird, where naebody gangs, I can easy get ither lodgings for mysel'. They'll meddle wi' naething, and I ken where to get wark for the lassie, when she's fit for it.'

Mr. Callendar considered. It was a good deal to ask, and he had no guarantee as to the honesty of his new tenants, but the good word of the son of a thief who happened to have squatted on his property.

'Weel, Cleg,' he said at last, with his quiet humoursome smile coming back to his lips, 'they can bide, gin ye are willing to come surety for them.'

Cleg jumped up with a shout and a wave of his bonnet, which brought the trim servant to the back of the door in consternation.

'I kenned ye wadna turn them awa'—I juist kenned it, man!' he cried.

Then Cleg realised where he was, and his enthusiasm subsided as suddenly as it rose.

'I shouldna behave like this on a carpet,' he said, looking apologetically at the dusty pads his bare feet had left on the good Kidderminster.

He was on the eve of departing when the builder called him back. He had been turning things over in his mind.

'I hae anither wood-yard doon by Echo Bank,'

he said. 'There's a cubby-hole there you could bide in, gin ye had a blanket.'

'That's nocht,' answered Cleg, 'in this weather. And thank ye kindly. I can do brawly withoot a blanket.'

And he sped out as he came, without troubling the maid, who was wearying for her master to be done with his dinner and take himself away to his office.

The good news was conveyed directly to Vara, and then she set Cleg's hut in order with a quieter heart. Cleg showed them where to get water, and it was not long before the three bairns were established in a safety and comfort to which they had been strangers all their lives.

But Cleg was not yet done with his day's work on behalf of the Kavannahs. He went down to the Hillside Works and saw the watchman there, after he had delivered his tale of evening papers.

'D'ye think,' he said diplomatically, 'that there's ony chance for a lassie to get wark here?'

The watchman shook his head.

'There's nae room for ony but the relations o' them that's workin' here already,' he replied firmly.

The watchman could be as diplomatic as Cleg. He had daughters of his own growing up, and, though he was willing to be a friend to the boy, it was against his principles to encourage the introduction into 'our works' of any alien blood. There was a tradition at Hillside that every old servant got his daughters 'in' as a matter of course. Indeed, matrimonial alliances were often arranged on this basis, and the blessing of children was looked upon as equivalent to the supreme blessing of money in the bank.

'But I dare say ye micht see Maister Donald,'

said the watchman, relenting. He remembered that after all he had no daughters that could be ready for a few years yet; and besides, Cleg was a very good friend of his. 'But what ken ye aboot lassies? My sang, but ye are early begun, my lad. Ye'll rue it some day.'

Cleg smiled, but disdained an answer. He was not 'argiebargiein'' at present, as he would have said. He was waiting to get a job for Vara Kavannah. In another minute he found himself in the presence of Mr. Donald Iverach, junior partner in the firm of Iverach & Company, whose distinguished position in the paper trade and whose special eminence in the production of the higher grades of 'foreign correspondence' were acknowledged even by rivals—as the senior partner always wrote when he was preparing the advertisement for the firm's yearly almanack.

Mr. Donald Iverach was not in the best of humours. He had hoped at this very hour to be playing 'pocket-handkerchief tennis,' of which he had grown inordinately fond, upon the lawn of Aurelia Villa. But it so happened that he had been required to supply his father upon the morrow with important data concerning the half-yearly balance. For this reason he had been compelled to remain in the dreary office in the South Back. This jumped ill with the desires of the junior partner, who was at present so very junior a partner that his share of the profits only amounted to a full and undivided fiftieth —'amply sufficient, however,' as his father said many times over, 'and much more than ever I had at your age, even with a wife and family to keep.'

'I wish *I* had!' said the reckless Donald, when he had heard this for the twentieth time—not knowing in his haste and ignorance what he said.

'Donald, you are a young fool!' said his father. Which, of course, materially helped things.

Now the temper of Mr. Donald Iverach was specially tried on this occasion, for he had good reason to believe that a certain picturesque cousin of Cecilia's from London, who had been invalided home from some ridiculous little war or another, was playing pocket-handkerchief tennis at Aurelia Villa that evening in place of himself.

So his greeting to Cleg was curt indeed, as he looked up with his pen in his fingers from the last estimate of 'goods returned damaged'—an item which always specially annoyed his father.

'What do you want, boy?' he said, with a glance at the tattered trousers with one 'gallus' strikingly displayed across the blue shirt, which represented Cleg's entire summer wear.

'Hae ye ony licht job ye could gie a clever and wullin' lassie the morn?' said Cleg, who knew that the way to get a thing is to ask for it.

'What lassie?' said the junior partner indifferently.

'A lassie that has nae faither or mither,' said Cleg —'worth speakin' aboot,' he added as an afterthought.

'We are full up,' said Donald Iverach, balancing himself upon one leg of his stool. For his father was old-fashioned, and despised the luxury of stuffed chairs in an office as not in keeping with a sound, old-fashioned, conservative business.

Cleg looked disappointed.

'It wad be an awsome graund thing for the lassie if she could get a job here,' said Cleg, sadly.

'Another time,' replied the junior partner, turning to his desk. To him the case and application were as fifty more. He only wished the manager had been at hand to refer the case to. Donald was like most of his kindly fellow-creatures. He liked to have his nasty jobs done by deputy. Which is one reason why the law is a lucrative profession.

Cleg went to the door, his head sunk so low that it was nearly between his feet. But at the very out-going, with the great brass handle in his fingers, he tried once more.

'Aweel,' he said, without taking his eyes off the brown matting on the floor, 'I'll e'en hae to gang and tell Miss Tennant aboot it. She wull be desperate vexed!'

The junior partner swung round on his stool and called, 'Hey! boy, stop!'

But Cleg was already outside.

'Call that boy back!' he shouted to the watchman, leaping to the door with sudden agility and astonishing interest.

Cleg returned with the same dejected mien and abased eyes. He stood, the image of sorrow and disappointment, upon the cocoa-nut matting.

'Whom did you say you would tell?' said Donald Iverach, with a tone in his voice quite different from his business one.

'Only Miss Tennant—a freend o' mine,' said Cleg, with incomparable meekness and deference.

'Miss Tennant of Aurelia Villa?' broke in the eager youth.

'Aye, juist her,' said Cleg, dispassionately. 'She learns us aboot Jacob and Esau—and aboot Noah,' he added, as if upon consideration. He would have mentioned more of the patriarchs if he could have remembered them at the time. His choice of names did not spring either from preference or favouritism. So he added Noah to show that there was no ill-feeling in the matter.

'And Miss Tennant is your friend?' queried the young man.

Cleg nodded. He might have added that sometimes, as in one noble ploy elsewhere described, he had been both teacher and friend to Miss Celie Tennant.[1]

'Tell your lassie to be here at breakfast-time to-morrow morning, and to be sure and ask for Mr. Donald Iverach,' was all the junior partner remarked.

And Cleg said demurely, 'Thank you, sir.'

But as Cleg went out he thought a great deal of additional matter, and when he said his adieus to the watchman he could hardly contain himself. Before he was fairly down the steps, he yelled three times as loud as he could, and turned Catherine-wheel after Catherine-wheel, till at the last turn he came down with his bare feet in the waist-belt of a policeman. The good-natured officer solemnly smacked the convenient end of Cleg with a vast plantigrade palm, and restored him to the stature and progression of ordinary humanity, with a reminder to behave—and to mind where he was coming if he did not want to get run in.

But even this did not settle Cleg.

'O Keelies!' he cried, as if he had been addressing a large company of his fellows, 'wasna it rare to see him loup off that stool when I mentioned Miss Celie, just like a yellow paddock into the canal.'

And Cleg, who scorned the eccentricities of love in more mature bosoms even when he traded upon the resultant weaknesses, went off into an ecstasy of mocking laughter.

[1] *The Stickit Minister*, 11th edit., p. 184.

ADVENTURE XV

THE FIRE IN CALLENDAR'S YARD

VARA KAVANNAH went daily to the factory at Hillside. She was but a slip of a thing, yet she soon learned the work that fell to her share, and developed marvellous quickness in passing the thin quires of foreign paper under her fingers, examining them for flaws and dirt, and rejecting the faulty sheets.

The girls were mostly very kind to her, though they teased her about her name. And, indeed, in a world of Maggies and Jeanies, her Christian name appeared somewhat strange. But Vara had a reverence for it, because it had been her single legacy from her father, the gentle and imaginative Sheemus, who had found married life so different from his hopes that he had been brought at last to try that bitter pass of flight, through which so many have fled to find a new life on the other side.

These were pleasant evenings in the wooden hut. Cleg generally dropped in to see his sub-tenants after his papers were delivered. Then he would potter about, watering the flowers, which now began to bloom bravely in spite of the city heat and the dust of the yard. Vara had a seam or a stocking, and sat at the outside of the door on a creepie stool.

Hugh learned to nurse Gavin on his knee or to

rock him in the old cradle which the kindly foreman of the yard, a recent widower, had lent to Vara, saying, 'I'm no needin' it the noo—no for a year or twa at ony rate.'

He might soon be a 'seeking' widower, and therefore he did not make the presentation absolute because he was a far-sighted man, and one never knew what might happen. As for Vara, she seemed to shoot up in stature every day, and the curves of her wasted and abused body filled out. Her face for the first time grew merry and bright, and she was ready to take her share in mirthful talk. But sometimes her eyes seemed sad and far away. Then she was thinking of her father, the gentle Sheemus; and she longed greatly to go to meet him in Liverpool, when the ill days would all be overpast and there was no mother any more in her life.

In the Works Vara gained the friendship of her companions, though she was younger than most of them. A tall girl, who was much looked up to in the mill because she sang in a choir (and was paid for it), stood firmly her friend. And these two, Agnes Ramsay and little Vara, used to walk home together. Vara was anxious that Cleg should apply for a situation for himself at the Works; but Cleg preferred his untrammelled freedom, and continued to deliver his papers and sleep in the yard at Echo Bank all through the summer.

It was mid-August and the sky shone like copper. There was a peculiar dunness in the air, and light puffs of burning wind rose up, hot and unrefreshing, from the walls and pavement in the afternoon. But when the girls came home 'on the back of six,' as they said, the air had grown cooler, and Agnes and Vara often lingered a little in the great 'saal,' or work-room, in order to let the press of girls well down the street before them, and so be rid of the rough chaff of the lads as they passed home.

But this evening, as they came leisurely out, arm linked in arm, Vara saw a great crowd blocking up the way in front of the clock which gave the time to the Works, and with a quick clutch at her companion's arm she would have drawn her away.

But Agnes Ramsay saw a woman furiously attacking the working manager, and pushed forward to get a better view. Vara knew too well what it meant. Her enemy had found her. She tried to steal away, but it seemed impossible to move. With a shriek of anger Sal Kavannah recognised her daughter, and threshed a way through the crowd to reach her. Vara stood still, white to the lips. Her mother seized her by the neck of her thin dress and began to shake her, striking her about the face and shoulders, with foul names and blasphemous words.

'Brazen besom,' she cried; 'you and your low "Keelie" stole my bairns frae me. Where have you hidden them? Ye think I canna find oot. But I can track them as I tracked you. Aff wi' that dress, you slut. It's ower guid for the like o' you, and me trapesin' in a gown like this. Take it off, I say, and give me back my children.'

Vara stood mute and silent under the succeeding storm of oaths. The manager would have sent for the police, but, knowing that Vara was a *protégée* of Mr. Donald's, he went within, leaving them (as he said) to fight it out.

Then Agnes Ramsay bravely pulled the shrinking girl away from her mother, and so turned the abuse upon herself. But Agnes was a well-grown girl, and, being supported by half a hundred of her companions, she stood her ground valiantly.

'Run,' she said, 'run, lassie, while ye can. She doesna ken yet where ye bide.'

So like a hunted hare Vara turned and ran. But when she reached the little wooden house, so trim and quiet, with its fragrant wood-yard about it, and the daisies and pansies in the plots and diamond-shaped patches which Cleg had made, the bitterness of her heart broke up within her, like the breaking up of the fountains of the great deep.

Little Hugh came trotting to her, waving a red flag, the latest gift of the widower foreman, in his hand. 'Vara, Vara,' he cried, 'Gavin can say "Dadda," and I nursed him good as gold all day.'

The tears were running down Vara's face. She went in without power of speech and sat down by the babe's cot. He was asleep, and she laid her wet cheek on the pillow beside his and sobbed. Hugh kept a little way off, not knowing what to make of such unknown and mysterious sorrow. Then he came softly up to her, and gave her sleeve a little pull.

'Vara,' he said, 'here's a seetie.'

For Hugh understood no sorrow which a sweetie would not make better.

'I can never go back to the Works,' sobbed Vara. 'I am disgraced before them all. I can never face them again—never!'

About seven Cleg came over the waste ground joyfully, having disposed of his papers. He sat silent while Vara told him of the terrible evening at the gate of Hillside, and of all her shame and terror. Cleg whistled very softly to himself, as he always did when he was thinking deeply.

'Wait here this ae nicht,' he said. 'I am watching with anither man at the corner o' the Grange, where they hae the road up. I'll think it oot in the shelter. Keep up your heart, Vara—we'll win through yet.'

But Vara would not be comforted. She did not even raise her head to bid him 'Guid nicht.'

So, whistling still more softly, Cleg departed.

He was not great company that night for the man in the shelter, one 'Tyke' Tweedie—a man who had once been a soldier for three months, before being bought off by his father, who had regretted the transaction ever since. 'Tyke' was a man of battles. By his own account he had been in the Crimea. He was great upon 'the Hichts o' Almy.' He described at length the joint career of himself and the victorious Sir Colin Campbell, concluding his epic with, 'Then him and me charged the enemy and carriet a' afore us, till we garred the Russian chiels rin like stour!'

But Tyke had a poor listener that night, though he never knew it. For Cleg sat silent, and only by a nod did he acknowledge his interest when Tyke had come to the crisis of one of his famous narrations.

The policeman on the beat would sometimes stop and look over the windward edge of the shelter. 'Hae ye gotten to the battle o' the Inkermann yet?' he would ask.

'Na, Rob,' Tyke would reply, 'we are aye on the Hichts o' Almy yet! Dear, sirce, but it was a sair, sair job. Ye see, there was me and Sir Colin, and wi' that we at them sword in hand——'

And then the policeman would stroll away from the glow of the fire, out under the stars—alone save for the transient rake-hell cat skirmishing across from area-railing to area-railing, and the tramp of a brother officer coming up sombre and subdued from far down the hill.

But about one of the clock, when the night was verging to its stillest, Cleg looked up and saw the stars overhead thinning out.

'It's never morning already!' he said, rubbing his eyes, for he had not half solved the hard problem of Vara Kavannah.

He stepped out of the shelter. All the heaven to the north was a-flicker with the skarrow of fire.

Without a word to the now drowsy Tyke, nodding over the blackening cinders in his grated brazier, Cleg Kelly set off at his top speed towards the fire, to be in at the death. 'It's surely in the Pleasance,' he said to himself as he ran. The flame towered mightily, clear and clean, without sparks or crackling as when houses burn.

'It's Callendar's yaird!' cried Cleg again, and never in his life had he run so fast. For there in the midst of the timber was the little wooden house in which were lying asleep little Vara Kavannah and her baby brothers.

It was indeed Callendar's wood-yard. When Cleg arrived whole regiments of firemen were playing upon the flames; but his experienced eyes saw at once that the case was hopeless. Indeed, the officer in charge had come to the same conclusion some time before, and he was now directing the solid streams of water towards such surrounding properties as seemed in danger of catching fire.

The crowds were kept back by police, and all was orderly. The owner of all stood patiently at the gate, talking matters over with his foreman. After all, it was the visitation of God, and, further, he was fully insured. It is a great thing to be prepared for affliction.

Into the dense, white-faced mass of the onlookers Cleg darted. He wormed his way round to the back. He crossed a wall on which three or four boys were roosting.

'Ye'll get nabbed if ye gang that road,' cried one of them, giving Cleg 'the office' in the friendliest way, though he belonged to quite another gang.

But Cleg sped on. He dived between the long legs of his former friend, the red-headed officer known as 'Longshanks.' He skimmed across the yard among the falling sparks, dodging the flames which shot out of the burning piles to intercept him, as if they had not been policemen.

The little wooden house lay before him in the red heart of the fire. He saw the daisies growing in his own garden plots. He even remembered that, in the hurry and distress of listening to Vara's story, he had not watered them that day.

But he dashed for the door, opened it eagerly, and fell forward across the floor. The hut was filled with the odour of burning. Shooting flames met him in the face as he rose; but nevertheless he groped all about the tiny room, getting his hands and arms burned as he did so. The children were not there—Vara, Hugh, and the baby—all were gone! He turned to the door. The thing he had stumbled over was a body. He turned the lump over with his bare foot. It was soft, heavy, and smelled of whisky. Cleg had found Sal Kavannah in the home he provided to protect her children from her persecution. He had little doubt that it was she who had set the yard on fire and stumbled into the hut afterwards.

Cleg stood a moment wondering whether he would not do better to leave Sal Kavannah where she was; and more than once since that night has the same thought crossed his mind. He still fears that in dragging her away by the feet from the burning hut, he interfered unduly with the working out of the designs of an all-wise Providence.

ADVENTURE XVI

IN THE KEY OF BOY NATURAL

IN process of time and under a new superintendent Cleg Kelly went back to Hunker Court Sunday School, some time after the loss of his friends the Kavannahs. This is equivalent to saying that Hunker Court became again an exceedingly lively place of instruction and amusement on Sabbath afternoons. It is true that Cleg was not always present, and when he was absent his teacher's heart sent up a silent thanksgiving. That was, of course, before Miss Cecilia Tennant took him in hand as a permanent scholar.

Cleg had several teachers before he found his fate. He was, in fact, the crux of the school, and every aspiring young neophyte who 'took a class' was provided with a nut to crack in the shape of Cleg. But he never cracked him.

The superintendent of Hunker Court at the date of this first pilgrimage was a somewhat ineffective gentleman, whose distinguishing characteristic was that he appeared to be of a pale sandy complexion all over. That is, all of him not covered by a tightly-buttoned black surtout. His name was Samson Langpenny. Why it was so, is historically uncertain—'Langpenny,' probably, owing to his connection with his father. But 'Samson' is wholly inexplicable, and was certainly exceedingly hard upon Master Langpenny as a boy.

For it procured him many lickings at that delightful season, owing to logic of the usual schoolboy vigour and cogency.

'Jock, ye dinna ken wha was the strongest man?'

'It's a muckle lee, I do ken. It was Samson!'

'Na, then it juist isna, for I lickit Samson this mornin' mysel'!'

The second boy thought this over a moment—saw it—considered it rather good.

'Dod,' he said, 'I wad like to could say that mysel'. I can lick Samson as weel as Pate Tamson!'

Whereupon he went and lurked for Samson till that unfortunate youth came along. Then he triumphantly established his claim to be the strongest man by once more thrashing 'Samson' Langpenny, even while the tears of the first combat were hardly yet dry upon the cuff of the coat-sleeve which Master Langpenny ordinarily used instead of a pocket-handkerchief.

It was quite in accordance with the contrariness of things, that Samson Langpenny should develop into the superintendent of the roughest Sunday School in all the South Side of Edinburgh. He had now a real handkerchief, as every one might see, for he wore about equal parts of it within his pocket and without. The lower and unseen portion was the working end. Now, there may be excellent moral purpose in a judiciously-used pocket-handkerchief. There was, indeed, in times prehistoric, a certain literary man whose wife averred that her husband's toilet consisted ordinarily of 'four paper knives, four smuts, and no pocket-handkerchief.' But this person has not usually been held up in Sunday Schools as a shining example. In fact, quite the contrary.

Now, Cleg Kelly had no great personal grievance

against his superintendent. But he said in his vulgar way (for there is no doubt that he was that kind of boy) that 'he did not cotton to that wipe o' Langpenny's!'

Cleg's present teacher was a young gentleman of the name of Percy Somerville, whose principal reasons for teaching in Hunker Court were that he might improve the minds of the youth of the district, and that he might have a fair chance of seeing Miss Cecilia Tennant home across the Meadows. This last was a pleasant thing to do at any time, but specially desirable in the summer season, after the heat and turmoil of Hunker Court. And, on this account, Samson Langpenny never lacked for recruits to his teaching staff at that time.

Now, Percy Somerville was 'a very nice boy'— these were Miss Tennant's own words. 'But, you know—well, you know—after all, he is only a boy.'

And, in addition, as they say in political circles, when the leadership of the party is in question, 'there was no vacancy.' The junior partner still lived.

Now Percy Somerville undoubtedly had his troubles, owing chiefly to Celie Tennant's hardness of heart; but they were as nothing to the difficulties which afflicted Samson Langpenny.

For instance, it was in this wise that Mr. Percy Somerville was greeted, as he appeared with a reluctant scholar who had been detected in trying to escape by the side door after the roll had been marked. (It was drawing near the time of the summer treat into the country, so it behoved the teachers to be careful in marking attendances.)

'Go it, Pierce-eye! Hit him one in the eye!'

This exclamation was afterwards traced to Cleg

Kelly's acquaintance in day-school with a baleful ballad included in the Royal Poetry Book, and intituled 'Chevy Chase.'

Mr. Somerville thereupon promptly lost his rightful and given name, and became to all eternity—or so long, at least, as he remained at Hunker Court—'Old One-in-the-Eye.'

But it so happened that, on this particular Sunday, Cleg's teacher with the pugnacious title was absent; and, in despite of the notice prominently placarded on the walls behind the superintendent's desk, Mr. Percy was absent without having provided a substitute.

There was nothing for it, therefore, but that Samson Langpenny should take the class himself. And he would as soon have faced a battery of artillery as a row of boys in which sat the Egyptian plague of his school, Cleg Kelly. It was, indeed, on this particular day that there came to Samson the resolution to try him with Miss Celie Tennant as a last resource, previous to a second and final expulsion.

Indeed, he would have chosen the latter alternative long ago, but for a well-grounded inward belief that, by the close of the hour after Cleg's compulsory exit, there would not be a whole pane of glass in all the many windows of Hunker Court Sunday School. He well remembered as a teacher the awful scene which accompanied the first expulsion under the reign of 'Pund o' Cannles'—a scene which, since his triumphant prodigal's return, had made Cleg almost idolised by the scholars of Hunker Court.

Samson Langpenny sat down uneasily to teach the Border Ruffians of the Sooth Back—Cleg Kelly's class. Now he was out of place, and he knew it. His true sphere in a Sunday School was in the infant department; where, with a packet of butterscotch and 'Hush-a-bye, Baby!' he might have been a great and shining success.

Why the minister did not see this was a standing problem in Hunker Court. But, as the teachers said one to another on their several ways home:

'It is so hard to get the minister to see anything —*and as for his wife*——'

'Can you say your Psalm—metrical version?' asked Samson Langpenny, as though for a certainty they were all letter-perfect in the prose version.

'*I* can,' said Cleg Kelly, promptly.

'Then,' said Samson, smiling well-pleased, 'we will take you last.'

With various hitches and shoves, the awkward and unruly class bored its way through the Psalm— 'metrical version.' An impartial observer might have noticed that the teacher contributed about ninety-five per cent. of the recitation in the form of hints and suggestions. Nevertheless, each boy, having completed his portion, sat back with a proud consciousness that he had done his duty with even needless promptitude and accuracy. Also it was an established canon of the place that so soon as a boy was released from the eye of the teacher, he instantly put his hand slyly under the bench. Then he either nipped his neighbour in a place which made the sufferer take an instant interest in the circumstance, or else he incontinently stuck a pin into him.

In either case the boy assaulted remarked: 'Ouch! —please, sir, Tam Rogerson's nippin' me. Wull ye speak to him?'

But this was only the usual routine, and provoked no remark.

When, however, the superintendent came to Cleg Kelly, and that diligent young student began at once to reel off the twenty-third Psalm with vivacity and despatch—the psalm which the entire body of Scottish youth learns long before the A, B, C—it was obviously time to interfere.

'If ye please, sir (or whether or no), that's no the richt yin!' said Tam Rogerson, who ran Cleg close for the place of honour as the 'warst loon i' the schule!' This was a post of as great distinction at Hunker Court as the position of clown in a circus.

Cleg's answer was twofold.

To Tam Rogerson he remarked—under his breath, it is true, but with startling distinctness—

'Wait till I get you oot, ma man; I'll warm you.'

And Tam Rogerson grew hot from head to foot, for he knew that he was as good as warmed already.

On the other hand, Cleg gave the answer of peace to his teacher:

'Please, sir, Maister Langshanks—penny, I mean —my faither is a Papish—an' he winna let me learn ony ither psalm but the three-an'-twunty. But I hae learned HER to richts!'

After this exhibition of the rights of the nonconforming conscience in strange places, Cleg continued his lesson in Hunker Court under the vague tutelage of Samson Langpenny. Now Samson was wholly unaware of the strong feeling of resentment which was gathering in the bosoms of his scholars, owing to the length of his 'introductory and closing exercises.' The Psalm and the 'questions' were all in the day's work, but Samson introduced a prayer in the middle of the teaching hour, which Cleg Kelly considered to be wholly uncalled for and indeed little short of impious.

IN THE KEY OF BOY NATURAL 121

So, as soon as Samson shut his eyes, Cleg silently joined the class nearest him, and the other scholars of the absent Mr. Somerville did likewise. When Samson opened his eyes and awoke to the state of the case, he found himself without a single scholar to whom instruction could be given.

Cleg had betaken himself to the class of Miss Robina Semple, an excellent maiden lady of much earnestness and vigour. She was so busy explaining the Scripture lesson, that she did not at first observe the addition to the number of her scholars in the wholly undesirable person of Master Kelly.

The lesson was the parable of the lame man at the pool of Siloam.

Now in Miss Semple's class there was a lame boy named Chris Cullen. He sat listening with strained attention and invincible eagerness to every word which fell from his teacher. Cleg, to whom all lessons were much alike, listened also—chiefly, it may be, because he saw the reflection of an angel's smile on the face of the lame boy, Chris Cullen.

'What gars ye hearken like that, Chris?' whispered Cleg, with some anxiety. Only the news of a prize fight would have brought such an expression of interest to his own face, or (it might be) the announcement that his father had got ten years.

'It's aboot a man that got a dook, an' then he could walk!' said Chris, speaking hurriedly over his shoulder, being anxious not to miss a word.

'What hindered him to dook before? Was the water ower cauld?' asked Cleg.

'He couldna get doon to the water-edge,' said Chris.

'Maybe the bobby was there?' persisted Cleg, to

whom the limit of where he might not go or might not do, coincided with the beat of the officers of Her Majesty's peace.

'*Wheesht*,' interjected Chris Cullen, 'she's telling it the noo!'

For the lame boy, his teacher existed for this purpose alone.

The calm, high voice of Miss Robina Semple went on—Robina Semple, whom some called 'a plain old maid'—

'And so the poor man, who had no one to carry him down to the edge when the angel troubled the water, had to stay where he was, and somebody else always got in before him! Are you not sorry for him?'

'Never heed, Chris Cullen,' broke in Cleg, 'I'll cairry ye doon on my back mysel'! There's naebody will daur to hinder ye dookin' in ony dub ye like, when I'm cairryin' ye!'

Cleg Kelly was certainly acquiring, by contact if in no other way, certain Christian ideas. For the rest he was still frankly pagan.

Now at this particular date Hunker Court Sabbath School was run under a misapprehension. It was the idea of the superintendent that a little sugared advice would tame the young savages of the courts and wynds. Hence the hour of instruction was largely taken up with confused sound and fury. Samson would have been wiser if he had suborned a prize fighter of moderately good moral principles, to teach the young idea of Hunker Court how to shoot head foremost out at the door. Under these circumstances it is conceivable that some good might have been done. But as it was, under the placid consulship of Samson Langpenny, teachers and scholars alike had a good deal of physical exercise of an interesting and healthful sort. But the moral and religious improvement of the pupils was certainly to seek.

Yet in the class of Miss Semple, that excellent woman and good teacher of youth, there was one scholar who that Sunday had heard to profit. It was Cleg Kelly. He carried home little Chris Cullen on his shoulders, and if no angel stirred the waters of the gutter puddles as these two went their way, and if no immediate healing resulted, both Chris and Cleg were markedly the better for the lesson of the troubling of the waters.

Even Samson Langpenny did not go to Hunker Court that day in vain, for he went along with Chris and Cleg part of the way home. Pride was not among Samson's failings, and, as we know, bashfulness was equally absent from the black catalogue of the sins of our small hero.

'What for are you carrying Chris?' asked Samson Langpenny, who, though he had many weaknesses, had also large and sufficient virtues of earnestness and self-sacrifice.

'Weel, ye see, sir,' said Cleg, trotting alongside cheerily, his burden upon his shoulders, 'it's true that Chris can gang himsel' wi' his stilt. But ye ken yersel' gin the laddies are verra ceevil when they get oot o' schule. They micht knock the wee yin ower. But when he is up on my shoothers, they juist darena'. My certes, but I wad like to fa' acquaint wi' the yin that wad as muckle as lift a "paver" to him. I wad "paver" him!'

The superintendent smiled, though as a general rule he deprecated an appeal to arms. Cleg had also a little sound advice to offer his superior.

'Ye dinna lick aneuch in your schule, Maister!' continued Cleg, for he was unselfishly desirous that everyone should succeed in the sphere of life to which Providence had called him. He did not, it is true, see any reason for a man's having taken to keeping Sunday School. Summer treats in the country might surely have been given without them—likewise tea *soirées*. But since these things had been mixed up together, the instruction part, however unnecessary, ought certainly be carried out in a workmanlike fashion.

'Not lick enough?' queried the superintendent, aghast. He thought that he could not have heard aright—the pest of Hunker Court counselling corporal punishment!

'Aye, an' div ye ken,' Cleg went on, 'div ye ken, I can tell ye wha ye could get to keep the laddies as quaite as pussy.'

The superintendent looked at the rebel Head Centre of Hunker Court, bending with the weight of Chris Cullen upon his shoulders. It did not strike him that Cleg might also be able to support his own crippled efficiency upon his willing heathen shoulders.

'What would you advise?' he asked at last, with a certain pathetic humility.

'There's a maister at oor day schule that's awsome handy wi' the taws, an' a' the laddies are feared o' him. He comes to your kirk—I hae seen him gang in the door. Ye micht get him for a teacher in your Sabbath schule! Then the boys wad hae to be quaite. His name's MacRobb.'

'Why would the boys have to be quiet, then?' said Samson Langpenny, who did not yet understand what his ragged mentor was driving at.

'Dinna ye see, sir,' said Cleg, eagerly, 'the boys daurna play their capers on Sabbaths at Hunker Court, an' then gang to his schule on Mondays. Na, he wad fair skin them alive. It wad mak' an awfu' differ to you, sir.'

'But I do not know Mr. MacRobb,' said Samson; 'how can I get him to give up his Sabbath afternoons to teach in such a noisy place? He will say that he gets enough of teaching during the week.'

'Gae 'way!' said Cleg in his vernacular, forgetting for the moment to whom he spoke, 'gae 'way, man! Get Bonny Miss Tennant, the lass in the yella frock, to speer at him. He'll come fast aneuch then. He does naething else in the kirk but glower at her a' the time the minister's preaching.'

Thus Cleg the Cynic jested with love, and used its victims at his pleasure.

ADVENTURE XVII

THE KNUCKLE DUSTERS

Soon after this Cleg Kelly became a member of a certain young lady's class, in a manner which has been elsewhere related.[1]

That young lady was Miss Cecilia Tennant, otherwise known as Celie—a young lady much admired by all who knew her (and by some who did not, but wanted to); and especially admired and assiduously courted by Mr. Donald Iverach, junior partner in the firm on whose premises the class was held. I have also related the tragical events which preceded the formation of the boys' class, organised under the guidance and tutelage of Cleg Kelly. But it soon became evident that something more than a night class was necessary, if any impression were to be made on the wild Arabs of the Sooth Back.

'Ye see, the way o' it is this, Miss Celie,' Cleg explained. 'Ye canna keep a boy frae ill-doing by juist telling him aboot Jacob for an hour in the week. There's a' day in the shop, wi' the gaffer swearin' blue murder even on, an' ill-talk, an' ither things that I juist canna tell ye. Then there's every nicht, when we drap work. What can we do but stand about the streets, or start the Gang and look aboot us for a

---
[1] *The Stickit Minister*, 11th edit., p. 172.

bobby to chivvy, or else for something handy for "liftin'?"'

'But, Cleg,' cried Celie, much alarmed, 'surely I do not understand you to say that you would *steal*?'

'Na,' said Cleg, 'we dinna steal. We only "nick" things whiles!'

Celie had heard, indeed, of the 'mobs,' the 'unions,' the 'gangs,' the 'crowds.' But she had always believed them to be simply entirely amiable but rather silly secret societies, such as her own cousins used to make a great deal of unnecessary secrecy about—calling themselves 'Bloody Bill of the Ranch,' 'Navajo Tommy,' and other stupid names. She had remarked the same mania in Cleg sometimes, and had some reason to believe that all boys are alike, whatever may be their station in life.

But Cleg soon put his friend out of the danger of any such mistake.

'Mind, say "*As sure as daith,*" an' ye'll cut your throat gin ye tell,' said Cleg, very earnestly, 'an' I'll tell yea—aye, an' make ye a member!'

Cleg was about to reveal state secrets, and he did not want to run any risks. Celie faithfully promised the utmost discretion.

'Weel, Miss Celie, I can see that ye are no gaun to do muckle guid amang us boys, if I dinna tell ye. An' I want ye no to believe ony lees, like what are telled to the ministers an' folk like them. There's mair ill in the Sooth Back than can be pitten richt wi' a track. I canna bide them tracks——'

The injudicious distribution of tracts was an old grievance of Cleg's. But Celie earnestly and instantly put him on the plain way again, for if he once began upon 'tracks,' there was no telling if ever she would get any nearer to her promised lesson on the good and evil of the boys' unions.

Celie found herself as eager as ever was her first mother Eve to eat of the tree of the forbidden knowledge.

'Gie us your han', Miss Celie, I'll no hurt ye,' said Cleg.

Celie drew off her dainty glove, and instantly extended a hand that was white and small beyond all the boy's imagining. Cleg took it reverently in his dirty, work-broadened paw. He touched the slender fingers as if they were made of thistle-down and might blow away accidentally. So he held his breath. Then he took out his knife, one with a point like a needle, which had been worn down in a shoe-factory.

Perhaps Celie winced a little as he opened the blade, but, if it were so, it was very little indeed. Yet it was quite enough to be perceptible to her very sincere admirer.

Cleg let her hand drop, and without a pause thrust the sharp point into the ball of his own thumb, squeezing therefrom a single drop of blood.

'It's no juist exactly richt, no to hae your ain blood, ye ken!' he explained gravely; 'but as ye dinna tell so mony lees as the boys, maybe mine will do as weel this time to take your oath with.'

With a clean new pen from Celie's desk, Cleg made on her palm the sign of a cross, and for her life the initiated dared not so much as let her hand quiver nor her eyelid droop.

She knew that the occasion was an entirely critical one. But in a moment it was over, and Celie Tennant was admitted a *bonâ-fide* acting member of the Sooth Back Gang, with full right in its secrets and to the disposal of one full and undivided share of its profits. No questions to be asked as to how these profits were come by. Indeed, from that moment there is little doubt that Celie Tennant might have been justly indicted for reset, conspiracy, and indeed for crimes infinitely various.

That night at Miss Tennant's class there was a full attendance, but the opening was delayed owing to necessity arising for the expulsion of a boy, apparently in no way offending against discipline.

Celie looked the question she dared not speak.

'*He's no yin o' us*,' explained Cleg in a whisper. 'He belongs to the Potter-raw gang—a low lot.'

Celie felt morally raised by the consciousness of belonging to a gang of the most high-toned 'nickums' in the whole city.

Then Cleg, after the briefest opening exercises had been endured, explained that there remained for that evening only the ceremony of reception of a new member who had already been sworn in. In this Celie had to concur with as good a grace as possible. She was then and there appointed, with acclamation, a full member of the honourable (or dishonourable, according to the point of view) society of the Knuckle Dusters of the Sooth Back. It was generally felt after this, that Jacob (the Patriarch of that name) could very well afford to wait over for a little.

But, after this ceremony was over, when Celie looked again at her class, she could hardly believe her eyes. Were these the lads who night after night had stood before her with faces sleeked and smugged with arrant hypocrisy, or had looked up at her after some bout of intolerable mischief, as demure as kittens after spilling a saucer of milk?

A certain seriousness and comradeship pervaded the meeting. But Cleg was not yet at the end of his surprises.

'I perpose,' he said, 'that we hae a Club a' for oorsels.'

The meeting with unanimous palm and hoof signified its approval of this grand proposal, obviously one which had been discussed before.

'We will hae it in here, and we'll pay to be members—an' that will do for the coals, and we'll hae smokin'——'

Celie sat aghast. Events were precipitating themselves with a vengeance. Indeed, surprise sat so manifest on her countenance that Cleg thought it wise to point out its genuine character to his brother members. It would never do for them to imagine that the great idea of the club had not originated with themselves.

'*She* kens nocht aboot it, but I ken fine she's gaun to stan' in wi' us!' he explained, putting her, as it were, on her honour and under the solemn seal of the bloody cross of the Knuckle Dusters.

In this Celie, bound by her oath, had indeed no choice.

She must of a surety stand by them. But a serious difficulty occurred to her.

'Lads,' she said, 'we have only the right to this place for one night in the week. How can we obtain permission to occupy it every night?'

All the boys laughed loud and long. The question was mightily amusing. Indeed, Celie was often most amusing to them when she had no intention of being so.

'Of coorse, we a' ken, ye hae only to ask *him!*' they said, with one solid voice of general concurrence.

Celie felt herself beginning to burn low down on her neck, and it made her angry to think that in a minute more she would blush like a great baby just out of the senior class of the Ladies' College. The boys watched her maliciously till she looked really distressed, and then Cleg struck gallantly into the breach.

'Chaps,' he cried, 'I think we should hae the pluck to ask for oorsels. We are gaun to elec' a commy-tee and run the show. Dinna let us begin by troubling Miss Celie. We'll gang an' ask oorsels. Gin ye are feared, I'm no!'

Crash! came a stone through the window. All leapt to their feet in a moment.

'It's that dirty scoondrel frae the Potter-raw. Oot and after him!' cried Cleg.

Whereupon the newly constituted Knuckle Dusters' Club tumultuously detached itself for police duty. There followed a scurry along the highway, a stubbornly resisted capture, and a fight at a street corner. Two boys got a black eye apiece. A policeman found himself assaulted in the half-humorous way peculiar to the district. A letter-deliverer sat down suddenly on the pavement, to the delay of Her Majesty's mails, and finally after five well-spent and happy minutes, the Club re-entered wiping its brow, and Cleg cried:

'Three cheers for the Knuckle Dusters' Club! Miss Celie to be the president for ever an' ever. Amen! We'll meet the morn's nicht to elec' the commy-tee. *And there's twenty meenits left for Jacob!*'

And so the Knuckle Dusters' Club sat patiently down to endure its Scripture lesson.

ADVENTURE XVIII

BIG SMITH SUBDUES THE KNUCKLE DUSTERS

THE reader of this random chronicle has not forgotten the Troglodytes—the Cave Dwellers, the Pailing Roosters—alien to the race of men, and with manners and customs darkly their own.

These are they with whom Cleg had mostly to do, when he amused himself all the summer day opposite the house of the sergeant. Of the Troglodytes the chief were Tam Luke, who for a paltry consideration gave his time during the day to furthering the worldly affairs of Tamson the baker; Cleaver's boy, who similarly conducted the butcher's business next door; and the grocer's boy, who answered to the name of 'Marg' —that is, if he who used it was very much bigger and stronger than himself. In other circumstances 'Marg' chased and hammered according to his ability the boy who called the name after him—for it was contracted from 'margarine,' and involved a distinct slur upon his line of business.

But each man of the Troglodytes was a sworn Knuckle Duster. In the Club they were banded together for offence and defence. In the days before Cleg took in hand to reorganise the Club, they had a good many things in common besides the fear of the constable.

Now, each boy was most respectable during his hours of business. There was no 'sneaking' the goods of their own masters. The till was safe, and they did not carry away the stock-in-trade to sell it. But that was pretty much all the way their honour went. Their kind of honesty, it is to be feared, was chiefly of the 'best policy' sort. Fun was fun, and 'sneaking' was the breath of life; but it was one thing to 'nail an apple,' and altogether another to be 'nicked' for stealing from one's master. The latter meant the loss of situation without a character. Now a 'character' is a valuable asset. It is negotiable, and must be taken care of. To steal does not hurt one's character—only to be found out. To break a plate-glass window with a stone does not harm a character as much as it damages the window; but to be an hour late three mornings running is fatal. So Cleaver's boy had a character; 'Marg' had a character, and even Tam Luke had a character of sorts. They were all beauties. Our own Cleg had half a dozen different characters in his various incarnations—most of them, however, rather indifferent.

But there is no mistake that, under the influence of Celie Tennant and the new Knuckle Dusters' Club, they were all in the way of improvement. The good character of their hours of work already began to lap over into their play-time. But thus it was not always.

Just before its re-inauguration as a law-abiding club the Sooth Back 'mob' had been rather down on its luck. Cleg was among them only intermittently. They had had a fight with Bob Sowerby's gang, which frequented the Pleasance lands, and had been ignominiously defeated.

Worse than all, they had come across 'Big' Smith, the athletic missionary of the Pleasance. He was so called to discriminate him from 'Little' Smith, a distinguished predecessor of the same name, who was popularly understood to have read every book that was. Big Smith was not remarkable in that way. All the same, he was both widely celebrated and immensely popular.

On this occasion he was addressing his weekly open-air meeting on the street underneath one of the great houses in the Pleasance. The Knuckle Dusters thought it good sport to ascend to the window of the common stair, and prepare missiles both fluid and solid. This was because they belonged to the Sooth Back, and did not know Big Smith.

Big Smith's mode of exhortation was the prophetic denunciatory. He was no Jeremiah among preachers— a Boanerges of the slums rather. He dealt in warm accusations and vigorous personal applications. He was very decidedly no minor prophet, for he had a black beard like an Astrakhan rug, and a voice that could outroar a Gilmerton carter. Also he was six feet high, and when he crossed his arms it was like a long-range marker trying to fold his arms round the target.

'Sinners in Number Seventy-Three!' cried Big Smith, and his voice penetrated into every den and corner of that vast rabbit warren, 'you will not come out to hear me, but I'll make ye hear me yet, if I scraich till the Day of Judgment. Sinners in Number Seventy-Three, ye are a desperate bad lot. I hae kenned ye this ten year—but——'

Clash! came a pail of dirty water out of the stair window behind which the Knuckle Dusters, yet completely unregenerate, were concealed.

Big Smith was taking breath for his next overwhelming sentence, but he never got it delivered. For as soon as he realised that the insult was meant for him, Big Smith pushed his hat firmly down on the back of his head, and started up the stair. He had his oak staff in his hand, a stick of fibre and responsibility, as indeed it had need to be.

The first he got his hands upon was Tam Luke.

Tam was standing at the back of a door, squeezing himself against the wall as flat as a skate.

'Come oot!' said Big Smith, in commanding tones.

' It wasna me ! ' said Tam Luke, who very earnestly wished himself elsewhere.

'Come oot ! ' said Big Smith, missionary.

Tam Luke came—not wholly by his own will, but also because the hand of Big Smith seemed to gather up most of his garments at once. And he grasped them hard too. Tam Luke's toes barely touched the ground.

' It wasna me ! ' repeated Tam Luke.

'What's a' this then ?' queried Big Smith, shaking him comprehensively, as the coal-man of the locality empties a hundred-weight sack into the bunker. Half a dozen vegetables, more or less gamey in flavour, dropped out of his pockets, and trotted irregularly down the stair.

Then Tam Luke, for the first time in his life, believed in the power of the Church militant. The Knuckle Dusters on the landing above listened with curious qualms, hearing Tam singing out his petitions in a kind of inappeasable rapture. Then, suddenly, they bethought themselves that it was full time they got out of their present invidious position, and they made a rush downstairs.

But Big Smith stood on the steps, still holding Tam Luke, and with a foot like a Sutton's furniture van he tripped up each one impartially as he passed, till quite a little haycock of Knuckle Dusters was formed at an angle of the stair.

Then Big Smith, in a singularly able-bodied way, argued with the heap in general for the good of their souls; and the noise of the oak stick brought out all the neighbours to look on with voluble approbation. They had no sympathy with the Knuckle Dusters whatever. For though these sinners of Number Seventy-Three continually troubled the peace of mind of Big Smith with their goings on, yet they were loyal to him in their own way, and rejoiced exceedingly when they saw him 'dressing the droddums' of the youth of the Sooth Back Gang.

'Lay on till them, Maister Smith!—bringin' disgrace on oor decent stair,' cried a hodman's wife from the top landing, looking over with the brush in her hand. And Maister Smith certainly obeyed her. Each Knuckle Duster crawled hurriedly away as soon as he could disentangle himself. And as each passed the lower landings the wives harassed his retreat with brushes and pokers, for bringing shame on the unstained good name of Number Seventy-Three in the Pleasance.

'It'll learn them no to meddle wi' oor missionary,' they said, as they retired to drink tea syrup, which had been stewing on the hearth since morning.

For they felt justly proud of Big Smith, and told their husbands, actual and attached, of the great doings upon their return at night. It became a standing taunt as far as the Arch of Abbeyhill for a month, 'I'll send Big Smith till ye!' And there was not a Knuckle

Duster who did not hang his head at the remembrance. The Pleasance was naturally very proud of its missionary, and offered long odds on him as against any evangelist in the town. 'He could lick them a' wi' his hand tied ahint his back,' said the Pleasance in its wholly reasonable pride.

Now this was one cause of the depression which for a long time had rested upon the Knuckle Dusters and tarnished the glory of their name. So low had they sunk that it was more than a month since any of them had been up for assaulting the police. So that, as you may see, things were indeed coming to a pretty pass. From all this the new club was to save them.

First of all, it re-established them in their own self-esteem, which is a great point. Then it gained them the respect of others as well, for Miss Celie Tennant was a much honoured person in the Sooth Back. Lastly, the Club fire burned half a ton of coals in the fortnight, and the fact in itself was fame.

So the Knuckle Dusters squared themselves up, and for the first time since the affair of Big Smith they looked a bobby in the face. More than that, they actually began to show some of their old spirit again.

Specially did they delight to tell the ancient story of the Leith chief of police and the apples. It was, indeed, enough to gild any 'mob' with a permanent halo of glory.

This is the tale at its briefest. But it took four nights to tell in the Club, working three hours a night.

The chief, in the plainest of plain clothes, was hastening down the shore to catch the Aberdour boat, for he was a family man, and also a most douce and home-loving citizen. He had taken a cottage near the shore at Aberdour, where he could have his bairns under his eye upon the beach, and at the same time be able to note how badly the Fife police did their duty in the matter of the Sunday excursionists.

But for all that, he ought to have had that packet of apples better tied up, for he had bought a whole shillingsworth on his way down to the pier. The chief was rather partial to a good apple himself; and, in any case, it is always advisable to be on the safe side of one's wife, even if you are a chief of police.

Now the chief reckoned without the Knuckle Dusters. These valiant youths chanced to be on the war-path, and as he was passing a point where the houses are few, along by the dock gates, Tam Luke came alongside and pulled the string of his parcel with a sharp and knowing twitch. Instantly it came undone, and the apples rolled every way upon the street. Thereupon every Knuckle Duster seized as many as he could reach, and the Club scattered like hunted hares down alleys and over fences.

For a moment the chief stood thunderstruck. Then he gave chase, selecting Cleaver's boy for his prey. But he found that he was not quite so supple as when he was a young constable fresh from the country. And besides, he heard the warning whistle blow from the 'Lord Aberdour.' He pictured his bairns on the quay and his wife looking out for him. After all, was it worth it? So he darted into a shop and bought chocolate instead, taking his anger out by saying 'I'll wager I'll make it warm for these young vagabonds.' He said it as many as forty times on the way over. He never minded the scenery one single bit. Among the Knuckle Dusters there was great jubilation. That night they told the whole to Celie

Tennant, who was horrified ; but she could only advise them to 'restore fourfold,' an unknown idea to the Club.

It was, however, a proposition ably advocated by Cleg Kelly, who, owing to absence, not honesty, had taken no part in the larceny. And, strictly as a humorous conception, the scriptural idea of fourfold restitution caught on wonderfully.

This is why a very dirty paper containing two shillings came to the chief of the Leith police, with the inscription thereon : 'FOR TO BUY MAIR AIPPLES.'

Celie wanted them to send four shillings, but the Club unanimously declined, because the grocer's boy said that the chief's apples were only second quality.

And the Club had every confidence in the grocer's boy being well-informed on the point.

ADVENTURE XIX

THE PILGRIMS OF THE PENNY GAFF

THE Junior Partner was, as he expressed it, 'down on his luck.' He was heartily sorry for himself, and indeed the fault was not all his own. It was now some considerable time since he began regularly to see home the lady member of the Knuckle Dusters' Club, and perhaps he had grown to some extent to presume upon his standing. He had, in fact, taken it upon him to warn her as to the difficulties of her position.

'It is not the right thing for a young lady to be about in this district at night—no girl ought to do it, whatever be her motive.'

He was sometimes a very short-sighted Junior Partner.

Celie Tennant fired up.

'And pray, Mr. Iverach, who made you my guardian? I am quite of age to judge where it is right for me to go, and what it is proper for me to do!'

The Junior Partner assumed a lofty attitude.

'I consider,' he began, 'that it is highly improper.'

But this was as far as he got. The pose judicial was not one to which Miss Cecilia Tennant was accustomed, even from her own father. She dropped her companion a very pretty courtesy.

'*I* consider that our roads separate here,' she said; 'and I wish you a very good evening, Mr. Iverach!'

And she gave the junior partner a look at once so indignant and so admirably provocative, that he turned away righteously incensed, but at the same time apostrophising himself for more kinds of idiot than his father had ever called him, even on his most absent-minded days in the office.

Nevertheless he endeavoured, by a dignified carriage as he walked away, to express his wounded feelings, his unquenchable sense of injustice, the rectitude of his aims and intentions, and the completeness with which he washed his hands of all consequences. It is not easy to indicate all this by simply taking off one's hat, especially when you have a well-grounded belief that you are being laughed at privately by one whom you—well, respect. And saying 'silly girl' over and over does not help the matter. For the junior partner tried, and it did not improve the situation so much as the value of a last evening's paper.

On the other hand, there was a decided sense of exhilaration about Celie Tennant's heart and a certain lightness in her head, when she had thus vindicated her independence. She stopped and looked into the window of a shop, in which nothing was displayed but a large model of a coal-waggon, loaded with something 'Jewels,' and bearing the sympathetic announcement that Waldie's Best Household Coal was down this week one penny a bag.

It is a curious thing, when you come to think of it, that the prettiest girls often stop opposite dark shop fronts where there is apparently nothing to interest them, and pass by others all aglow with the blanched whiteness of feminine frilleries. There is some unexplained optical problem here. The matter has been mentioned to Miss Tennant, but she says that she does not know the reason. She adds that it is all nonsense. Perhaps, when Professor Tait has found out all about the flight of the golf-ball, he will give some attention to this question. He can accumulate facts and statistics on any well-frequented street by keeping the shady side.

So Celie stood a moment—only a moment, and was then quite ready to turn away, assured in mind and at peace with all men—with the doubtful exception of Mr. Donald Iverach.

Her bonnet was indeed 'straight on.' But she gave her foot a little stamp when she thought of the junior partner.

'The idea!' she said.

But she did not condescend to expound the concept which troubled her, so that an idea it has ever since remained, and indeed must be left as such.

Then Celie became conscious that some one was gazing at her—some one not a woman, I mean. She turned. It was only Cleg Kelly. But she was glad to see even him, for, after all, one does need some support even in well-doing. It is so difficult to be independent all by one's self.

'Where are you going, Cleg?' she said.

'To the penny shows aff o' the Easter Road,' replied Cleg.

'Will you take me, Cleg?' said Celie, with a sudden clearing of her face, her eyes beginning to blaze with excitement.

A great thought took possession of her. This appeared to be quite a providential chance to prove all that she had been advancing to Mr. Donald Iverach, who, indeed, had nothing whatever to do with the matter.

'Take you, Miss Celie?' stammered Cleg, aghast. 'Ye wadna gang to the penny shows?'

And he laughed a little laugh of wonderment at the jest of his goddess, for of course it could only be a joke.

'I *will* come with you, Cleg, if you will take me!' said Celie.

'But ye ken, Miss Celie, it's no for the like o' you. It's a' weel aneuch for boys and common folk, but no for you!'

Thus Cleg urged prudence, even against the wild hope which took possession of him.

'Come on, Cleg!' said Celie Tennant, rushing into flagrant rebellion at the thought of having her independence called in question, even by one of the Knuckle Dusters.

'It's all *his* fault!' she said to herself.

Which it very clearly was—Cleg's, of course, for he ought not to have followed her home.

Now, some distance along the Easter Road, then only a somewhat muddy country track, there was a small quarry which has been filled up, and a vacant acre or two of land where the show-folk took up their stances, and waged mimic but not bloodless wars in the mornings for the best positions.

Great sheets of canvas were stretched above, flaring cressets were being lighted below. For some of the largest shows were dark inside, being those where the mysteries of 'Pepper's Ghost' were shortly to be unveiled.

Celie Tennant was greatly excited by the prospect of eating of the tree of knowledge at a penny a go.

'Let us try in here,' she said, pointing to the wondrous 'Ghost Illusion' bearing the name and style of

Heddle. She drew out her purse to pay, but Cleg stopped her with his hand. He had grown quite dignified.

'Na,' he said, 'ye canna do that. It's my treat the nicht, when ye are walkin' oot wi me.'

Then for the first time it dawned upon Celie that she was assisting at a well-understood function—no less than the solemn treating of a lady fair upon the evening of a pay-day. The thought nearly overcame her, but she only said, 'Thank you, Cleg,' and was discreetly silent.

For the time being she was simply Cleg Kelly's 'young woman.'

They went in. A fat lady, with large silver rings in her ears of the size of crown pieces, took Cleg's money and looked with great sharpness at them both. Cleg paid for the best places in the house. They cost him sixpence, and were carpeted—the seats, not the floor. To such heights of extravagance does woman lead man! The play was already proceeding as they sat down. Presently, after some very moral observations from an old gentleman in trouble with a dying child (he said 'choild') the curtain dropped and the roof of canvas was drawn aside, in order to let in the struggling daylight and save the flaring naphtha cressets.

Instantly upon the return of the lights Celie and Cleg became the sole centre of attraction—a doubleted courtier in tights, with an unruly sword which scraped the curtain, having no chance whatever in competition with their grandeur. Cleg folded his arms with a proud disdain and sat up with a back as straight as an arrow.

'Glory be—if 'tisn't Cleg Kelly wid the Quane of Shaeba,' said a compatriot in the pit. (The house was divided into pit and carpet.) And this was the general opinion. It was the proudest moment of Cleg's existence—to date, as he himself said.

Celie sat all the while demure as a kitten and smoothed her gloves as if she had been in church. Several Knuckle Dusters passed Cleg the private wink of the society, but none dared intrude on that awful dignity of responsibility. Besides, none of them were 'on the carpet,' and Heddle of the Silver Rings possessed a quick eye and a long arm.

The curtain went up. This time it was a haunted room. A haunted clock ticked irregularly in the corner, and the villain sat alone in his quite remarkable villany, on a solitary chair in the middle of the room. It was very dark, owing to the murky cast of crime all round. Suddenly the gentleman on the chair shouted out the details of his 'croime' at the pitch of his voice, as if he had been the town crier. He told the audience how much he regretted having left his victim weltering in his gore, whereupon the aforesaid victim abruptly appeared, 'weltering,' it is true, but rather in a white sheet with the lower part of which his legs appeared to be having a difficulty.

The villain hastened to rise to the occasion. Once more he drew his sword, with which he had been making gallant play most of the time. Again he informed the next street of his 'croime.' Then he pulled a pistol out of his belt and solemnly warned the spectre what would happen if he did not clear out and take his unruly winding-sheet with him.

But the spectre appeared to be wholly unimpressed, for he only gibbered more incoherently and fluttered the bed-quilt (as Cleg called it) more wildly. The villain continued to exhort.

'He's an awfu' blatherumskite!' said Cleg, contemptuously. He knew something of real villains. He had a father.

Again the spectre was impressively warned:

'Your blood be upon your own head!' shouted the villain—and fired the pistol.

The ghost remarked, *Br-r-r-r-r! whoop!*—went up to the ceiling, came down again wrong side up, and then set about gibbering in a manner more freezing than ever. Whereupon the villain seized his crime-rusted sword in both hands and puddled about in the spectre's anatomy, as if it had been a pot and he was afraid it would boil over. But soon he satisfied himself that this was not the game to play with a spirit so haughtily indifferent. And with a last wild shriek of despair he cast the sword from him on the floor.

'Ha, baffled! foiled!' he remarked, clasping his hands suddenly upon his brow: 'COL-LD FIRE IS USELESS!'

This was summing up the situation with a vengeance, and tickled Celie so much that she laughed joyously—whereat the audience clapped and cheered with appreciation, and Cleg rose to come out.

'What comes after that?' said Celie, who was quite willing to stay to the end.

'After that the devil gets him. We needna wait for that!' said Cleg, simply. He had an exceedingly healthy and orthodox belief in the ultimate fate of ill-doers. But he did not choose that his goddess should witness the details.

ADVENTURE XX

THE DIFFICULTIES OF ADONIS BETWIXT TWO VENUSES

BUT we must hasten to do our hero justice. After the spiriting away of Vara Kavannah and the children from the burning house in Callendar's yard, Cleg did not submit to their loss without making many attempts to find them. His friend, the sergeant's wife, set the machinery of the police in motion. But nothing could be heard of Vara nor of Hugh, nor yet of little Gavin. Cleg went the round of the men who drive the rubbish-carts, each man of whom was a personal and particular friend. Now a persevering ash-man knows a lot—more even than a policeman, having a wider beat, and not so much encouragement to tell officially what he knows. But, as Cleg could tell you, an ash-man's temper needs watching. Like the articles of diet he empties out of the baskets into his great sheet-iron covered carts, it is apt to go both high and bad. A policeman patrolling his beat is, according to his personal deservings, stayed with flagons, comforted with apples. But what maid in all the areas thinks upon the poor dustman?

Nevertheless, Cleg went the round of the ash-cart men, and from each he inquired circumspectly about the Kavannahs. Not one had seen them in any part of the city. But, indeed, there had been many people, even women and children, awake and abroad that morning of the great fire in Callendar's woodyard. Cleg next looked up the morning milkmen who converge upon the city from every point, summer and winter alike. They have risen to the milking of the cows during the small hours of the morning, and thereafter they have set their barrels with care and circumspection upon a light cart, before spinning cityward between the hedges. The milkmen can tell as much of the country roads as the dustmen of the city streets. But to none had a vision of three pilgrim children, setting forth from the city of persecution, been vouchsafed.

So Cleg had perforce to abide ill-content, with his heart unsatisfied and sore. Perhaps, so he thought, some day hidden things would come to light, and the shadows which had settled upon the fate of the Kavannahs break and flee away.

In the meantime the ancient Society of the Knuckle Dusters flourished exceedingly in its new incarnation of 'The Club.' The deputation which approached Mr. Donald Iverach having by the intervention of the watchman chosen a good time for their visit, was most graciously received. The watchman, a man of some penetration, gave Cleg the word to come at six o'clock on a day when the junior partner had brought his tennis shoes to the works.

'You want to use the old store-room every night?' said Donald Iverach, looking at the shamefaced deputation, every man of whom itched to draw triangles on the floor with his toe and yet dared not.

'Except Sundays,' answered Cleg, who, as ever, was ready of speech, and not at all shamefaced.

'What does Miss Tennant say?' asked the Junior

Partner, who wished to see where he was being led. He was not a selfish young man, but, like the rest of us, he wanted to be sure what he was going to get out of a thing before he committed himself.

'Miss Tennant's a memb——' began Tam Luke, who had no discretion.

Cleg kicked Tam Luke on the shin, severely. Tam promptly coughed, choked, and was led out by unsympathetic friends, who expressed their opinion of him outside with pith and animation.

'Miss Celie wants us to look after this club oorsels,' said Cleg. 'We are the commy-tee—except Tam Luke,' he added. Tam Luke had *de facto* forfeited his position by his interruption.

The commy-tee hung its head, and looked about for possible exits.

'And who is responsible?' asked Mr. Donald Iverach, smiling a little and shaking his head.

'Me an' Miss Celie,' answered Cleg, promptly.

The Junior Partner stopped shaking his head, but continued to smile.

'Come away, chaps,' said Cleg, who knew when a battle was won; 'guid nicht to ye, sir, an' thank ye kindly. Miss Celie *wull* be pleased!'

Thereafter the Knuckle Dusters' Club was formally organised. The prominent feature in the management was the House Committee. Its powers were unlimited, and were chiefly directed to 'chucking out.' This was the club's sole punishment. Fines would certainly not be collected. Privileges were so few that it was not easy to discriminate those which pertained to members of the club in good standing. But the members of the House Committee were chosen on the principle that any two of them, being 'in charge,' should be qualified to 'chuck' the rest of the club—members of the House Committee itself being of course excepted. It was a singularly able-bodied committee, and willing beyond all belief. So long as it held together, the situation was permanently saved. Its average measurement round the forearm was eleven inches.

There were difficulties, of course. And, strange as it may seem, these arose chiefly from the ravages of the tender sentiment of love. The Knuckle Dusters had laid it down as a fundamental condition that no girls were to be permitted, or even encouraged in the vicinity. Miss Celie had insisted upon this. Perhaps, woman-like, she desired to reign alone, and could brook no rivals near her throne. But in practice the rule was found difficult of enforcement. For there was no maidenly backwardness about the girls of the Sooth Back. It was indeed a rule that each Keelie, beyond the condition of a schoolboy, should possess himself of a sweetheart—that is, so soon as he was capable of 'doing for himself.' Sometimes these alliances resulted in singularly early and improvident marriages. Oftener they did not.

Cleg, of course, was much too young for 'nonsense' of this kind, as he described it. But Cleaver's boy, and Tam Luke, and indeed most of the Knuckle Dusters, being 'in places,' were from the first equipped with a complete working outfit of sweethearts, pipes, and navy revolvers. They got them all about the same time, not because they wanted them, but because it was the fashion. Yet I do them no more than justice when I allow that they thought most highly of the pipes. They treated their pipes with every consideration.

It is true that each Knuckle Duster spoke of his

sweetheart as 'my young lady,' but this was only between themselves. To the 'young ladies' themselves their words were certainly not the ordinary and hackneyed terms of affection, such as generations of common lovers have used.

But the girls were not to be daunted. With such cavalier and disdainful knights, ordinary methods were put out of court. It was clearly necessary that someone should do the wooing. If not the Knuckle Dusters (haughty knaves), why then the 'young lady' herself. It was always Leap Year in the Sooth Back. There were but two unforgivable crimes in the bright lexicon of love, as it was then consulted in the lower parts of the Pleasance. On the side of the Knuckle Dusters the one unpardonable fault was 'going with a swell.' On the part of the 'young ladies' it was 'taking up with another girl.' Blows, disdain, contumely, abuse, all fell alike harmless—mere love-pats of the gentle god. 'Another' is the one fatal word in love.

So, then, it was quite in keeping with the nature of things, and especially with the nature of untrammelled youth, that the Knuckle Dusters' Club should have its amatorious difficulties. Part of each evening at the club was now devoted to the sciences. Arithmetic and writing were the favourites. There was also talk of forming a shorthand class. For shorthand has a mysterious fascination for the uneducated. It is universal matter of faith among them, that only the most gifted of the human race can learn to write shorthand. This is strange enough, for both observation and experience teach us that the chief difficulty lies in reading the shorthand after it is written.

The entrance to the club-room of the Knuckle

Dusters was through a vaulted 'pend,' which, having no magistrate of the city resident within it, was wholly unlighted. It was no uncommon thing, therefore, for the solemn work of scientific instruction to be interrupted by the voice of the siren outside—a siren with a towse of hair done up loosely in a net, a shawl about her head, and elf locks a-tangle over her brow. The siren did not sing. She whistled like a locomotive engine when the signals are contrary and the engine-driver anxious to go off duty. At first the Knuckle Dusters used to rise one by one and quietly depart, when, in this well-understood fashion, the voice of love breathed shrilly up the store-room stair. But after a little, Celie, who, from an entirely superfluous sense of delicacy, had hitherto suffered in silence, felt that it was time to remonstrate.

It was Cleaver's boy who caused most trouble. Now this was by no means the fault of Cleaver's boy, who, to do him justice, was far more interested in the adventures of 'Sixteen String Jack' or 'Deadshot Dick, the Cowboy of Coon County,' than in a dozen Susies or Sallies. But Cleaver's boy was a youth of inches. Besides, he had a curly head and an imperious way with him, which takes with women—who, gentle and simple, like to be slighted and trodden upon when the right man takes the contract in hand. Cleaver's boy was, in fact, just Lord Byron without the title and the clubfoot. Cleaver's boy had also genius like the poet. Here is one of his impromptus, written after a current music-hall model :

> I met my Sal a-walkin' out, a walkin' on the street,
>   I says to Sal, ' Why do you walk upon them clumps of feet ?'
> Says Sal to me, ' None of your lip. I've got another chap !'
>   *So I hits Sal a slap, and I sends her back*
>   *To her ain countrie.*

Cleaver's boy could do any amount of this kind of thing. But it was not popular in the Sooth Back. The article in demand there was a song about a little child who softly faded away after bidding farewell —a long farewell—to all his friends so dear, in a verse apiece. Like King Charles, this boy was quite an unconscionable time a-dying. But then he did not know it. He was a popular boy in the Sooth Back, and Tam Luke warbled about him till the assembled Knuckle Dusters snivelled secretly, and looked hard down between their knees so as to pretend they were only spitting on the floor. But Cleaver's boy, who in early youth had come from England with his father, the slaughterman, said it was 'Bully-rot!' He swore that he could make a song about Sal Mackay that would be worth a shopful of such 'tripe.' The verse quoted above is part of the song he made. Cleaver's boy has repeated the whole poem to me more than once, but the above is all that I can bring myself to print. For Sal Mackay has able-bodied relatives, and, besides, there is a law of libel in this country, which is provided for in my agreement with my publishers.

Sal Mackay and Susy Murphy were rivals for the affections of the handsome 'boy' of Cleaver the butcher. But for long the swain was coy and gave no final evidence of preference. So that day by day in the factory, where they worked side by side, neither could exult over the other.

'Ye needna think he cares a buckie for you, ye tow-headed crawlin' ferlie!' said Sue, who was of the dark allure, to Sal, who was fair.

'He wadna look the road ye are on, ye ill-grown, cankered-faced, jaundice hospital!' was the retort elegant of Sal Mackay.

So it happened nightly that when Celie Tennant was at the most impressive portions of the Scripture lesson, or, as it might be, engaged in elucidating the mysteries of compound division (and pardonably getting a little tangled among the farthings), that there would come a long whistle at the door, and then a smart rapping at the window. Another blast like a steamer signal was blown before the dark tower, the Knuckle Dusters would throw their heads back to laugh, and then look at Cleaver's boy. He would stand it a little while, and then, to escape from their meaning looks, he would throw down his slate and books and go quietly out at the door.

At last Celie plucked up courage to speak to him.

'It is not so much that I mind,' said Celie, for she had been learning many things since she came down to the Sooth Back—things that she did not mention when she went home to Aurelia Villa, or even repeat to the Junior Partner.

'It is not that I mind so much myself,' she said, 'but it is a very bad example for Cleg and the younger boys.'

'I ken, I ken—but faith, I canna help it, Miss Celie,' said Cleaver's boy, in desperation. 'As sure as daith, it is no my faut. Thae twa lasses will juist no let me alane. I canna gang alang the street for them.'

And Celie, blushing for her sex, believed him and condoled. For, next to Cleg, she had a weakness for Cleaver's boy. He was so good-looking.

'Wait till they come the nicht!' said Cleaver's boy, darkly.

It was the hour of the vesper writing lesson. Cleaver's boy was seated at the long desk which Mr.

Donald Iverach had found, as he said, 'about the premises'—but for which he had, curiously enough, previously paid out of his own pocket. Cleaver's boy had his head close down to the paper. His elbows were spread-eagled over the table. His shoulders were squared with determination, and his whole pose gave token of the most complete absorption and studious intentness. He was writing the line, 'Kindness to dumb animals is a sign of nobility of character.' As his pen traced the curves, his tongue was elaborating the capitals, so exactly that you could almost tell by watching the tip whether Cleaver's boy was writing a K or an N. This kind of expressive caligraphy has not been sufficiently studied. But Cleaver's boy was undoubtedly a master of it.

There came the sound of angry voices at the door.

'What are you doin' here ? I tell ye he's my chap !' said a voice sharp and shrill.

'It's a black lee. I tell ye he's naething o' the kind !' cried another yet louder and rougher.

Sue Murphy and Sal Mackay were at it again. So said the Society of the Knuckle Dusters, as it winked amicably and collectively to itself. Celie Tennant was at that moment looking over the copy-book of Cleaver's boy. As she stood behind him, she could see the scarlet swiftly rising to his neck and brow. Adonis was becoming distinctly annoyed. It was going to be a rough night for Venuses.

'I tell ye it was only on Saturday nicht that he knocked my bonnet off my head, an' kickit it alang the street--an' ye will hae the impidence to say after *that* that he is your lad !'

It was the voice of Sue Murphy which made this proud declaration.

'That nocht ava', ye Irish besom,' retorted Sal Mackay; 'yestreen nae farther gane, he pu'ed a handfu' of the hair oot o' my heid. Aye, and rubbit my face wi' a clabber o' glaur, forbye!'

It was the last straw. Cleaver's boy rose to his feet with a look of stern and righteous determination on his face. The assembled Knuckle Dusters watched him eagerly. Celie stood aghast, fearing that murder might be done, in the obvious endeavour which Cleaver's boy was now about to make, to excel all his records in the art of love-making, as practised in the previous Sooth Back and the Tinklers' Lands.

He walked slowly to the corner of the store-room, where on a little bench stood two very large watercans of tin, painted a dark blue. They were the property of the Club and contained the drinking water for the evening. They had just been filled.

Cleaver's boy took one in his hand and opened the door. Then he swung the heavy can, and, tilting it up with the other hand, he arched the contents solidly and impartially upon the waiting Juliets. Returning, he seized the other, and from the shrieking down the passage it was obvious to Celie that he had been equally successful in cooling the ardour of the rivals with that.

Cleaver's boy came back with the empty cans in his hand, panting a little with honest toil, but there was no shamefacedness in his eyes now. He looked straight at Celie like a man who has done his full duty, and perhaps a little over.

'I pit it to yoursel', Miss Celie, can a man do mair than that?'

And with no further word, Cleaver's boy dusted the drops from the knees of his breeches, and sat down to write six more lines of 'Kindness to dumb animals is a sign of nobility of character.'

But next night he came to Celie in the blackness of despair.

'I will hae to resign, after a', Miss Celie,' he said, 'I canna bide here to be a disgrace to ye.'

'Why, what's the matter, James?' said Miss Tennant, who did not yet know everything; 'are the girls going to prosecute you in the police-court for throwing the water over them last night?'

Cleaver's boy opened his mouth in astonishment and kept it so for some time.

'Prosecute me?—I wish to peace they wad!' cried he, after he got his breath. 'Na, faith, Miss Celie; will ye believe me, they are fonder o' me than ever. They were baith waitin' for me at the stairfit this mornin' when I cam doon to gang to the shop.'

And Miss Celie, sighing for her sex, again believed him.

ADVENTURE XXI

AN IDYLL OF BOGIE ROLL

PERHAPS it was in sheer desperation that Cleaver's boy (whose name, by the way, was James Annan, though the fact was hardly ever mentioned except in the police court) at last resolved to make a desperate cast.

'They canna baith hae me,' he said, 'an' Guid kens I want neither o' them. But gin I had yin o' them, she micht maybe keep the ither off.'

So Cleaver's boy scratched his head to find out a way of settling the difficulty. He could, he thought, be indifferently happy with either. It was only having both of them perpetually 'tearing at his coat-tails' that made him miserable.

At last he dashed his hand against his thigh with a cry of joy, and fell to dancing a hobnailed fandango in the gutter.

'Dod, man, the verra thing,' he said; 'I'll toss for them!'

So with that Cleaver's boy took out his lucky penny, and, selecting a smooth space of the unpaved roadway of a new street, where the coin would neither stick edgeways nor yet bounce unfairly on the stones, he spun the coin deftly upwards from his level thumb-nail.

'Heads Sal—tails Susy!' he said, very solemnly, for his life was in the twirl of the penny.

'Heads she is—Sal has got me!' exclaimed the ardent lover.

They were engaged that night. The next day they were photographed together—Sal with a very large hat, a great deal of hair, and a still larger amount of feather; Cleaver's boy with a very small hat, an immense check suit, and a pipe stuck at a knowing angle with the bowl turned down. That same night Sal had still a lover, indeed, but the glory of her betrothal attire was no more. Her hat was a mere trampled ruin. Her fringe was frayed and patchy. She had a black eye; and all that remained of Susy Murphy was in the lock-up for assault and battery. Without doubt it had been a stirring time for James Annan, and it is to be feared that Mr. Cleaver and his customers did not get quite their fair share of his attention while it lasted.

Susy Murphy got off under the First Offenders' Act. But immediately upon re-encountering her successful rival she hilariously became a second offender, and as such was summarily fined thirty shillings or seven days. And it added to the bitterness of Cleaver's boy, that he had to come good both for the hat ruined in the first battle and the dress torn to shreds in the second.

Then in addition it became his duty to take out Miss Mackay every evening, and so frequent were the demands upon his purse, that Cleaver's boy perceived that nothing but marriage stood between him and financial ruin.

'If I was only marriet,' he soliloquised, 'I could stop the lemonades and ice-creams. They're juist terrible expensive. I declare Sal thinks naething o' a dozen bottles. And then gin ye stickit a preen until her ony place, I declare she wad fizz.'

It occurred to him, however, that as a temporary alternative it might be possible to increase his earnings. And, like his friend Cleg, Cleaver's boy was not above asking for what he wanted.

'Guid jobs wants finding nooadays!' was a favourite expression of his.

Now there was a certain Bailie Holden among the customers of Mr. Cleaver. This dignitary had succeeded to the responsible position of Convener of the Cleaning and Lighting Department—a division of the city's municipal business which has always been associated with excellent eating and drinking, and a good deal of both.

Bailie Holden was reputed to have the finest taste in the light wines of his country of any man on the council. In his happier moments of inspiration he could tell the age of Long John to within a year. Now Bailie Holden possessed, among other excellent domestic properties, a kitchenmaid who was not above casting soft eyes at spruce James Annan of Cleaver's, so *débonnaire* with his blue apron and his basket over his arm. And James had cultivated the acquaintance according to his opportunity, without, of course, thinking it necessary to say anything about it to Sal Mackay—or, for the matter of that, to Sue Murphy either. So that, in the course of conversation at the area door, it fell out that Cleaver's boy mentioned his desire to be no more Cleaver's boy, but a servant of the city corporation in the department of Cleaning and Lighting. And the kitchenmaid answered, keeping her bright eyes on James Annan and adjusting her tumbled cap at the same time,

'I'll speak to the maister when he comes through the back kitchen, to smoke his pipe in the yaird after dinner-time.'

For it was the use and wont of Bailie Holden, when he was without company, or could shunt the entertainment of it upon his wife, to put on a seedy garden coat and slip off quietly round by the greenhouses. Here he took from the edge of a heating tube a short clay pipe of excessive blackness; then from a well-hidden canister he extracted a snaky twist of Bogie roll. Bailie Holden was renowned for keeping the best cigars in the city, and he also smoked them regularly indoors. His wife, indeed, did not allow anything else. But he came outside for his real smoke—in his shirt-sleeves in the warm evenings, and in his garden coat when it was colder. For though to all men he was now Havannah of the most exclusive brand, and all his appointments like unto that dignity, yet at the heart of him he was still kindly Bogie roll.

The Bailie thought on many things out there in the dark, as he nuzzled down the glowing ash in the comfortable pipe-bowl close under his nose. He thought, for instance, of the year Elizabeth and he were married, when they started at the foot of Morrison Street in one room at the back of the gasfitter's shop. They did not keep a servant then, and Elizabeth had not yet learned to object to the smoking of Bogie roll. Indeed, her father and her three brothers (all honest masons) incessantly smoked nothing else. But when there was need to find a place in the little back-room for another person with no experience in Bogie roll where he came from, then the Bailie had gone out every night to the backyard, sat down on a roll of lead tubing and smoked a black pipe, with a

M

babe's little fretful complainings tugging at his heart strings all the while. And the memory of the Bogie roll outside the window across which the black shadows went and came, had somehow kept his heart warm all through the years.

And, strange it is to say it, but though he was in many ways a difficult man to serve, yet many a servant had remained another term, simply because the master slipped out by the back door to take his smoke away from every one in the evening. This is the whole idyll of the life of Bailie Holden, Convener of the Committee on Cleaning and Lighting and proximate Lord Provost of the city. It is curious that it should be an idyll of Bogie roll.

ADVENTURE XXII

THE SEDUCTION OF A BAILIE

So it was at this most favourable of times that Cleaver's boy's kitchen-maid approached her master with her request. It was just at the critical moment when the Bailie was laying aside the Convener and host, and donning the Morrison Street plumber with the garden coat which carried so strong an atmosphere of Bogie roll.

'If ye please, sir, there's a young man——,' the voice of the kitchen-maid broke upon his dreams.

'Ah, Janet,' said the Convener, getting helped into the garden coat, for he was not now so slim as once he had been, 'there always *is* a young man! And that's why the world goes on!'

'But,' said Janet, the kitchen-maid, 'this is a very nice young man. You may have seen him, sir. He comes here twice every day, from Mr. Cleaver's, the butcher's, sir.'

'No, Janet,' said the Bailie, amicably, 'I do not know that I have observed him. You see my duties do not compel me to be cleaning the kitchen steps when nice young men come from Cleaver's!'

'Sir,' said Janet, with a little privileged indignation, 'James Annan, sir, is a most respectable young man.'

'And he asked you to speak to me?'

'Oh no, sir! Indeed, no, sir! But I thought, sir, that in your department you might have need of a steady young man.'

'I have, indeed, Janet. You are as right as ever you will be in your life,' said the Convener of Cleaning and Lighting, thinking of the ravages which the traditional hospitality of the department sometimes made among his steadiest young men.

'What are his desires, Janet?' said the Bailie; 'does he want a chief inspectorship, or will he be content to handle a broom?'

'Oh, not an inspectorship—at least, at first, sir. And he can handle anything, indeed, sir,' said Janet, breathlessly, for the Convener had endued himself with his coat and showed signs of moving gardenwards.

'Including your chin, my dear,' said the Bailie, touching (it is very regrettable to have to state) one of Janet's plump dimples with the action which used fifty years ago to go by the name of 'chucking.' He had dined, his wife was safely upstairs out of harm's way, and Bogie roll glowed cloudily before him. Let these be his excuses.

'James Annan, nor no one else, has more to do with my chin than I like to let them, sir,' said Janet, who came from Inverness, and had a very clear idea of business.

The Bailie laughed and went out.

'I will bear it in mind, Janet,' said he, for he felt that he was wasting time. He did not mean Janet's dimpled chin.

'Better put it down in your notebook—I'll fetch it, sir!' And Janet promptly fetched a black leather

THE SEDUCTION OF A BAILIE   165

case, round-shouldered with importance and bulgy with business.

So the Bailie stood in the half-light which came from the kitchen window, and wetted the stub of a lead-pencil, which Janet had carried for years in the pocket of her working-dresses without ever needing it. He hesitated what to write.

'The young man's name, sir, is James Annan, and you can send the letter in care of me, sir,' said Janet, with a subtle suggestiveness. She tiptoed round till her cheek touched his sleeve, so as to look over at what he was writing.

'Thank you, Janet; anything else?' asked the Bailie.

'No, sir,' said Janet, hesitating with her finger at her lip, 'unless, sir, you could think to put him on this district.'

So it happened that in due time Mr. Cleaver lost the services of Cleaver's boy. These valuable assets were simultaneously taken over by the city corporation in the department of Cleaning and Lighting. This has been the immemorial method in which subordinate positions have been filled, according to the best traditions of the municipal service. The great thing is, of course, to catch your Convener, as it were, between dinner and Bogie roll.

James Annan was placed on the southern district, and his duty was to mark in a notebook, less important but a good deal cleaner than the Bailie's, the names of the streets which were attended to in their order, and also the exact moment when each final ash-basket was heaped upon the cart.

What precise benefit trim Janet of Inverness got

from the arrangement is not clear. For, being occupied during the night, Cleaver's boy could no more come for the orders early in the morning, nor yet trot whistling down the area steps an hour later with the laden basket swinging upon his arm. So that Janet, supposing the matter interested her at all, seemed definitely to be the loser.

Yet one never knows. For the ways of girls from Inverness are deep as the sea is deep in those unplumbed places in the middle, which are painted the deepest indigo on the atlases. James Annan continued to be called Cleaver's boy, in spite of the fact that a successor at six shillings a week had been appointed, who now wore Cleaver's boy's discarded blue aprons. In several other ways he would have been glad to succeed to the perquisites of Cleaver's boy. But he was a sallow-faced youth with straight hair, who used his tobacco without the aid of a pipe. So Janet did not deign to bandy a single word with the new boy. He was no more than a penny-in-the-slot machine, wound up to deliver so many pounds of steak every day. The kitchen steps were now always cleaned in the early dawn, and Janet went about in her old wrapper all the morning and most of the afternoon.

She had taken a saving turn, she said, as if it had been the measles. It was all very well for the table-maid always to wear a black frock.

But though she saw less of Cleaver's boy (the original and only genuine article), it is possible, and indeed likely, that Janet of Inverness knew more of the romance of Susy and Sal than Cleaver's boy gave her credit for. Let those who try to run three or four love affairs abreast, like horses in a circus ring, take warning. Janet of Inverness had never heard of either Sal or Susy from the lips of Cleaver's boy. Nevertheless, there was not much of importance to her schemes which was not familiar to the wise little head set upon the plumply demure shoulders of Janet of Inverness.

ADVENTURE XXIII

THE AMOROUS ADVENTURES OF A NIGHT-SHIFT MAN

An interview which Cleaver's boy had to endure may throw some light upon this. By some strange law of contrary, the undisputed possession of James Annan's affections damped Sal's ardour. She became flighty and difficult in her moods. Cleaver's boy could not take her to enough places of resort, or at least, not to the right ones. So long as he slighted her and rubbed her face with snow as a regular method of courtship, she could not love him enough. But now, when she was formally engaged to him, and the alliance had been acknowledged by Providence and Miss Cecilia Tennant, Sal suddenly found that she did not care so much about Cleaver's boy after all. This happened in the second week of the new situation in the department of Cleaning and Lighting.

Sal came home from the mill at six. James went on duty at eight. Consequently it was now usually about seven when James called. It was an unhappy and ill-chosen time, as anybody but a man would have known. For Sal appeared to be in some undress, and was indeed engaged in frizzling her front hair with a pair of hot knitting needles, occasionally burning her fingers and her forehead in the process.

'Hoo are ye the nicht, Sal?' said James, standing at the cheek of the door and crossing his legs comfortably. Someone (he forgot who) had told him he looked well that way.

'Naething the better for seein' you!' retorted Sal over her shoulder. She never took her eyes off the fragment of mirror which was secured to the wall by two long nails and the broken end of another knitting needle.

'Wy Sal, what's wrang wi' ye?' began Cleaver's boy, anxiously. For though in the affairs of men, as between boy and boy, his voice was most for open war, yet in the things of love he desired peace and sacrificed much to secure it.

Sal humped up the shoulder next him and turned sharply away with a gesture indicative of the greatest disdain—without, however, taking her eyes from the faint blue smoke which went up from the left side of her fringe, to which she had at that moment applied a fresh pair of red-hot knitting needles.

''Tell me what's the maitter wi' ye, Sal,' said James humbly. For the spirit seemed to have departed out of him.

Sal tossed her head and made a sound which, though inarticulate, indicated that much might be said upon that subject. She could and she would.

Slowly Cleaver's boy extracted from his pocket a neat parcel done up in paper.

'Hae, Sal!' he said, going forward to her elbow and offering it to her; 'hae, here are some sweeties I fetched ye.'

They were her favourite brandy-balls, and on a suitable day, with a light wind and strong sun, their perfume carried fully a quarter of a mile. James had never known them fail of their effect before. But now, with a swift half-turn, Sal snatched them out of his hand

and flung them behind the fire. Cleaver's boy stood aghast. They had cost him fourpence-halfpenny at Tam Luke's shop, and would have cost twice as much but for Tam's good offices in the weighing department.

'What's wrang wi' the brandy-balls, Sal?' he cried in despair. The like of this had never happened before in all his experience. Thus Time works out its revenges.

'Did ye get them oot o' an ash-backet?'[1] at last cried Sal, breaking her indignant silence.

'No,' said innocent James. 'I got them at Tam Luke's for fourpence-halfpenny.'

'So ye say!' returned Sal, who was determined not to be appeased.

The brandy-balls were now flaming up the chimney, and fast dissolving into their elements with a sickly smell and a fizzling noise.

'Tell us what ye hae against us, Sal; oot wi' it!' said Cleaver's boy, who recognised the great truth that with a woman it is always better to be at the bottom of what she knows, and that at once.

'I'm no meanin' to keep company wi' ony man that gangs on the nicht shift!' cried Sal, turning with the needles in her hand and stamping her foot. 'I'll let ye ken that Sal Mackay thinks mair o' hersel' than that. I hae some pride!'

The murder was out. But poor James, who thought that he had done a fine thing in attaining promotion, knew not what to reply.

[1] The local technical term. It seems to have resulted from an attempt to say 'bucket' and 'basket' at the same time, though doubtless experts will tell us that it is a pure French word which came over with Queen Mary.

'And what differ does that make, Sal?' asked Cleaver's boy in astonishment.

'What differ does it make? Hear to the cuddy. Differ—juist this differ, that ye'll walk oot wi' some dafter lass than Sal Mackay. I hae mair respect for mysel' than to bemean mysel' to gang wi' a nicht-shift man!'

'But,' said James, 'I get far better pay. Think o' that, Sal!'

'I'm no carin' for that, when I canna be there when ye spend it,' retorted the mercenary Sal, with, however, commendable straightforwardness.

'But I fetched ye the brandy-balls, Sal,' persisted the once proud boy of Cleaver's.

'Brandy-balls! *That* for your brandy-balls!' cried Sal, pointing to the fire-place, in which a little blue flame was still burning, at the spot where the Tam Luke's sweetmeats had been so irregularly consumed. 'D'ye think that Sal Mackay is to be dependent every nicht on a chap that has to gang on duty at half-past seven?——'

'Eight o'clock!' said Cleaver's boy, eagerly.

'At half-past seven,' said Sal, jerking her head pugnaciously at each syllable, 'he pits on claes that are a disgrace to be seen, forbye smelled. And what's to come o' the lemonades noo, I wad like to ken—or o' the gallery at the theaytre?'

'There's Saturday afternoon, Sal,' said James placably, with a sudden access of cheerfulness. He felt that he had scored a point.

'Aye, there's Saturday afternoon,' replied Sal, with chilling cynicism, 'and what will ye do with your Saturday afternoon? Ye'll maybe tak' me ower to Aberdour again in the boat, and be sae dazed and sleepy-like that ye'll faa asleep on the road, as ye did the last time. And hae everybody sayin', " My word, Sal, but ye hae a blythe young chap there for a lad! Ye maun hae been fine heartsome company to him!" D'ye think ony lass that thinks onything o' hersel' wad stand the like o' that?'

Sal stamped her foot and paused for a reply. It was certainly an awkward question. Sal, like most women (thought James) was a demon at 'casting-up' when she began.

Cleaver's boy scratched his curly head and advanced towards Sal. He felt that in the war of words he was very distinctly going to have the worst of it. But he thought that he might fare better nearer at hand. It was one of his favourite axioms that 'it is aye best to argue wi' the weemen at close grips.' Which, whether it be true or not, at least shows that Cleaver's boy was a youth of some experience—but Sal Mackay chose to misinterpret his action.

She turned instantly, and, snatching up an iron goblet of hot water which stood on the hearth, she advanced to meet him, crying, 'I'll gi'e ye your fill o' throwin' water on decent folk. An' this will keep ye fine and warm on the nicht shift, my lad!'

At this Cleaver's boy turned and fled. But as he scudded down the stairs, bent nearly double, the boiling water from Sal Mackay's pan fell in stinging drops upon the back of his neck, and, what was worse, upon his suit of new clothes, bought with his last week's wages and donned for the first time.

When Cleaver's boy reached the pavement, he dusted off the water splashes as well as he could, and walked thoughtfully and determinedly across Nicholson Street.

'It'll be an awesome savin' in lemonade,' he said, 'an' yon dreadfu' expensive bottle lemonade too!'

A tramcar was passing. A wild thought ran through his brain.

'Dod,' he said, 'I declare I'll save that muckle by giein' up Sal—I'll risk it.'

And he hailed the car and walked very slowly towards it when it stopped. The conductor waved to him to come on.

'Could ye no hae run, man, an' no wasted a' this time?' he said, when Cleaver's boy had at last got himself upon the platform.

'I was gettin' my twopence-worth,' said James Annan, with dignity; 'I am an inside passenger!' And he went through the glass door and sat beside Bailie Holden, who was going home to dinner and already thinking of Bogie roll.

The Bailie and Cleaver's boy got out at the same place. They made their way to the same house. The Bailie let himself in quietly by the front door. Cleaver's boy went equally unannounced to the back. But Cleaver's boy knew that he had pretty Janet of Inverness waiting for him, whereas the Bailie only had his wife. And in these circumstances most people would have preferred to enter by the back door with James Annan.

Janet of Inverness was standing by the kitchen-window polishing a brass preserving pan in which she could admire her pretty dimpled chin, and the hair which, curling naturally, did not need the intervention of red-hot knitting needles to be beautiful.

Janet ran hastily to the door.

'Do ye want to see the maister?'

'No,' said James Annan; 'wull ye hae me, Janet?'

Janet of Inverness looked Cleaver's boy a moment in the eyes. What she read there, Janet only knows. At any rate it seemed to be satisfactory enough, for, with all the ardour of love's young dream, she fell on his neck, and murmured, 'Aye, Jamie, when '—(here Janet of Inverness sobbed)—'when ye get a rise o' wages!'

ADVENTURE XXIV

THE CROOK IN THE LOT OF CLEAVER'S BOY

I SHOULD have mentioned before that Inverness Janet's other name was Urquhart, but for the fact that second names do not seem to matter anywhere, except in those grades of society where persons require calling cards to remind them of each other's names.

It was only a natural precisian like Mr. Cleg Kelly who always insisted on the second name. But Cleg had a reason for that. He was himself in the curious position of having no definitely ascertained first name. There was a tradition in the family that he had been baptized Bryan, but his mother had never used the name. And since his father and everyone else had always called him Cleg, Cleg Kelly he has remained all his life—or, at least, as they say commercially, 'to date.'

But it is with Inverness Janet and the faithless and easily consoled James Annan, late assistant to Mr. Cleaver, butcher, that we have presently to do. Janet's conditional acceptance of his devotion seemed in a fair way to being made absolute. For Cleaver's boy proved a success at the night work. But in spite of this, and of his apparently assured position, both in the fields of practical sanitation and in those of love, James Annan was clearly not happy.

Judging by some past experience of his own, Cleg thought he must be pining for his old freedom.

'What for do ye no rin away, if ye want to be rid o' Janet?' was Cleg's contribution to the problem.

'Haud your tongue! I dinna want to get rid o' Janet!' said Cleaver's boy, loyally, but without indignation. Such things had been, and might be again.

'It's aboot Janet onyway,' said wise Cleg, shaking his head; 'hae Sal or Susy been botherin' her?'

'Na,' said Janet's lover, 'they ken better. My certes, Janet wad gie them the door in their faces and then send for a polissman.'

'Ye had better tell me, at ony rate,' said Cleg.

And with a little pressing, James Annan did unburden his sore heart.

'Ye see,' he said, 'Janet's bonny—or I think sae——'

'It is the same thing exactly!' interjected Cleg.

'She's bonny, an' easy to be doin' wi'. She's no sair ava' in the way o' expense. She is a natural saver hersel', an' she's aye at me to be puttin' by the siller. O, in some ways it is juist like heaven—nae leemonades, nae swing rides, nae merry-go-rounds, nae shows! I declare she cares no a buckie for Pepper's Ghost. In that respect there's no a mair agreeabler lass in the toon. Janet is aye pleased to tak' a walk on the Calton, or maybe in the Gardens, or to the Museum, or doon the shore to Leith to see the ships, or, what pleases her best, juist doon to the Waverley station to see the Heelant train come in. O, Cleg, she is sic a weel-dooin', couthy, kindly lass, that ony man micht hae been prood o' her.'

'What is't then,' said Cleg, 'since she's sae perfect? Is't the poetry?' To Cleg 'the poetry' was a trouble which might unaccountably seize a victim at any moment, like toothache. 'And then where are ye?' he would add, cogently.

But it was not the poetry. It was a deeper grief. It appeared from the tale which Cleg laboriously extracted from the reluctant and deeply wounded suitor, that Janet, though a well-doing lass in every respect, had one grave fault.

All day she was at work in her kitchen quietly and willingly. It was the nature of James's occupation that he should be in the neighbourhood in the early morning. At that hour Janet, in her sprigged working gown, was all that heart could desire. But when Cleaver's boy chanced to go round in the afternoon, or met Janet by appointment, some malicious pixie had wrought a sea-change in the lass of Inverness.

She would then tell, with the greatest candour and engaging innocence, tales which even a faithful lover could not otherwise characterise than as 'whoppers.' This mania appeared to come upon her as soon as she had taken off her morning wrapper and put on her company dress. She was going (so she declared) to 'the mistress' to ask for a few evenings off, in order to fulfil her innumerable social engagements. Every house where at any time she had been engaged (as kitchen-maid) opened wide its doors to her as a welcome guest. She told the cook, who listened with unconcealed scorn, how she had been at balls and suppers galore in 'the best houses' in Melville Street and Princes Street. She must really, she said, begin to remodel and refashion some of her many silks and satins for the approaching season.

Only the evening before, she had entertained the servants' hall at Bailie Holden's with an account of a dinner she had been at the night before in the Grange.

She even got off early in order to have her hair done by the hairdresser.

'The hairdresser, as a great favour, is going to arrange it in the latest style for five shillings, instead of ten-and-six, his usual charge,' said Janet of Inverness, with a glance like an angel's for innocence. Then she described her drive to the house in a four-wheeler. 'My hair would have got so blown about, or I should have gone in a hansom, which is much more distinguished.' Her former master had, it appeared, come into the hall to receive her. Two gentlemen had almost quarrelled as to who should see her home. A handsome and distinguished gentleman and a member of Parliament for the city, celebrated for his gallantry to ladies, had, however, forestalled them both, arranged the shawl deliciously about her shoulders with well-accustomed fingers, and had thereafter driven home with her in a hansom!

'It did not matter about the hair then, you know,' said gay Janet of Inverness, looking daringly at Cleaver's boy.

At this the cook laughed out loud. She then said that it was all lies, and that she had seen Janet walking along the Bridges with another girl at the supposed hour of the dinner. Thus was shame brought upon Cleaver's boy and upon the pride and good name of his sweetheart.

'An' what do ye think I should do, Cleg?' asked James Annan.

'I wad gie her a lickin' and gar her stop,' said Cleg, who held prehistoric notions as to the discipline of women.

'Na,' said Cleaver's boy; 'I hae thocht o' that. But, man, she's no like Susy or Sal. Ye couldna lift a hand to her when she looks at ye wi' yon e'en, an' tells ye that her faither was either a Highland Chief or a Toon Councillor o' Inverness. I couldna do it, Cleg.'

'Hoot,' said Cleg, 'then I wad try no to heed. She may grow oot o't. An' thae Heelant folk are aye leein' onyway. Think on a' the terrible lees they tell aboot their Bonny Prince Chairlie!'

'I hae tried no to mind,' answered Cleaver's boy, sadly; 'but when I see the ither yins a' laughin' at her an' her no seeing it, but gaun straight on wi' her daft-like story, I tell ye, Cleg, it pits me fair wild. There'll be murder dune, Cleg, gin it's no stoppit.'

'Weel, Cleaver,' said Cleg philosophically, 'I think I see the reason on't. She disna gang to shows an' theaytres, to save the siller; but she says she gangs, an' that costs naething. I dinna see what ye hae to complain o'!'

'If that's a' ye can tell me,' said Cleaver's boy, indignantly, 'I wadna hae missed muckle if ye had stayed at hame.'

'Hoots, butcher,' said Cleg, with indulgence, 'dinna gang aff like the fuff o' a match. There's little sense and nae siller in that. But I'll tell ye what, butcher: I'll speak to Miss Celie. She will ken what ye had better do.'

It was thus indirectly that Providence was appealed to in the Sooth Back.

ADVENTURE XXV

A COMELY PROVIDENCE IN A NEW FROCK

CLEG was as good as his word. He went that very night to call on Miss Tennant at Aurelia Villa. He found her in a philanthropic frame of mind. She had received from the dressmaker a dress of the latest mode, and she was conscious that the new fashion suited her like a garment fashioned by the fairies in a dream. Also (what was even better) she knew that it would make other girls whose shoulders were not so good and whose figure was less slim and graceful, look perfectly hideous. Yet for all that they would have to wear it. Celie felt that evening that there was little left to wish for in this sinful world. She looked out of the window toward the west. There was also (it seemed on purpose) a beautiful sunset which glorified the purple cliffs of Arthur's Seat—a quiet, providential sunset, for it went so well with the colour of her new dress. Besides, here was Mr. Donald Iverach walking slowly up the Avenue. And yet some people complained that this was not a good world! What would folk say next?

But Cleg forestalled the Junior Partner. He came by the back door, and when in a strait betwixt two, a serving maid will always answer a knock at the back in preference to a ring at the front door. The back door is more variously interesting.

A COMELY PROVIDENCE

So Cleg had the floor of the house, and was just finishing his tale, when Mr. Donald Iverach was announced.

Celie held out her hand to him, with a motion which signified at once a welcome and a desire that he should not interrupt. So the Junior Partner, who had for some time been accustomed to devote more time to the study of her moods and tenses than he had ever done to his Bible (and he had not neglected that either when nobody saw him), sat down upon a sofa and became interested in the pattern of some crochet work, which Miss Celie had tossed on a chair with characteristic impetuosity when she rushed across the room to greet Cleg.

'Are ye gaun to pit on that dress on Sabbath at the Sunday School?' asked Cleg, when he had time to think a little about his own affairs.

Celie looked at him with a small start of ingenuous wonder. It was a good little start in its way, and expressed amazement that anyone should notice so plain and simple a thing as her new dress. It is an undoubted fact that she was a truthful girl, and it is also a fact that she was quite aware how instantly the summer dress had riveted the attention of both Cleg and the Junior Partner. Yet the little start expressed as plainly as words her surprise, even her sorrow, that in the midst of so serious a world the minds of men and boys should dwell upon so vain a thing as a girl's new gown. Perhaps Celie's little start was her way of telling stories. For the sage sayeth that all women tell stories habitually and unintentionally, whereas men tell them only occasionally but generally intentionally.

At any rate, whether it was the start or whether it was merely owing to her sympathetic nature, after a moment's consideration of the sad failings of Janet of Inverness, Celie lifted her eyes to those of the Junior Partner.

'Poor girl,' she said, 'I quite understand; don't you?'

'You see, I have not heard,' said the Junior Partner, hesitating.

Celie instantly withdrew her eyes from his. She looked at once hurt and disappointed. He set up for being sympathetic and kind, and yet he failed to understand a simple thing like this. He was clearly unworthy of confidence. Celie Tennant turned to Cleg for assistance. He was looking at her with wide eyes of boyish adoration. Cleg at any rate understood. She turned half round in her chair, and the profile which she presented to Mr. Donald Iverach struck a chill through the room like that part of Greenland which looks towards the Pole. Celie's lovers did not lack varied interests in their lives; and perhaps that was why she had so many. For in the affairs of the heart most men like good sport and a run for their money.

'Come, Cleg,' she said, rising, 'I want to speak to you. My father is in the garden, Mr. Iverach!' she added, pointedly.

What Mr. Iverach said under his breath of his excellent friend Mr. Robert Greg Tennant at that moment, it is perhaps better not to write down. He rose and went to the window. From the wide space of its oriel, he watched with furtive sidelong gloom the confabulation of Celie and Cleg which was taking place in the porch. Celie was explaining something with great animation to the boy, who looked down and seemed a little doubtful. Then, with inimitable archness, which seemed thrown away upon an Arab of the city (if it were intended for him), Celie explained the whole matter over again from the top of the steps. She went a little way back towards the house.

'Now you quite understand?' she cried with impressive emphasis. And lest he should not yet comprehend, she turned ere she reached the door, ran back once more to Cleg at the gate with still more inimitable daintiness, and, with her hand upon his arm, she explained the whole thing all over again. The Junior Partner felt a little string tighten somewhere about the region in which (quite erroneously) he believed his heart to lie. He clenched his fist at the sight.

'O confound it!' he remarked, for no very obvious reason, as he turned away.

But Celie was full of the most complete unconsciousness. Yet (of course also without knowing it) she quite spoilt the game of two young men, who were playing lawn tennis on the court of a neighbouring house. Their returns grew wilder and their services were beneath contempt. Their several partners (attractive young women whom the new style of dress did not suit) met casually at the net, and one of them remarked to the other, 'Isn't she a minx? And her pretending to be good and all that!' Which was perhaps their way of clenching fists and saying, 'Confound it!'—or worse.

Then in a little while Cleg went down the Avenue with a sense that the heavens had fallen, and that angels were getting quite common about the garden gates of the South Side. He carried the arm on which Celie had laid her hand a little apart from him. It was as blissfully sensitive as if he had been ten years older.

Celie stood a moment at the gate looking after him. She shaded her eyes from the sunset and gazed down the long street. It is a charming pose when one is sure of one's arms and shoulders. At this moment one of the young men in the garden sent a ball over the house, and the eyes of his partner met those of the other girl. Peace was upon the earth at that sweet hour of sunset, but good-will to women was not in their two hearts. Celie felt that the light summer silk had already paid for itself.

'I don't believe a bit in religion—so there!' said the girl next door to her friend over the net.

At that moment Celie gave a little sigh to think that her first night in the new garment was so nearly over. 'And father wanted to give me a black silk,' said Celie Tennant to herself. Celie felt that she was not the girl to waste either her own time or her father's money. He ought to be a very grateful parent.

So to show her gratitude she went and found her father. He was slowly walking up and down the little plot of garden, meditatively smoking his large evening pipe. He stopped now before a favourite row of cabbages, and now at the end of the strawberry bed. He regarded them equally with the same philosophical and meditative attention. He was a practical man and insisted on growing vegetables in his own private domains at the back, leaving his daughter to cultivate roses and the graces in the front garden.

Celie elevated her nose and sniffed as she came out. 'O father, what a horrid smell of tobacco you are making!'

'It is almost inevitable,' he said, apologetically; 'you see it is tobacco I am smoking.'

If it had been assafœtida, Celie could not have appeared more disgusted.

'I thought your young thieves smoked at that club of yours,' said her father.

'Oh, yes; but that is different,' she answered.

'Yes, it *is* different,' chuckled her parent, thinking of what his tobacco cost him.

Then Celie went on to explain all about Cleaver's boy and his trouble, telling the sad tale of the 'failing' of Janet of Inverness, as, well—as I should like to have the tale of my weaknesses told, if it were necessary that they should be told at all.

Her father smoked and listened. Sometimes he lifted a snail from the leaf of a cabbage with care. Sometimes he kicked a stone sideways off the path, and ever he smoked, listened, and nodded without comment.

'These are all your orders, ma'am?' he asked slowly, when his daughter had finished.

'I'll pull your ears, father, now I will,' affirmed Miss Tennant, with equal want of connection.

And did it.

'Oh, I had forgotten Mr. Iverach!' she cried, running off towards the house with a little gesture of despair; 'what shall I do?'

'Give him his orders, too!' her father called after her, as the last flutter of the new dress flashed through the twinkling poplars.

ADVENTURE XXVI

R.S.V.P.

A GREAT event happened in the back-kitchen of Bailie Holden. The postman had brought a letter with a fine monogram—a very stiff, square letter, for Miss Janet Urquhart. The table-maid, who considered herself quite as good as a governess, examined it as though there must needs be some mistake in the address. The housemaid turned it about and looked at it endways and upside down, to see if there might not be another name concealed somewhere. She rubbed it with her apron to discover if the top would come off and something be revealed beneath. The cook, into whose hands the missive next passed, left a perfect tracing of her thumb and forefinger upon it, done in oils, and very well executed too.

In this condition it reached the back-kitchen at last, and the hands of Janet of Inverness. As she took the letter in her little damp fingers, she grew pale to the lips. What she feared, I cannot tell—probably only the coming true of some of her dreams.

In a cluster round the door stood the housemaid, the table-maid, and family cat—the one which went habitually on four legs, I mean. The cook moved indignantly about the range, clattering tongs, pans, and other instruments of music, as it is the immemorial use of all cooks when the bird in the breast does not sing sweetly. She was, of course, quite above curiosity as to what Janet's letter might contain.

'Likely it's an invitation!' sneered the housemaid.

'Aye, frae the police!' added the table-maid from the doorway. She was plain, and Cleaver's boy never stopped to gossip with her. Not that she cared or would have stood talking with the likes of him, anyway.

The cook banged at the top of the range, like Tubal Cain when Naamah vexed him in that original stithy, near by the city of Enoch in the land of Nod.

Janet of Inverness opened the letter. Scarcely could she believe her eyes. It was a formal invitation upon a beautifully engraved card, and contained a wish on the part of Mr. Greg Tennant and Miss Tennant that Miss Janet Urquhart would favour them with her company at Aurelia Villa on the evening of Friday the 17th, at nine o'clock. R.S.V.P.

Janet sank into a seat speechless, still holding the invitation. The table-maid came and looked over her shoulder.

'Goodness me!' she exclaimed, as she read the card.

'She's been tellin' the truth after a',' said the housemaid, who, having some claims to beauty, was glad of Janet's good fortune, and hoped that some day the like might happen to herself.

'I dinna believe a word o't!' said the cook indignantly. 'I'se warrant she wrote it hersel'!'

But Janet had not written it herself. She could not even bring herself to write the answer, though she had received a sound School Board education. But the three R's do not contemplate the answering of invitations upon thick cardboard, ending 'R.S.V.P.' They stop at the spelling of 'trigonometry' and the resolution of vulgar fractions into decimals.

In spite of her silks and satins and her vaunted experience, Janet did not know the meaning of 'R.S.V.P.' But the housemaid had not brushed clothes and 'done' bedrooms ten years for nothing.

'It means "Reply shortly, very pleased"!' said she. Which, being substantially correct, settled the question.

Nevertheless, poor Janet was in great perturbation. When Cleaver's boy went to see her that evening before going on duty she showed him the card.

'What shall I do?' she said. 'I hae nothing fit to wear, and I am feared to gang.'

Cleaver's boy looked up at the ceiling of the back-kitchen, as he sat on the edge of the sink, unconscious that a tap was running behind him and that the plug was in.

'There was that purple brocade ye telled me aboot, wi' the auld lace and the pearls that belonged to your grandmither, the Earl's dochter,' said James Annan, meditatively.

'O aye,' said Janet. 'Yes, of course there is that one.' But she did not look happy.

'Or there is the plain white muslin wi' the crimson sash aboot the waist, that the twa gentlemen were for stickin' ane anither aboot, yon nicht they quarrelled wha was to see ye hame.'

'Aye,' said Janet, piteously, 'there's that one too.'

'An' what say ye,' continued James Annan, remorselessly, ' to the yellow sattin, trimmed wi' flounces o' glory-pidgeon roses and—— ?'

Cleaver's boy suddenly stopped. He had been

feeling for some time a growing coolness somewhere. But at this point the water in the sink ran over on the floor, and he turned round to discover that he had been sitting in a full trough of excellent Moorfoot water, with the spigot running briskly down his back all the while.

'O James,' cried Janet, pleased to get a chance to change the subject, 'what for did ye do that, James? And your new breeks, too!' she added, with an expression of supreme pain.

'I didna do it for naething,' remarked Cleaver's boy, tartly. 'I didna do it ava'. It was you that left the spigot rinnin' and the plug in!' he added, after a thoughtful pause, while he realised how cool a sitz-bath can be even on a summer evening when one stands by an open window.

Now, nothing is more provoking, when you are performing a high and noble work in the reformation of another person's morals, than to have the thread of your weighty discourse broken by something so ridiculous as sitting down in a bucket of water. There was every reason why Cleaver's boy should be annoyed.

Especially when Janet broke out in a sobbing ecstasy of laughter, which irritated her lover more even than her wrong-doing.

'I wonder at you,' he said, 'telling a' thae lees when ye haena a dress to your back, forbye the black alpaca that ye pit on on Sabbaths!'

It was a mistake, and Cleaver's boy knew it as soon as he had the words out of his mouth.

Janet instantly stopped in the midst of her laughter.

'I would have you know,' she said with dignity, 'that I shall accept the invitation. And I will never speak to you again. I'll thank you to take yourself out of my presence, James Annan!'

'And out of Bailie Holden's back-kitchen!' continued her lover, whose anger did not diminish with the growing coolness consequent upon standing in a draught. Then, as he went up the steps from the area, he cried, 'Be sure and put on the brocade, Janet!'

It was an unbearable affront, for Janet had told her stories so often, and with so much innocent feeling, that though, of course, she could not quite believe them entirely herself, she had nevertheless all the feelings of an indignant moralist insulted and outraged in her tenderest susceptibilities.

ADVENTURE XXVII

JANET OF INVERNESS TASTES THE HERB BITTER-
SWEET

JANET duly arrived at the house of Mr. Robert Greg Tennant at the hour named in the invitation. She had had a great struggle with herself, but pride had ultimately triumphed. Her fellow-servants had given her no peace. She had, indeed, to dress in her black alpaca. But, sure enough, her hair had been done in the latest fashion by her only friend, the girl with whom the cook had seen her walking, who was an assistant in a hair-dresser's shop. It was so twisted and tortured that Janet felt 'as if she had slept on it the wrong way for a week,' as she expressed it to herself. She passed and repassed the end of the Avenue half a dozen times, but her courage would not let her ring the bell of the corner house. For there were lights in nearly every window, and a cab had just driven away from the door.

Poor Janet's heart leapt within her, and she had half a mind to turn homeward and confess that she had been romancing after all. But another cab stopped before the gate, and through the open door she saw a glimpse of lights and flowers that looked to her like

Paradise—as she imagined it from the hymn-singing at the Salvation Army meetings.

So as the last cabman came slowly out of the Avenue, Janet called to him. The man was arranging his rugs about him for a long drive back to his stand in the centre of the town.

'I'll give you a sixpence if you will turn about and drive me up to that door you have just been at,' said Janet.

'Done,' said the man; 'and good money for the job.'

So, without betraying the least surprise or curiosity, the man turned about his vehicle, and Janet tripped daintily inside. They drove up to the door with prodigious rattle and ceremony. The cabman jumped from his seat and rang the bell in form. When the door was opened, Janet Urquhart paid the man his easily earned sixpence. He touched his hat, and she went leadenly up the steps.

A trim maid-servant was at the door, who evidently had received very definite orders, for only the faintest curl of the nostril betrayed her own opinion of the affair.

When Janet was shown into the cloak-room her troubles began. Should she take off her hat, or should she not? She looked about to see if the ladies had left their hats. None were to be seen. Yet she had never seen ladies in the evening except bareheaded. After long consideration she resolved to keep her hat on. But when she was in the doorway to go up to the drawing-room she saw a lady coming through the outer door with a shawl of soft gauzy wool over her head.

Janet shrank back instantly and turned cold with

the thought of her escape. With trembling hands she took off her hat and pinned her veil to it as she had once seen her mistress do. The lady came in, bustling a little like one who knows she is late.

'It is cold to-night,' she said affably to the shy girl standing in the doorway, but without looking at her.

'Yes, ma'am,' said Janet, and the next moment she could have bitten her tongue out for the mistake.

'Oh, how I wish I had never come,' she said a score of times to herself as she went up the stairs.

But it was too late to turn back.

'What name?' said the daintily-capped maiden, with the curl of her nostril a little more accentuated.

For a moment Janet was so taken aback that she could not even remember her own name.

'Janet,' she stammered; 'Janet—from Bailie Holden's.'

The maid's face broadened into a smile, at sight of which poor Janet's lip quivered, and for a moment she thought that she must burst out crying. Scarcely was she able to keep back the welling tears. But the door was a little open, and she saw Miss Celie, whom she already knew and loved. The sight of that pleasant face, dimpling and flashing all over with bright kindness, reassured her.

'Say "Janet Urquhart"!' she said, with a little faltering return of assurance in her voice.

And the trim maid-servant, with a strong protest in her tone, announced in accents of terrifying distinctness, 'Miss Janet Urquhart.'

Then she shut the door, and Janet was left standing aghast and speechless in the bright humming place.

'I would not have done it,' soliloquised the indignant maid outside, 'unless my place had depended on it.'

But within Celie Tennant's drawing-room, poor silly little Janet of Inverness was being most pleasantly and charmingly entertained by her hostess. Celie had, in fact, asked only a few of her most intimate friends, whom she could trust with the momentous secret of the loves and sorrows of Cleaver's boy. The fascinating cousin from the tented field was there, ready alike for love or war. But it was to Donald Iverach that the principal work of the evening had been allotted.

It was he who first asked Janet to dance with him. It was he who sat out with her after her desperate failure, for she had lacked the courage to say that she had never learned to dance. It was he who found her a handkerchief, when, with the bitterness of disappointment, the tears at last would not keep down, but welled piteously up from the underlids of Janet's blue and childish eyes. It was Mr. Donald Iverach who took her down to supper, where she suffered agonies over the use of fish-knives and the management of a plate upon her knees. It was he who finally took her aside into an alcove, and there so fervidly pursued his wooing that, had Janet Urquhart been mercenary, he might without doubt have had a suit for breach of promise of marriage successfully brought against him. So far did the wooing proceed, and so fervently persistent was this wicked Junior Partner, that, bewildered and dazzled, poor Janet found herself being pressed to name the happy day, and, what is more, in some danger of doing it. As for the Junior Partner, that young man was obviously excited, but seemed quite unconscious of the risks he was running. Had the Senior Partner heard him, he would undoubtedly have considered his son to be rapidly qualifying for a strait-jacket. But the infatuated youth held on his way. Janet and he were sitting in the little alcove at the top of the stairs, which was cobwebbed with the latest artistic Japonaiseries of the period.

'And now,' urged the reckless wooer, when he had sealed in due form the silent acquiescence he had won, 'let us go back and tell them all that we are going to be married.'

Mr. Donald Iverach was certainly quite mad. But Janet of Inverness was madder still, for instead of accepting this very eligible young man with modest reluctance, she burst out crying all at once without the least warning, and ran downstairs, leaving Donald Iverach standing spellbound looking after her. Down the stair and through the hall she ran. She opened the door and flew out into the night, crying, 'James! James! I want you, James!'

And the strangest part of the whole is that even as she opened the door, two dark forms separated at the outer gate.

'There noo, look you after her,' said Cleg Kelly to Cleaver's boy. And James Annan went to do his duty even as he was bidden. The girl's wild cry of 'James! James!' hushed into quite another way of saying the same words, when she found herself clasped in the arms of Janet's boy—late Cleaver's. For James Annan not only had the root of the matter in him by nature, but, as we have seen, he was a lad of some little experience in affairs of the heart.

'What did I tell you, sir?' said Cleg to the Junior Partner, as they stood together on the step, and looked after the pair who had vanished into the darkness.

'It came out all right, I know,' said Mr. Donald Iverach, 'but I want no more games with pretty kitchenmaids. I will tell you what—for three full minutes I thought she was going to take me!'

And the Junior Partner went down the street at the rate of five miles an hour, without so much as stopping to say good-night.

ADVENTURE XXVIII

THE ENGINE-DRIVER WITH THE BEARD

WHAT James Annan said to little Janet of Inverness on the way home, and what Janet of Inverness said to James Annan, I know. But since it concerns only themselves, with themselves I will leave it. At all events, it was no long season before they were at one. Miss Cecilia Tennant's exact share in the plot is a harder matter to apportion. But that she had a share in it far beyond the mere issuing of the invitations is certain, for the very next evening Mr. Donald Iverach was heard saying to the arch-conspirator in the semi-privacy of the dusky angle of the stairs, 'But what I want to make out is, what *I* am to get out of it.'

'Virtue is its own reward,' replied Miss Celie, sententiously, 'and, besides, you make love to that sort of person so well, that it is evident you must have had a great deal of practice.'

'Now I call that a little hard on me,' said the Junior Partner, who felt that he had made a martyr of himself all the night before, and that he had, indeed, narrowly escaped the sacrificial altar.

'Wait,' he said threateningly, 'till you want me to do anything else of the kind for you.'

Celie Tennant set her pretty head the least bit to the side. It could not be called a cock, but it was the very nearest thing to it. Next she pursed up her mouth till it looked like a cherry.

'You would do it just as quick if I asked you to do it all over again,' said Celie Tennant, looking pins and needles at Donald Iverach, till the very palms of his hands pingled.

The Junior Partner stamped his foot.

'Oh, hang it all!' he cried, 'I believe it's the God's truth—I would.'

That night as he walked home, the Junior Partner, who had no gifts for the imparting of religious instruction, but who respected those who had (especially if they were pretty), wondered what could make a Sunday-school teacher act in such a perverse manner. He could not understand how it was that Celie Tennant, who upon occasion would weep over the crushing of a fly, and who was all the time worrying her life out over these young rascals of hers, could yet take pleasure in so tormenting a fellow-creature, and making his very existence a burden to him.

But when he came to think of it afterwards, he had to confess that on the whole he rather liked it. In fact, he thought that he would rather be made unhappy by Celie Tennant than that anyone else should give him the happiness of Paradise. He was a rankly foolish young man, and he would have hugged his follies if he had had any hope that this particular folly would have permitted him.

The present chronicler has, be it understood, undertaken to relate the adventures of Cleg's companions as well as those which immediately concern that hero. But these adventures of Cleaver's boy and his Janet of Inverness were not without direct bearing upon the fates of Cleg and of his lost friends the Kavannahs.

For it so happened that Duncan Urquhart, the uncle of Janet of Inverness, came one night to see her in the kitchen of Bailie Holden. The cook was pleased with him, for he was a single man and well bearded ; in fact, the very kind of man whom all cooks adore. Housemaids, on the other hand, like clean-shaven or moustached men, and as a rule prefer to catch them younger. And this is the reason why cooks marry gardeners while housemaids marry coachmen. Whereas nurses, having in their youths had enough of other peoples' children, live to a good old age in picturesque cottages, with assured pensions and uncertain tempers, and eventually die old maids. At least, so sayeth the philosopher.

Duncan Urquhart was not the chief of a clan. He was an engine-driver in the goods department of the Greenock and South-Eastern Railway. In the course of conversation the engine-driver, chiefly for the sake of the applause of the cook, cast about him for moving tales of the iron road on which his working hours were passed. He had settled in his mind that the cook was a wonderful woman. She could, to his certain knowledge, watch a roast, turn an omelette, taste a soup, and cast a languishing glance over her shoulder at him, all at the same time. He could not help thinking how excellent a thing it would be to come home to such a wife after a grimy run on the footplate. And then, having washed, how delightful it would be to sit down in his own house to the soup, the omelette, and the joint, with (so little did he know) as many of the languishing glances as ever he could wish for, thrown in as a permanent asset of his home ! So overcome was he by the idea, that for the moment he forgot that matters had proceeded even further with another cook in the town of Netherby, which formed his alternate stopping-place. It was a pity, he sometimes thought (for an instant only), that the laws of his country did not permit two such homes to be set up, one at either end of his daily journeyings.

Now, as one good effect of Duncan Urquhart's visit to Bailie Holden's kitchen, the position of Janet of Inverness as kitchenmaid was made a far more tolerable one. It is indeed a thing strongly advisable, that if the junior domestics of a house have presentable brothers or even uncles, unmarried and eligible, they should make haste to produce them. Janet of Inverness quite understood this. She knew, of course, that Duncan was to marry his cousin Mary in the Black Isle. But she was far too wise a little girl to say anything about a family arrangement like that. And then the cook always allowed her to walk in much pleasanter places for several days after the visits of her Uncle Duncan, who, as has been said, was a handsome man with a beard, and in habit very well put on and desirable.

But it is with Duncan's story that we have to do. Duncan spoke the speech of the north, crossed with the dialect peculiar to the Greenock and South-Eastern—a line whose engines are apple-green and gold, but the speech of whose engineers is blue, with purple patches. Not that Duncan swore before ladies, though Bailie Holden's cook certainly would have forgiven him because of his beard. It was indeed a habit she was rather partial to, thinking it a mighty offset to the conversation of bearded men. There is no denying that Duncan's speech was picturesque. But Cleg could not help feeling that swearing of Duncan's sort was altogether roundabout and unmanly. For himself, when he had need and occasion, he simply said 'Dam' and had done with it. Anything more savoured of superfluity to a boy of his simple tastes.

Duncan the engine-driver was talking about feats of strength.

'In my young days,' he said, 'I could toss the caber with any man. The Black Deil o' Dumfries tak' me, gin I couldna send a young tree birlin' through the air as if it had been a bit spale board. But ye should see Muckle Alick doon at Netherby Junction, where I pit up for the nicht. He's the porter there on the passenger side. An' the mid steeple is no better kenned for twenty miles round Netherby. Hands like the Day o' Judgment comin' in a thunder-cloud—heart like a wee white-faced lammie on the braes o' the Black Isle—that's Muckle Alick o' Netherby.

'As braid across the breast as if he was the gable end o' a bakehoose coming linkin' doon the street its lane. Lord bless me, when the big storm blew doon the home signals last spring, I declare gin Muckle Alick didna juist stand on the railway brig that sits end on to the Market Hill, and signal in the trains wi' airms like the cross trees o' a man-o'-war!

'I declare to conscience it's a Guid's truth!

'Aye, an' when that puir trembling chicken-hearted crowl, Tam Mac Wheeble, that drives the Port Andrew local passenger, stood still, wi' the bull's-eyes o' his wee blue engine juist looking roond the corner, an' whistled and yelled for the proper signal, pretendin' that he didna see Muckle Alick (him belongin' to anither kirk), Alick cried doon at him off the brig, so that they could hear him half a mile, "Ye donnert U. P., come on wi' your auld blue steam-roller an' your ill-faured cargo o' Irish drovers, or I'll come doon an' harl ye in mysel'!"

'Fac' as daith! I was there, talkin' to a nice bit lass that stands in the Refresh'!

'You weakly toon-bred loons' (here Duncan Urquhart looked from Cleg to Cleaver's boy) 'thinks me a strong man. But Alick, though his shooders are gettin' a wee bowed and his craw-black hair is noo but a birse o' grey, could tak' half a dozen like me and daud our heads thegither till we couldna speak. True as the "Reason Annexed" to the Third Commandment! I hae seen him wi' thae een that's in my head the noo!'

'Tell us mair,' said Cleg, standing with his mouth open, for the relation of feats of strength is every unlearned man's 'Iliad.' So Duncan went on to tell mighty things of the wrath of Muckle Alick.

'But, lads, ye maun ken Alick is no a ramblin' wastrel like the rest o' us aboot Netherby Junction. He's an elder amang the Cameronians. Haith! a weel-learned man is Alick, an' guid company for a minister—or ony other man. And never an ill word oot o' the mouth o' him. Na, no even when yince there was twa trains at different platforms, an' the station-maister cried to Alick to tak' the tickets frae baith o' them at the same time. "Juist tak' the Port Road train yoursel', gin ye are in sic a fidge!" quoth Alick. An' it was the station-maister that swore— Alick was even mair pleased-like than usual.

'But nae man ever saw Muckle Alick angry. The ill-set callants o' the Clearin' Hoose tries whiles to provoke him. Alick, he says little—only looks at them like a big sleepy dog when the pups are yelping. Then after a while he says, "Ye are like Tam Purdy's cat, when it ate the herrin' he had for his breakfast the time he was askin' the blessin', ye are 'gettin' raither pet!'"

'And then, if they winna take a telling, Alick will grip them in his loofs, gie them a shake and a daud thegither as if he was knockin' the stour aff a couple o' books, syne stick their heads in a couple o' bags o' Indian meal, an' leave them there wi' their heels in the air. But Alick is never oot o' temper. And ceevil —fresh kirned butter is no sweeter at eighteenpence a pund!'

ADVENTURE XXIX

MUCKLE ALICK'S BANNOCKBURN

'But what was I gaun to tell ye? Oh, aboot the Irish drovers. Ye maun ken they are no a very weel-liked class doon aboot Netherby. For they come in squads to the Market Hill on Mondays, and whiles their tongues and their sticks are no canny. Though some, I'm no denyin', are ceevil chiels. But them that I'm gaun to tell ye aboot were no that kind.

'It was the middle o' the day and Alick was away for his denner. There had been a bad market that day. Baith the marts were through hours afore their usual. So the drovers swarmed up to the station to get the afternoon train for Port Andrew. And on the platform the drinkin' frae bottles an' the swearin' was fair extraordinar'! So I am telled. Then, when the train cam' in, there was eight or nine o' the warst o' them that wadna be served but they maun a' get into a first-class compartment. And oot o' that they wadna get!

'The station-maister was a young man then and newly gotten on. He thocht a heap o' himsel'—as a young station-maister aye does when he first gets on the stemmed bonnet, and comes oot frae the office like Lord Almichty wi' a pen ahint his lug.

'Weel, at ony rate, the Netherby station-maister

was that sort. An' he was determined that naebody should cross him in his ain station.

'"I'll juist lock them in and let them fecht it oot," said the guard, "and by the time we are through the big cutting at the Stroan they'll hae shuggled doon as quaite as a session."

'It was doubtless good advice. But the station-maister was mainly angered. He gaed to the door o' the compartment and threatened the drovers wi' the law. And they juist pelted him wi' auld sodjers and ill talk. Then he cried for a' the porters and clerks, till there was a knot o' ten or a dozen o' them aboot the door—and a' the folk in the train wi' their heads oot o' the windows, askin' what on earth (an' ither places) was keepin' the train. And doon the main line the express was whustling fair blue-fire and vengeance because the signals were against her. But nae farther could they get. The station-maister he was determined to hae the drovers oot. And they were as set no to come—being gye and weel filled wi' the weedow's cheapest market whusky, that she keepit special for the drovers, for faith it wad hae scunnert a decent Heelant sow! I tried it yince and was I the waur o't for a for'nicht. But ony whusky is guid enough for an Irishman, if only ye stir plenty o' soot amang it! They think they're hame again if they get that.

'So here the hale traffic o' Netherby Junction was stelled for maybe a quarter o' an hour, and the station-maister was nearly daft to think what he wad hae to enter on his detention sheet. A' at ance somebody cries, "Here's Muckle Alick coming up the street." And sure enough there he was, slidderin' alang by the hill dyke wi' his hands in his pooches. For ye see this wasna his train, and he had ten minutes to spare. So wi' that the station-maister and the guard and half a dozen lads frae the offices rins to the far side o' the platform, waving on Alick and crying on him to come on. Alick he juist looks aboot to see wha was late for the train. But no' seein' onybody he steps leisurely alang, drawin' on his weel-gaun pipe, proud-like as ye hae seen an elephant at the head o' a show.

'And the mair they cried and waved, the mair cannily Alick looked aboot him for the man that was late for the train.

'"It maun be the provost at the least, wi' a' this fuss," said he to himself; "he'll be gaun up to Loch Skerrow to fish!"

'At last a wee upsettin' booking-clerk, the size o' twa quill pens, cam rinning and telled Alick a' aboot the drovers and the state the station-maister was in.

'"I'm no on duty at this train," said Alick, "but I'll come and speak to them."

'So they made way for him, and Alick gaed through the crowd at the platform like a liner through the herring-fleet below the Tail o' the Bank.

'"Lads," says he to the drovers, "what's this?—what's this?"

'Then they mocked and jeered at him. For it so happened that nane o' them had been often at Netherby Market, and so no a man o' them was acquaint wi' Muckle Alick. Providence was no kind to the Paddies that time whatever.

'"Boys," says Alick, as canny as if he had been courtin' his lass, "this wull never do ava', boys. It's no nice conduck! It's clean ridiculous, ye ken. Ye'll hae to come oot o' that, boys!"

'But they were fair demented wi' drink and pridefulness at keepin' the trains waitin', and so they miscaa'ed Alick for a muckle nowt-beast on stilts. And yin o' them let on to be an auctioneer, and set Alick up for sale.

'" Hoo muckle for this great lumbering Galloway stirk ? " says he.

'" Thrip ! " says another, " and dear at the money."

'" Boys," says Alick again, like a mither soothin' her weans when she hears the guidman's fit, " Boys, ye'll hae to come oot ! "

' But they only swore the waur at him.

'" Aweel," says Alick, " mind I hae warned ye, boys——"

' And he made for the carriage-door in the face o' a yell like a' Donnybrook broken lowse. Then what happened after that it is no' juist easy to tell. Alick gaed oot o' sicht into the compartment, fillin' the door neatly frae tap to bottom. There was a wee bit muffled buzzing like a bee-skep when a wasp gets in. Then presently oot o' the door o' the first-class carriage there comes a hand like the hand o' Providence, and draps a kickin' drover on the platform, sprawlin' on his wame like a paddock. Then, afore he can gather himsel' thegither, oot flees anither and faa's richt across him—and so on till there was a decent pile o' Irish drovers, a' neatly stacked cross-and-across like sawn wood in a joiner's yaird. Certes, it was bonny to see them ! They were a' cairded through yin anither, and a' crawling and grippin' and fechtin' like crabs in a basket. It was a maist heartsome sicht !

' Then, after the hindermost was drappit featly on the riggin', oot steps Muckle Alick—edgeways, of course, for the door wasna wide aneuch for him except on the angle. He was, if onything, mair calm and collected than usual. Muckle Alick wasna angry. He juist clicked his square key in the lock o' the door and stood lookin' composedly doon at the crawlin' pile o' drovers. Folk says he gied a bit smile, but I didna see him.

'"Ye see, boys, ye had to come oot!" said Muckle Alick.'

ADVENTURE XXX

HOW GEORDIE GRIERSON'S ENGINE BROKE ITS BUFFER

'Hoo-r-ray!' shouted Cleg Kelly and Cleaver's boy together, till the cook and little Janet of Inverness smiled at their enthusiasm.

'But there's mair,' said the engine-driver.

'It canna be better than that!' said Cleg, to whom the tale was as good as new potatoes and salt butter.

'It *is* better!' said the engine-driver, who knew that nothing holds an audience and sharpens the edge of its appetite better than a carefully cultivated expectancy.

'It was that same day after the Port Andrew train got away, when the cowed drovers were sent to the landing-bank to wait for their cattle train and the carriage that was coupled on to it for their transport. The driver o' the main line express was Geordie Grierson, an' he was no well-pleased man to be kept waitin' twenty minutes, with his engine-whistle yellyhooin' bluefire a' the time. He prided himsel' special on rinnin' to the tick o' the clock. So as soon as the signal dropped to clear he started her raither sharp, and she cam' into the station under a head of steam some deal faster than he had intended. Ye could hae heard the scraichin' o' the auld brakes a mile an' mair. But stop her they couldna. And juist as Geordie Grierson's engine was turnin' the curve to come past the facing points to the platform, what should we see but a wee bit ragged laddie, carryin' a bairn, coming staggerin' cross the metals to the near bank. Every single person on the platform cried to him to gang back. But the laddie couldna see Geordie's engine for the way he was carryin' the bairn, and maybe the noise o' the folk cryin' mazed him. So there he stood on the four-foot way, richt between the rails, and the express-engine fair on him.

'It cam' that quick our mouths were hardly shut after crying out, and our hearts had nae time to gang on again, before Muckle Alick, wha was standin' by the side o' the platform, made a spang for the bairns—as far as we could see, richt under the nose o' the engine. He gripped them baith in his airms, but he hadna time to loup clear o' the far rail. So Muckle Alick juist arched a back that was near as braid as the front of the engine itsel', and he gied a kind o' jump to the side. The far buffer o' the engine took him in the broad of his hinderlands, and whammeled him and the bairns in a heap ower on the grass on the far bank.

'Then there was a sough amang us wi' the drawing in o' sae mony breaths, for, indeed, we never looked for yin o' them ever to stir again. Geordie Grierson managed to stop his train after it had passed maybe fifty yairds. He was leanin' oot o' the engine cubby half his length an' lookin' back, wi' a face like chalk, at Muckle Alick and the weans on the bank.

'But what was oor astonishment to see him rise up wi' the bairns baith in his ae airm, and gie his back a bit dust wi' the back o' the ither as if he had been dustin' flour o' it.

'"Is there ocht broken, think ye, Geordie?" Muckle Alick cried anxious-like to the engine-driver.

'"Guid life, Alick, are ye no killed?" said the engine-driver. And, loupin' frae his engine, Geordie ran doon, if ye will believe it, greeting like a very bairn. And 'deed, to tell the truth, so was the maist feck o' us.

'"Killed?" says Alick; "weel, no that I ken o'!"

'And he stepped across the rails wi' the twa weans laughin' in his airms, for a' bairns are fond o' Alick. And says he, "I think I'll pit them in the left luggage office till we get the express cleared." So he did that, and gied them his big turnip watch to play wi'. And syne he took the passengers' luggage over and cried the name o' the station, as if he had done nocht that day forbye eat his denner.

'Then there cam' a lassie rinnin', wi' a loaf in her airms, and lookin' every road for something.

'"Did ye see twa bairns? Oh, my wee Hugh, what's come to ye?" she cried.

'"Ye'll find them in the luggage office, I'm thinkin', lassie," says Alick.'

And here the engine-driver of the goods train rose to depart. But his audience would not permit him.

'And what cam' o' the bairns?' cried Cleg, white with anxiety, 'and what was their names, can ye tell me?'

'Na, I never heard their names, if they had ony,' said Duncan Urquhart. 'They were but tinkler weans, gaun the country. But Alick could tell ye, nae doot. For I saw him gang doon the street wi' the wee boy in his hand, and the lass carryin' the bairn. An' the folk were a' rinnin' oot o' their doors to shake hands wi' Alick, and askin' him if he wasna sair hurt ?'

'"Na," says he; "I'll maybe a kennin' stiff for a day or twa, but there's nocht serious wrang—except wi' the spring o' Geordie's engine buffer! That's gye sair shauchelt!"'

'And guid nicht to ye a', an' a guid sleep. That's a' I ken,' said Duncan Urquhart from the kitchen door, where he was saying good-bye to the cook in a manner materially calculated to advance the interests of his niece, Janet of Inverness.

'And I'm gaun the morn's mornin' to see Muckle Alick!' cried Cleg. And he went out with the engine-driver.

ADVENTURE XXXI

THE 'AWFU' WOMAN'

A SORE heart had Vara Kavannah as she sat in the hut in Callendar's yard the night her mother had appeared at the gate of Hillside Works.

'I can never go back among them—no, never, never!' Vara said to herself again and again.

And already she saw the sidelong glance, and heard the sneering word thrown over the shoulder, as the companions from whom she had held herself somewhat aloof reminded her of her mother's disgrace. 'O father, father, come back to us—come back to us!' she cried over and over again till it became a prayer.

She sat with her hands before her face so long that little Hugh repeatedly came and stirred her arm, saying, 'What ails sister? Hugh Boy not an ill boy!'

Vara Kavannah's thoughts ran steadily on Liverpool, to which her father had gone to find work. She remembered having seen trains with carriages marked 'Liverpool' starting from the rickety old station at the end of Princes Street. She knew that they went out by Merchiston and Calder. That must, therefore, be the way to Liverpool. Vara did not remember that it must also be the way to a great many other places, since many carriages with other superscriptions passed out the same way.

As it darkened in the little construction hut, Vara listlessly rose to set the room to rights, and to give the baby its bottle. Nothing now seemed any use, since her mother had come back into her life. Yet Vara did not cry, for that also was no use. She had lost her place at the works, or at least she could never go back any more. Her world was at an end.

Hugh Boy still lingered outside, though it was growing latish, and the swallows that darted in and out of the stacked rafters and piled squares of boards began one by one to disappear from the vaulted sky. Hugh was busy watering the plants, as he had seen Cleg do. And he kept one hand in his pocket and tried to whistle as like his model as possible. Vara was just laying the baby in its cot when she heard a scream of pain from Hugh at the door.

'Mercy me!' said she, 'has the laddie tumbled and hurt himsel'?'

She flew to the open door, which was now no more than a dusky oblong of blue-grey. A pair of dark shapes stood in front of her. Little Hugh lay wailing on the ground. A hard clenched hand struck Vara on the mouth, as she held up her hands to shield the baby she had carried with her in her haste, and a harsh thick voice screamed accumulated curses at her.

'I hae gotten ye at last, ye scum, you that sets yourself up to be somebody. You that dresses in a hat and feather, devil sweep ye! Come your ways in, lad, and we will soon take the pride out of the likes o' her, the besom!'

The man hung back and seemed loth to have part in the shame. But Sal Kavannah seized him by the hand and dragged him forward.

'This is your new faither, Vara,' she said; 'look at him. He is a bonny-like man beside your poor waff wastrel runnagate faither, Sheemus Kavannah!'

The man of whom Sal Kavannah spoke was a burly, low-browed ruffian, with the furtive glance of one who has never known what it is to have nothing to conceal.

But Vara thought he did not look wholly bad.

'Come in, mother!' she said at last in a low voice. Then she went out to seek for Boy Hugh, who had run into the dark of the yard and darned himself safely among the innumerable piles of wood which stood at all angles and elevations in Callendar's wide quadrangle.

'Hugh! Boy Hugh!' she cried. And for a long time she called in vain. At last a low and fearful voice answered her from a dark corner, in which lay the salvage of a torn-down house.

'Is she gane away?' said the Boy Hugh.

'No, but ye are to come hame,' said Vara, holding the babe closer to her bosom.

'Then Hugh Boy is no comin' hame the nicht till the "awfu' woman" is gane away!' said the lad, determinedly.

'Come, boy, come,' she said again; 'my heart is wae for us a'. But come wi' your Vara!'

'Na, Hugh Boy is no comin'. Ye will hae to *hist* me oot wi' big dogs afore I will come hame to the "awfu' woman,"' said Hugh Boy, who was mightily set when his mind was made up.

So Vara had perforce to drag her feet back to the horrors which awaited her within the construction hut. The man and her mother had been pledging one another when she entered. A couple of black bottles stood between them, and Sal Kavannah looked up at her daughter with a fleering laugh.

'Aye, here she comes that sets up for being better than her mother! But we'll show you before we are through with you, my man and me, you———'

However, it does not enter into the purpose of this tale to blacken so much as a page with the foul excrement of a devilish woman's hate of her own child. The Scripture holdeth—the mother may forget. She may indeed have no compassion on the child of her womb. And Vara Kavannah sat still and listened, till the burning shame dulled to a steady throbbing ache somewhere within her. The woman's threats of future torture and outrage passed idly over her, meaningless and empty. The man drank steadily, and grew ever silenter and more sullen; for, to his credit be it said, the situation was not to his taste, and he looked but seldom at Vara. The girl sat clasping the babe to her bosom, with a secret sense that in little Gavin she had her best and indeed her only protector. For even the very bad man in his senses will hardly hurt an infant— though a bad woman will, as we may read in the records of our police courts.

So Vara sat till the man reeled to the door carrying the unfinished bottle with him, and Sal Kavannah, her orgie logically completed, sank in a fœtid heap on the floor with the empty one beside her.

The man as he stumbled out left the door open, and in a little while Vara could hear Boy Hugh's plaintive voice, asking from the wood-pile in the corner whether the 'awfu' woman' was gone yet.

As Vara sat and listened all through the short hours of that midsummer night to the clocks of the city churches, the stertorous breathing of her mother and the babe's occasional feeble wail were the only sounds within the hut itself. But Boy Hugh's plaint detached itself fitfully from the uneasy hum of the midnight city without. A resolve, new-born indeed, but seemingly old and determinate as the decrees of the God she had learned about in the Catechism, took hold upon her.

It seemed to Vara that it did not matter if she died—it did not even matter whether Hugh and Gavin died, if only she could find her father, and die far away from her mother and all this misery.

The girl was so driven to the last extremity by the trials of the day and the terrors of the night, that she rose and put on her hat as calmly as though she had been going for a walk with Cleg and the children across the park. As calmly also she made her preparations, stepping carefully to and fro across her mother on the floor. She put all the scraps of bread that were left from Cleg's windfall into her pocket, together with the baby's feeding bottle and a spare tube. Then she added Hugh's whistle and a certain precious whip with a short bone handle and a long lash, which Cleg had given him. Vara was sure that Hugh Boy would cry for these, and want to go back if she did not take them with her. She had nothing of her own to take, except the indiarubber umbrella ring which Cleg Kelly had given her. So she took that, though she had never possessed an umbrella in her life. Groping in Gavin's crib, she found her shawl, and wrapped it about her with a knowing twist. Then she deftly took up the baby. The shawl went over her left shoulder and was caught about her waist at the right side, in a way which all nurses and mothers know, but which no man can ever hope to describe. The babe was still asleep, and Vara's tender touch did not awake it as she went bravely out into the night to walk to Liverpool to find her father.

But as a first step she must find Boy Hugh. And that young man was exceedingly shy. He had got it in his obstinate little head that his sister wished to drag him back to the 'awfu' woman.' It was not, therefore, till Vara had managed to persuade him in the most solemn way that she had no intention of ever going back, that he consented to accompany her upon her desperate quest.

At last Boy Hugh took her hand, and the three bairns left Callendar's yard behind them for ever. What happened there that night after they left we already know. It is with the children's wanderings that we now have to do.

ADVENTURE XXXII

MAID GREATHEART AND HER PILGRIMS

IT was already almost grey day when the children fared forth from the city. Vara's chief anxiety was lest they should not be able to escape out of the town before the light came, so that some officious neighbour might be able to direct her enemy upon their track. It was not long before they emerged out of the side-alleys upon a broad paved street which led towards the south.

Vara paused and asked a policeman if this was the way to Liberton.

'And what are you going to do at Liberton so early in the morning?' said the policeman. He asked because he was a Lothian man, who always puts a second question before he can bring himself to answer the first.

'We are gaun to see our faither,' said Vara, speaking the truth.

'Weel,' said the policeman, 'that is the road to Liberton. But if I was you I would wait till the milk-cairts were drivin' hame. Then I could get ye a lift to Liberton fine.'

He was a kind-hearted 'poliss,' and in fact the same officer who had looked over the screen by the watch-shelter behind which Tyke was spinning his yarns to Cleg Kelly.

So that—thus strange is the working of events when they take the reins into their own hands—at the very moment when Cleg Kelly was sleeplessly turning over in his mind the problem of the life-fate of Vara and the children by the dying fire at the Grange crossing, Vara herself with the baby on her arm was trudging down the pavement opposite. As she passed she looked across, and only the timbered edge of the shelter prevented her from seeing Cleg Kelly.

Thus, without the least hindrance or observation, the three children escaped out of their thrice-heated fiery furnace into the cool of the country hedges and upon the clean hard surface of the upland roads.

With the inevitable instinct of hunted things Vara turned aside whenever she heard the brisk clapper of the hoofs of a milk-cart pony, or the slower rumble of a market waggon. For she knew that it was of such early comers into the city that questions would be asked. So, when Cleg set about his inquisition among the milkmen and market gardeners, he was foiled by the very forethought which had only desired to defeat an enemy, not to mystify a friend.

Thus hour by hour they left behind them quiet, kindly, red-tiled villages, set in heartsome howes and upon windy ridges. And, as they went ever onward, morning broadened into day; day crept dustily forward to hot noon; noon drowsed into afternoon, with a scent of beanfields in the air, dreamily sweet. Vara's arm that held the baby grew numb and dead. Her back ached acutely from the waist downwards as though it would break in two. Sometimes the babe wailed for food. Little Hugh dragged leadenly upon her other hand, and 'whinged' on, with the wearisome iteration of the corncrake, that he wished to go back to Callendar's yard, till Vara had to remind him, because nothing else would stay his plaining, of the 'awfu' woman' waiting for him there.

Vara did not rest long that whole day. They sat down as seldom as possible, and then only for a few minutes. Vara poured a little of the water from a wayside spring upon the crumbs that were left, and gave them to little Gavin, mixing them with the remaining milk in his bottle. Hugh begged incessantly that Vara would let him take off his boots and walk barefoot. But his sister knew that he would certainly become lame in a mile or two. Yet there must have been pleasure in their journey too, for they sat down in the pleasantest places all that fine, warm, bough-tossing day. The shadows were sprinkled on the grassy hillsides, like a patchwork quilt which Vara had once seen in their house when Hugh was very little, but which had long ago become only a memory and a lost pawn-ticket.

Never before had the children seen such quaint woodland places—nooks where the rabbits tripped and darted, or sat on the bank washing faces pathetically innocent and foolish. Little runnels of water trickled down the gullies of the banks and dived under the road. But for Vara, at least, there was no true enjoyment, no resting all that day. They soon spent their store of food. By noon Hugh had eaten all the cold potatoes. The babe had taken, at first with difficulty, then under the pressure of hunger greedily, the thin water and milk with the crushed crumbs in it which Vara had made at the brook-side. So that also was finished. Hunger began, not for the first time, to grip them.

But still they could not rest long. In a little, just

as Hugh Boy was beginning to drop asleep and lean heavily against Vara, there came again upon her without warning a terrible fear. She looked down the road they had come, and she seemed to see the cruel eyes of her enemy, to hear again the foul threats of the life she was to be compelled to lead for 'setting herself up to be better than her mother,' all the words which she had listened to during those last hours of terror and great darkness in the old construction hut.

So Vara shook Hugh awake, stroking his cheeks down gently till his eyes opened. She settled the shawl over her other shoulder, and the bairns were soon on their way again. The dusty road beneath appeared to stream monotonously between their feet, and so weary did they grow that sometimes they seemed to be only standing still. Sometimes, on the contrary, they appeared to be going forward with incredible speed. Vara bore the aching of her carrying-arm till it became agony unspeakable, and the weight of Gavin dragged on her very brain. Then, for a treat, she would shift him to the other arm, and for a few minutes the keen twinging ache deadened to a dull pain, as the tired wrist and elbow dropped to her side. But soon in the other arm the same stounding agony began.

Still the children fared on, spurred forward by the fear of that which they had left behind them. The thought and hope of their father had greatly died out of Vara's mind, though not altogether. But the mighty instinct of hiding from days and nights like those which had gone over her head recently, drove her restlessly forward. Yet she began sadly to acknowledge that, though she herself might be able to stumble on a little longer ere night fell, Hugh and Gavin could not go much further. The former began to lag behind at every turn, and whenever they stopped a moment he fairly dropped asleep on his feet, and his head fell flaccidly against her side.

The bells of a little town on the slope of a hill were just striking six and the mill-folk were streaming homeward, when the children had their first great piece of luck. They were just by a stone watering-trough at the curve of a long brae, when a smart light cart with yellow wheels came past. It was driven by a young man, who sat, looking very bright and happy, with his sweetheart beside him. As the pair came slowly up the brae they had been talking about the children, whom they could see dragging on before them weary-foot, sick with pain and drowsiness.

Perhaps the young man's heart was touched. Or mayhap his sweetheart asked him to give them a penny, and he wished to show his generosity. But in either case certain it is that as he passed up the hill he nodded brightly back to the children and threw them a coin. It rolled on its edge to Vara's feet, who stooped and picked it up, solacing her independent soul as the precious silver lay apparent in her hands by telling herself that she had not asked for it. Her mother had found all her savings the night before, and had emptied them into the hand of her companion, out of the cup in which they had stood on the shelf which served for the mantelpiece of the old construction hut. So that but for this happy young man's sixpence Vara and her charges were absolutely penniless.

ADVENTURE XXXIII

THE BABES IN THE HAYSTACK

But even Hugh brightened at the sight of the silver, and when Vara proposed to go back and buy something for them while he stayed with Gavin and gathered him flowers to play with, the lad said determinedly, 'Hugh Boy come too!'

So they all went back to the village. They stood looking long and wistfully into the shop windows, for what to buy was so momentous a question that it took them some considerable time to decide. At last Vara made up her mind to have twopence-worth of stale bread at a baker's. She was served by the baker's wife, who, seeing the girl's weary look, gave her a fourpenny loaf of yesterday's baking for her coppers, together with some salt butter in a broad cabbage leaf into the bargain. Vara's voice broke as she thanked the woman, who had many bairns of her own, and knew the look of trouble in young eyes. Then at another shop Vara bought a pennyworth of cheese, which (as she well knew) satisfies hunger better than any other food. Then came a pennyworth of milk for the baby, with which she filled his bottle, and gave what was over to Hugh Boy, who drank it out of the shopkeeper's measure.

When the children came out, Vara took Hugh

by the hand, and they marched past the baker's without stopping. For the boy had set his love upon a certain gingerbread lion with a pair of lack-lustre eyes of currants, and as they passed the baker's shop he set up a whining whimper to have it. But his sister marched him swiftly past before the dews in his eyes had time to fall. The baker's wife had come to the door to look after them, and, seeing Hugh Boy's backward dragging look, she sent her little girl after them with the very gingerbread lion of Hugh's dreams. Hugh Boy stood speechless, open-mouthed with thankfulness. The little girl smiled at his surprise.

'We hae lots o' them at our house,' she said, and hurried back to her mother.

They mounted the hill once more and sat on the grassy bank by the side of the watering trough, into which a bright runlet of water fell, and in which little stirring grains of sand dimpled and danced.

Never was anything sweeter than the flavour of yesterday's bread, except perhaps the gingerbread lion, from which Hugh had already picked one black currant eye, leaving a yellow pitted socket which leered at him with horrid suggestiveness of stomach-ache. But hunger-ache was Hugh Boy's sole enteric trouble, so that the suggestion was lost upon him.

The water of the hill spring, splashing into the stone trough, sounded refreshing beyond expression. The baby dreamed over his bottle, and lay with his eyes fixed on the clear heavens above—from which, if all tales be true, he had come to a world of whose kindness he had had so little experience since his arrival in it.

For the first time that day Vara took a bite for

herself and many a draught of the dimpling spring-water, whose untiring crystal rush into the basin it was so pleasant to watch. Then Vara washed Hugh's feet and her own in the overflow of the trough, just at the place where the burn ran under the road. On Hugh Boy's feet was a painful pink flush, but no blister appeared. On her own feet, however, there were two or three. Vara was glad that Hugh was fit for his journey.

They started again, and, with the refreshment of the food and the brief rest, they managed to make two or three miles before the dark fell. But soon it was evident that the three wanderers could go no further that night. The babe's eyes were long closed with sleep, and poor little Hugh could only keep awake and stagger on by constantly rubbing his knuckles into the corners of his eyes.

They were now on a high wild moor, and there was no house within sight. They still went onward, however, blindly and painfully. The roadsides trailed past them black and indistinct till they came to a farmhouse. They could see tall buildings against the skies and hear the lash of an unseen mill-stream over a wheel into a pool. A blackcap sang sweetly down in some reeds by the mill-dam.

Vara did not dare to knock at the door of the house. She was just about to go into the farmyard in search of a shed to lie down in, when she remembered that she had heard from Cleg how there were always fierce dogs about every farmhouse. For Hugh's sake she could not risk it. Instead of going forward, therefore, she groped her way with one hand into a field where there were many stacks of hay and corn. Vara could tell by the rustling as her hand passed over them.

Soon she came to a great haystack in a kind of covered shed, which stood between wooden posts like trees. One end of it was broken down and cut into platforms. Vara mounted upon one with the baby, and reached down a hand for Boy Hugh. For the last few miles, indeed ever since it grew dark, Hugh had been more than half asleep, and his weariful sobbing had worn down to a little clicking catch in his throat, which still recurred at intervals. It was by the sound that Vara found him. She leaned over as far as she dared, and drew him up beside her. He was asleep in her arms before she could lay him down.

Vara thought the people of the farm would not be very angry in the morning if she pulled out a little of the hay.

'It is for the baby's sake!' she said, to excuse herself.

So she scooped out of the higher step of the stack where it was broadest a little cave among the hay, and into this she thrust Boy Hugh gently, putting his legs in first and leaving only his head without. Then she rolled the babe and herself in the shawl and crawled in beside him. She drew the hay close like a coverlet about them. She listened awhile to Hugh Boy's breathing, which still had the catch of bygone tears in it. She kissed Gavin, closed her eyes, and instantly fell asleep herself. Vara said no prayers. But the incense of good deeds and sweetest essential service went up to God from that haystack.

ADVENTURE XXXIV

MARY BELL, BYRE LASS

The morning came all too soon, with a crowing of cocks and the clashing hurrahs of the rooks, circling up from their nesting in the tall trees about the steading. But the tired children slept on. The life of the farm began about them, with its cheerful sounds of clinking head-chains as the cattle came in, and of tinkling harness as the teams went afield. But still the children did not wake. It was not till Mary Bell, byre lass, came to get an armful of fodder from the stack that they were found.

'Lord, preserve us! what's that?' she cried when, with her knees upon the step of the stack, she saw the children—Vara's wearied face turned to the babe, and the dew damp on the white cheeks of Boy Hugh.

'I maun fetch the mistress!' said Mary Bell.

And then these two women stood and marvelled at the children.

'Mary,' said the mistress of the farm, 'd'ye mind the text last Sabbath?'

Mary Bell looked indignantly at her employer.

'How do ye think I can mind texts wi' as mony calves to feed?' she asked, like one of whom an unfair advantage is taken.

'O Mary!' said her mistress, 'how often hae I

telled you no to set your mind on the vainities o' this wicked world?'

'An' whatna ane do ye pay me for?—to keep mind o' texts or to feed the calves?' asked the byre lass, pertinently.

'Mary,' said the other, ignoring the argument, 'the text was this: "I will both lay me down and sleep"—dod, but I declare I forget the rest o't,' she concluded, breaking down with some ignominy.

'In the land o' the leal,' suggested Mary Bell, either wickedly or with a real desire to help. Her superior promptly accepted the emendation.

'That's it!' she said. 'Is it no bonny to look at thae bairns and mind the text, "I will both lay me down and sleep, in the land o' the leal,"?'

'I'll wauken them,' said practical Mary Bell, 'and bring them into the hoose for some breakfast.'

'Na, na,' said her mistress, 'ye maunna do that. What wad the guidman say? Ye ken he canna be doin' wi' folk that gang the country. A wee drap o' yestreen's milk noo—or the scrapins o' the parritch pot!'

'Aye,' said Mary Bell, '"in the land o' the leal." Ye had better gang ben and look up the text, mistress; I'll attend to the bairns.'

'Aye, do that,' said the good wife, with perfect unconsciousness of Mary Bell's sarcasm, 'but be sparin'. Mind ye, this is hard times for puir farm folk! And we canna spend gear and graith recklessly on unkenned bairns.'

'Ye will be free o' that crime, mistress,' murmured Mary, as her mistress took her way into the house; 'gin ye could tak' a' the siller that ye hae saved wi' ye, what a bien and comfortable doon-sitting wad ye no hae in heeven ! Itherwise, I'm nane sae sure—in spite o' your texts.'

Then Mary sat down and took the children one by one, touching their faces to make them waken. Vara sat up suddenly, with wild eyes and a cry of fear. In her terror she clasped the baby so hard that it also waked and cried. With the other hand she brushed away the elf locks about her own eyes. But her heart stilled its fluttering as she caught the kindly eyes of Mary Bell, set in a brown sun-coarsened face of broad good humour.

'O,' said Vara, 'I thought ye were my mother!'

And Mary Bell, who, though a byre lass and daughter of toil, was born with the gentle heart of courtesy within her, refrained from asking why this wandering girl should be so greatly afraid of her own mother.

'Are you hungry?' she said, instead.

And little Boy Hugh awoke, rolled out of the hay, and shook himself like a young puppy. He stretched his arms wide, clasping and unclasping his fingers.

'I'm *that* hungry!' he said, as if he had heard Mary Bell's words in a dream.

'That's answer enough!' said the byre lass. 'Certes, ye are a bonny laddie; come here to me.'

And Mary Bell, who was born to love children and to bear them, snatched him up and kissed him warmly and roughly. But Hugh wriggled out of her arms, and as soon as he found himself on the ground he wiped his mouth deliberately and ungratefully with the back of his hand.

'Hae ye ony pieces and milk for wee boys?' he said.

The byre lass laughed.

'Ye like pieces and milk better than kisses,' said she. 'Hoo does that come?'

'Pieces and milk are better for ye!' said Boy Hugh, stating an undeniable truth.

'It's a peety,' said Mary Bell, sententiously, 'that we dinna aye ken what's guid for us.' And she was thoughtful for some moments. 'Come awa', bairns,' she said, taking Gavin from Vara, and carrying him herself into a milk house, which was filled with a pleasant smell of curds and cheese.

Hugh Boy went wandering about, wondering at the great tin basins filled with milk to the brim, some fresh and white, and some covered smoothly with a thick yellow coating of cream.

'I never thocht there was as muckle milk in a' the world!' said Boy Hugh.

So here the children ate and drank, and were infinitely refreshed. And as she set before them each new dainty—farles of cake, thick soda scones, milk with the cream generously stirred amongst it, fresh new milk yet warm from the cow for Gavin, Mary Bell said: 'This is better than mindin' a text! Sirce me, heard ye ever the like o' it—"To the land o' the leal"? An' she took it a' in. She reads a' the Bible ever she reads between her sleeps in the kirk, I'se warrant. Wait till I see Jamie Mailsetter; I'll hae a rare bar to tell him!'

It was an hour after, much comforted and refreshed with a back-load of provisions and one of Mary Bell's hardly-earned shillings, that the wanderers set out. They continued to wave her their farewells till they were far down the loaning.

And they might well be sorry, for there were not many people so kind and strong-hearted as Mary Bell to be met with between the entering in of the Land of Pilgrimage and the City of the Twelve Foundations. And some of these are rough-handed and weather-beaten men and women, who work out their Christianity in feeding calves and wandering bairns instead of parading texts—keeping the word of God in their hearts according to the commandment.

ADVENTURE XXXV

THE KNIGHT IN THE SOFT HAT

AND so their second day was a good day, as most days are that are well begun with an excellent breakfast. For, together with a good conscience, that makes all the difference. And especially when you are Hugh Boy's age, for then even the state of the conscience does not so much matter.

Hugh Boy had never been in the country before, and, being a lad of much observation, he had to watch all that there was to see. And there were many things for Hugh Boy to observe that day. Robin Redbreasts peeped with their summer shyness upon them from the low bushes on the banks. Sparrows pecked about among flowery patches, instead of at the mud in the streets, as Hugh Boy had always seen them do before. There was a big bird which floated above the farmyard of one of the farms they passed. Hugh wondered what sort of creature it could be. He heard a motherly hen, which had been scraping and clucking among the dust as they came round the corner, suddenly give a strange screech, just like the noise which Vara had made the other night when the 'awfu' woman' came to their door. He saw the hen droop her wings and crouch in the dust, keeping her beak up in the air, her timid watchful eyes now glittering with anger.

Hugh Boy questioned Vara, but Vara had the baby to attend to, and answered that it was 'just a bird.' But soon the big shadow on the sky with the outstretched wings floated away, and the hen went back to its contented picking. The children also went along the wayside to-day with many more rests and lingerings. For they had no longer the sharp instant spur of pursuit driving them on.

They stopped to take their meal by a little bridge, under which a moorland burn ran bickering down to join a big river which flowed to the distant sea.

They sat down in the dark of the arch to be out of the sun, and Vara had spread out all the provision which her kind friend, Mary Bell, had given her before she saw that at the other end a young man was crouching close in by the wall. At sight of him Vara started, and would have put her bread and milk back again. But the man cried out to her, 'Not so fast, my pretty dears; there's another hungry stomach here.'

'You are welcome to a share o' what we have,' said Vara, who had been too often hungry herself not to know the pain it meant.

The youth came and sat down by them. He was a lean and unwholesome-looking vagrant. The whites of his eyes had turned an unpleasant leaden colour, while the pupils were orange-coloured, like the stripes on a tiger's skin.

Vara gave him one of the largest of Mary Bell's scones, and some of the butter they had got from the baker's wife the day before. The young man ate these up greedily, and reached out his hand for more. Vara offered him some of the loaf which she had bought.

'None o' that dry choko-tuck for me; gimme the soft bread!' said he, rudely snatching at it.

Vara told him civilly that it was not for herself that she wanted to keep it, but to break up in the baby's milk.

In spite of her pitiful protest, however, the young man snatched the scone and ate it remorselessly, looking at Vara all the time with evil eyes, and smiling a smirk of satisfaction. There was no snivelling weakness about him. Hugh Boy never took his eyes off him. Then, when he had finished, the lout rose, coolly stuffed the remainder of their provision into his pocket, and came over towards Vara with his hand stretched out. He caught her by the wrist and sharply twisted her arm.

'Shell out your tin,' he said. 'Out with it now, and no bones about it!'

Vara bore the pain as well as she could without crying out. Suddenly, however, the rascal dropped her hand, and snatched Gavin from her arms. He stood on the edge of the ravine over which the bridge went, holding the child, and threatened to throw him over if she did not give him all the money she had. He was, of course, as he told himself, only 'kidding' her, but Vara was in wild terror for Gavin. Her own particular evil genius had never hesitated to carry out such threatenings.

'I will! I will!' cried Vara. And she took the byre lass's shilling out of her pocket and gave it to the man.

'Any more?' said he. 'Yes, I see there is. Out with it!'

And Vara drew out the remainder of the sixpence which the young lover had thrown to her from his cart yesterday.

Then the cruel hobbledehoy tossed her the child

with a laugh, and sprang sharply round the parapet of the bridge. Pale as ivory, Vara ran after him to watch. The rascal was quite at his ease, for he stopped a little way off to light his pipe and to take a drink out of a little square bottle. This he stowed away in the tails of his coat, which were very long. Then he waved his hand humorously to Vara and Boy Hugh as they stood by the arch of the bridge.

A tall, well-built young fellow was coming down the road towards them, and a hope sprang up in Vara's mind that he might do something for her. The stranger's round soft hat and dark clothes marked him for a clergyman. But he swung his stick and whistled, which were new things to Vara in one of his cloth.

At sight of him the thief pulled down the corners of his mouth and put on his regulation mendicant's whine.

'For the love o' God, sir, help a poor fellow that's dyin' o' hunger. I've walked fifty miles without a bite —hope to die if I haven't, sir. I wouldn't tell you a lie, sir.'

The stalwart young minister smiled, and gave his stick another swing before he spoke.

'You have not walked five miles without drinking, anyway, as my nose very plainly tells me. And your pipe is setting your coat on fire at this very moment!'

The hobbledehoy plucked his lighted pipe out of his pocket and set his thumb in the bowl.

'You are one o' the good kind,' he persisted; 'you are not the sort that would deny a poor chap a sixpence because he takes a draw of tobacco when he can get it?'

'Not a bit,' said the minister, good-humouredly; 'I can take a whiff myself. But I don't ask anybody else to pay for it. It's a fine business, yours, my lad. But I'm not keeping a free rum and tobacco shop. So you had best tramp, my man.'

At this the tramp began to pour forth a volley of the most foul-mouthed abuse, cursing all parsons as rogues, liars, and various other things. The minister listened patiently for some time.

'Now,' he said, when at last there came a pause, 'I have given you your say—away with you! And if I hear another foul word out of your mouth, I will draw my stick soundly across your back.'

'Oh!' said the other, impudently, 'I thought you were one of the softish kind—the sort that when you smote them on the one cheek, turned the other also.'

The young man in the round hat squared his shoulders.

'Did anyone smite me on the one cheek?' he asked. 'If they did, I didn't know it. Perhaps you would like to try?'

And he came nearer to the rascal, who drew off as if not at all inclined to make the experiment. He made no reply.

'But,' said the minister, 'since you are so ready with your Scripture, you will not object to another text—just as good, and more suitable for application to the like of you. It is—"A rod for the fool's back!"'

And with that he lifted his stick and brought it down on the young rough's shoulder with the swing of a cricketer cutting a high ball to the boundary.

Never was there in the world a more astonished scoundrel. He turned on the instant and ran. But Vara was close beside them by this time.

'He stole my money!' she cried; 'catch him! O dinna let him away!'

The young minister clapped his hat firmly on the back of his head and gave chase. The thief was for the moment the swifter, but he had not the wind nor yet the training of his opponent.

'Stop!' cried the pursuer, imperiously.

The thief glanced about, and seeing the stick he had tasted once before hovering in the air, he dropped in a heap across the path to trip his pursuer. The minister cleared him in his stride and turned upon him. The rascal kept perfectly still till his captor approached. Then suddenly he shot out his foot in a vicious kick. But the young fellow in the round hat had been in France, and knew all about that game. He caught the foot in his hand and turned the fellow over on his back. Vara came panting up.

'Give this girl her money,' said the minister. 'How much was it, my lassie?'

'It was a shilling and twopence,' said Vara.

'Out with it or I'll go through you!' said the minister. And the thick stick again hovered an ultimatum.

So Vara got her money, and without so much as a parting curse the cowed and frightened rascal took himself off down the road at a slow trot, keeping his eyes on the ground all the way.

Vara was left alone with her knight of the soft hat.

ADVENTURE XXXVI

THE MADNESS OF HUGH BOY

THE young minister put out his hand to Vara, and the two walked quietly back to where Boy Hugh was kneeling on the grass, and baby Gavin was sitting grasping a dandelion with one hand and looking with wide deep-set eyes of philosophic calm upon the world.

'Tell me all about it,' said her champion. And Vara told the tale, with her heart again beginning to beat with terror. 'But how is it that you are here?' said he. And Vara explained as much as she could.

'To look for your father in Liverpool?' he said. 'It is a long, sad way—a terrible journey.' He mused.

He had a passion for setting things right, this young fellow, and it occurred to him that it would be a good thing if he could get these children into a home of some kind, and then communicate with the police on the subject of their father.

But as soon as the young man began to speak in his low, persuasive tones of a home where they could be safe and quiet, Vara stood up.

'O no, sir, I thank you, but we cannot bide. Somebody might come and find us.'

At the mere thought she began to tremble and hastily to put her scattered belongings together. The young minister made no further objection. He walked with them a little along the way, and before he parted from them he put another shilling into Vara's hand. Then he leaped over the stone dyke on his way to a farmhouse where there was a sick man waiting for him. From the other side of the fence he told Vara shyly to remember that she had another Father somewhere else to care for her, One who could always be found. But he was shy about saying so much, this remarkable young man. However, he had a high sense of duty, and he felt that the circumstances justified the observation.

'Thank ye,' said Vara; 'I'll no forget.'

This, their second day of wandering, had become one of brooding heat, and Vara was glad to have enough to buy a good meal for them all at the next little town they passed through. They were fortunate also in the afternoon, for at a little house by the wayside, a cottage with red creepers growing all along the wall, the mistress took them all in and gave them a cup of tea and some of the fresh white scones she was baking. There was milk too for little Gavin. And as they went away a thought seemed to strike the woman. She bade them wait a little while. She climbed up into the attic, and presently returned with a shawl, which she wrapped about Vara, and settled the baby into the nook of it with her own hands.

'But this is a good shawl. We must not take it from you,' said Vara.

'Nonsense,' said the good woman; 'it is a fair exchange. Leave me the auld ane; it will make very decent floor-clouts.'

So it was on the whole a good day for them. And it was not till late in the evening that misfortune again befell them. Vara's hands were usually so full of Gavin that she had little thought for anything else. But at one resting-place she put her hand into her pocket and her heart stood still because she failed to find the slim coins upon which she had put her trust. She felt the pennies, but not the shilling or the sixpence. She laid Gavin down on the grass and turned the pocket inside out. There was nothing whatever there. But Vara found instead a little slit in the lining, and the thought of her loss, together with what it meant to them all, turned her faint and sick.

'The man might just as well have had them, after all,' she said.

Night fell with them still upon the road. They had found no friendly shelter, and indeed they seemed to be alone on a wide moor, through which the road ran unfenced, like a tangle of string which has been loosely thrown broadcast. Hugh Boy cried bitterly to be allowed to lie down. Vara looked about her anxiously and long. But she could see nothing except wild moorish hilltops girdling the horizon, too like one another to give her any idea of the direction in which a habited house might lie. She saw only the slow twilight of midsummer in the north creeping down over the brown moors, and in the moist hollows of the boglands shallow pools of mist gathering.

From a great distance the sound of a voice was borne upon the still air.

'Hurley, hurley, hie away hame!' it said. And Vara went to the top of a heathery knowe and called loudly. But only the moorbirds, making ready for bed, answered her. They flew round and round, circling and complaining, especially the peewits, which, being reassured by the small size of the three, came almost offensively near.

Boy Hugh filled his pockets with stones to drive them away. He also got out his whip. He had heard of the Babes in the Wood, and, being a sensible boy, he did not want any Robin Redbreast nonsense. It was not so much that he objected to die, but he felt the humiliation of being covered with leaves by silly whaups. He complained bitterly to Vara, who was preoccupied with Gavin, that the day before their flight the Drabble had stolen from him the iron barrel of the pistol which Cleg Kelly had given him. Had it not been for that felony, they would not now have found themselves all defenceless in that wild place.

'Boy Hugh thinks that there's sure to be lions an' teegers here!' he said.

It was not long before Vara decided that they must spend another night out of doors, and looked about for a suitable spot where they could get water and shelter.

At last she settled under the lee of a large boulder, and began to give Gavin what remained of his milk. Boy Hugh thought this was his opportunity to make sure that they were well defended against their enemies. The moon was rising, and he remembered that Cleg Kelly had told him how lions and tigers always hunted by moonlight. That widely-read journal, 'The Bully Boys of New York,' was Cleg's authority for this statement.

There was certainly an appalling silence on the face of the moorland. Boy Hugh could see, indeed, the rock behind which Vara and Gavin were crouched. But he tried to forget it. He yearned for the sensation of perfect loneliness. Then the devil entered into Boy Hugh, and he wanted to explore. The moon looked out from behind a cloud, and everything became bleached and flat, melting away into vague immensities and nerve-shaking mysteries which, in their turn, vanished sideways as you approached. Of course that was not the way Boy Hugh put it to himself. It only made him want to run deeper into the wilderness. But suddenly a vague fear struck him to the heart, and he started to run back (as he thought) towards Vara and Gavin. He imagined that he could hear the sound of some ferocious animal trampling about the moss in search of little wandering boys. And it occurred to him that he had no means of defence except the whip, and even that served him not so well now, for the lash was broken from the handle. So this was the reason why Boy Hugh finally ran away.

Though, indeed, his progress could hardly be called running. For at every few steps he tripped in some intricate twist of heather, tough as wire, and, falling forward, he instinctively bent his body into a half-hoop, like a young hedgehog. Thus he rolled down the braes, often coming upon his feet at the bottom and continuing his flight with energy unabated, and without pausing a single moment even to ascertain damages.

Then so soon as she missed him Vara stood up, with Gavin in her arms, and cried, 'Come back, Boy Hugh!' But Boy Hugh continued his wild flight, driven by the unreasoning terror of the vast and uncomprehended night which had seized him suddenly and without warning.

At last Boy Hugh paused, not so much because he wished it, as because he had fallen into a moss-hole up to the neck, and so could run no further. He sustained himself by grasping a bush of blaeberry, and he dug his toes into the soft black peat.

Then Boy Hugh, who had not gone to Hunker Court for nothing, bethought him that, since there was nothing else that he could do, it was time to say his prayers. 'O Lord!' he prayed—'O Lord, forgive us our sins, and remember not our trans-somethings against us! Look down from heaven and help'—(so far his supplications had run in the accustomed groove in which Samson Langpenny conducted the 'opening exercises' of Hunker Court, but at this point Boy Hugh diverged into originality, as Samson himself did sometimes when he stuck in the middle of the Lord's prayer)—'Look down from heaven and help—a—wee laddie stickit in a moss hole. Keep him frae teegers and lions, and bogles and black horses that come oot o' lochs and eat ye up, and frae the green monkeys that hing on to trees and claw ye as ye gang by. And gie me something to eat, and Vara and Gavin after me. For I'm near dead o' hunger, and I want nae mair day-before-yesterday's bread, and help me to find my whup-lash. And make me grow up into a man fast, for I want to do as I like—and then, my certes, but I'll warm the Drabble for stealin' my pistol. And bless Vara and Gavin, my faither and Cleg Kelly, and a' inquirin' freends. Amen.'

And if anybody knows a more comprehensive prayer, let him instantly declare it, or, as the charge runs, be for ever silent.

ADVENTURE XXXVII

BOY HUGH FINDS OUT THE NATURE OF A KISS

VARA always looks back upon that night of fear and loneliness as the worst in all their wanderings. She wrapped Gavin tightly in the shawl, till only a little space was left for him to breathe. Then she ran from knowe-top to knowe-top to look for Boy Hugh, and to call him to come back to her. She dared not go far from the boulder lest she should miss her way, and so not be able to return to the baby.

While Vara was wandering distracted over the moor, calling pitifully to him, Boy Hugh was comfortably asleep beneath a heather bush. The June nights are brief and merciful in Scotland. It was not long before a broad bar of light lay across the eastern hills. In fact, the pale sea-green lingering in the west where the sun had gone down, had not altogether faded into the ashy grey of uncoloured night ere the eastern sky began to flame.

The clouds of sunrise are like ocean-rollers on a wide beach—long, barred, and parallel—for the sun rises through them with a certain majestic circumspection. But the clouds of sunset are apt to converge to a point, like a wake which the sun draws after him in his tumultuous downward plunge.

But the sun rose quite sharply this morning, as

though he must be businesslike and alert, in spite of the fact that he had a whole long summer day before him. As he did so the shadows of every bush of bog-myrtle and each tuft of heather started westwards with a rush. And the cool blue image of a lonely boulder, like a Breton menhir, lay for half a mile across the moor. On the sunny side of this landmark the red rays fell on a bare and curly head. There were drops of dew upon the draggled hair, just as there were upon the yellow bent grass upon which the head pillowed itself.

Boy Hugh lay curled up, like a collie drowsing in the sun. He continued to sleep quietly and naturally the undisturbed sleep of childhood. Nor did he waken till the dew had dried from the bent and from off the tangles of his hair.

At last he awoke, when the sun was already high. He uncoiled him like a lithe young animal, and started to find himself under the open heaven instead of under a roof. With a shake and a toss of his head he made his toilet. Then suddenly he remembered about Vara, and hoped vaguely that he would soon find her. But, alas! the day was bright. The sunshine began to run in his veins, and all the moorland world was before him. He did not think much more about her at all. For the moment he was as merry as the larks singing above him. He hallooed to the plovers, and occasionally he threw stones at them, just as the mood took him. By-and-by Boy Hugh came to a wide burn, and at once proceeded to cross it, as many a time he had crossed a plank in Callendar's yard—upon all-fours like a monkey.

The burn was fringed, like many of the watercourses of the southern uplands, with a growth of sparse and ill-favoured birches. Hugh Boy found one of these which leaned far over the water, having had its roots undermined by the winter spates. He crawled out upon its swaying top without hesitation till it became too slender to bear him. He counted upon the slender trunk bending like a fishing-rod and depositing him near enough to the opposite bank to drop safely to the ground. But just when Hugh Boy was ready to leap, the treacherous birch gave way entirely, and fell souse into the water, with the small human squirrel still clinging desperately to it. The birch lay across the pool, and Boy Hugh held fast. He was up to the neck in water. He wondered how he would get out. As a first step he managed to kick his legs free of the twigs which clutched him, and tried to drag him down.

'Here, nice little boy!' a voice above him cried suddenly. 'Take hold of my hand, and I will pull you out of the water.'

It was the clearest little voice in the world, and it spoke with a trill which Boy Hugh seemed to have heard somewhere before. It conveyed somehow, indeed, a reminiscence of Miss Celie Tennant. But the little lady who spoke was only a year or two older than Boy Hugh himself, and she was dressed in the daintiest creamy stuff, fine like cobweb. Boy Hugh looked at her in such amazement that he came near to letting go the birch-tree altogether. She seemed to him to be altogether wonderful, with yellow hair like summer clouds, and blue eyes full of pity.

Boy Hugh recalled certain things which he had heard at Hunker Court.

'Are you an angel?' he said, quite seriously.

'Oh no, silly!' cried the maiden gaily, shaking her fleece bewilderingly at him. 'Of course, I am only a little girl. I just tooked my parolsol and comed a walk. And you are the very nicest little boy that ever I saw—quite a teeny-tiny child, of course,' she added patronisingly. ' But take hold of my parolsol. Be careful not to splash me when you shake yourself. And after that I'll give you a kiss. I like nice little boys ! '

' What is a kiss ? ' asked Boy Hugh.

They did not deal in the commodity in the Tinklers' Lands. And even if his sister Vara did kiss him in his sleep every night, and was for ever kissing the baby as if its mouth had been a sweetmeat, she did not think it becoming or menseful to mention the word. So that, quite sincerely, Boy Hugh asked again, ' What is a kiss, little girl ? '

' Come up here, nice boy, and I will show you ! ' replied the maiden promptly.

And somehow or other Hugh knew that this was an invitation by no means to be declined.

ADVENTURE XXXVIII

MISS BRIGGS AND HER TEN CATS

'Now then, how do you like it?' asked this frank young person. But Hugh Boy was silent as to what he thought of his first knowledgable kiss. Not that it mattered, for the gay lady of the curls rattled on regardless. 'And what is your name, little boy? You are very ragged, and you have come a long way. But you are clean, and Aunt Robina can't scold me, for she tells me to be kind to the poor, especially when they are quite clean.'

Boy Hugh bashfully answered that his name was Hugh Kavannah. 'And a very nice name it is, nice little boy!' the maid rattled on, heeding her companion little, but altogether enamoured of the sound of her own twitter.

The children went over the moor together, till it began to feather into sparse birch-woods and thicker copses towards the plain. Sometimes as they went the little girl's hair whipped Boy Hugh's brow. He had forgotten all about Vara and the baby.

'Do they make you say your prayers in the morning as well as at night?' she asked; 'they do me—such a bother! Aunt Robina, she said last week that it was self-denial week, and we must give up something for the Lord. So I said I did not mind giving up saying my prayers in the morning. "Oh but," said cousin Jimmy, "you must give up something you *like* doing." Horrid little boy, Jimmy, always blowing his nose—you don't, well, I don't believe you have any handkerchief—and Aunt Robina, she says, "Well, and what do you think God would say if you gave up saying your prayers?" "God *has* said already," I told her. "What has God said?" she wanted to know, making a face like this—. So I told her that God said, "Pray don't mention it, Miss Briggs!" My name is Miss Briggs, you know. I have ten cats. Their names are Tom and Jim, and Harry and Dick, and Bob and Ben and Peter. But Peter's an awful thief.'

She paused for breath and shook her head at the same time. Hugh Boy listened with the open mouth of unbounded astonishment.

'Yes, indeed,' said Miss Briggs, 'and I fear he will come to a bad end. I've thrown him into the mill-dam three times already, like Jonah out of the ship of Tarshish. Aunt Robina says I may play Bible stories on Sundays, you know. So I play Jonah. But he always gets out again. Next time I'm going to sit squash on him till he's dead. Once I sat on a nestful of eggs because I wanted some dear wee fluffy chickens—but I need not tell you all about that. It was a horrid mess. I got whipped, but Aunt Robina had to buy me a new pair of—oh, I forgot, I was telling you about wicked Peter. Peter is not a house-cat like the rest, you see. He is a bad, wicked cat. He lives in the barn or in the coach house and eats the pigeons. And he lies on the cows' backs on cold nights. But in the daytime Peter sleeps on the roof of the outhouses, and when any one of the other cats gets anything nice to eat, Peter comes down on him like a shot——'

'Oh aye!' cried Boy Hugh, excited to hear about something he understood, 'I hae seen them do like that. Then there's a graund fecht, lying on their backs and tearing at ane anither wi' their claws, and spittin' and rowin' ower yin anither like a ba'——'

'My cats are not horrid creatures like that!' said Miss Briggs in a dignified manner, 'as soon as ever they see Peter coming they take to their heels and—oh, you should see them run for the kitchen door! And their tails are just like the fox's brush that Aunt Robina dusts the pictures with. And then in a minute after you can see wicked Peter sitting on the rigging of the barn eating my poor darling house-cat's nice breakfast.'

'Three cheers for Peter!' cried Hugh, who did not know any better than to express his real sentiments to a lady.

Miss Briggs instantly withdrew her hand from his. Her nose turned up very much, till its expression of scorn became almost a religious aspiration.

'I am afraid you are not such a nice little boy after all,' she said, severely.

As they went on together the children came to the very edge of the moorland. They ascended a few steps to a place where there were many tumbled crags and cunning hiding-places. From the edge of these they looked down upon a plain of tree tops, from the midst of which peeped out the front of a considerable mansion. The lower windows and the door were hidden in a green haze of beech leaves.

'That is where I live, little boy,' said Miss Briggs, grandly. 'The propriety will belong to me some day. And then I shall send Peter away for good.'

For a moment Miss Briggs looked down on the

house and gardens with the eye of the future possessor of a 'propriety.'

'Tissy, wissy—tissy—wissy!' she cried, suddenly forgetting her dignity.

There was a stirring here and there among the trees. And lo! from off the roofs of the barn and the byre, out of the triangular wickets, from off round-topped corn-stacks and out of different doors in the dwelling-house, there sprang a perfect host of cats. 'See them,' said Miss Briggs, impressively, 'every one of them comes to meet *me*. That's Peter, wicked Peter,' she said, pointing to a large brindled pussy which led the field by half a dozen lengths. Over the bridge they came, all mewing their best and all arching their tails.

'Their ten tails over their ten backs!' said Miss Briggs, unctuously, as if she found much spiritual comfort in the phrase.

The cats rubbed themselves against her. Some of them leaped upon her shoulders and sat there, purring loudly. Hugh Boy was unspeakably delighted.

'I wish Vara could see,' he said, remembering for the first time his sister and Gavin.

A harsh voice broke in upon them.

'Elizabeth Briggs! Elizabeth Briggs! What is all this play-acting? And what gangrel loon is this that ye are bringing to the door by the hand? Is there not enough wastry and ruination aboot the house of Rascarrel already, without your wiling hame every gypsy's brat and prowling sorrow of a gutter bluid? Think shame o' yoursel', Elizabeth Briggs!'

Hugh Boy dropped the hand which held his. He would not bring disgrace on the friend who had helped him.

'Aunt Robina, you forget yourself,' interposed the young lady with prim dignity, 'and you forget "what sayeth the Scripture."'

She took Boy Hugh's hand again, and held it tighter. 'Forget the Scripture,' cried a tall darkbrowed woman who came limping out from a seat under a weeping elm. She was leaning heavily with both hands upon a staff, which she rattled angrily on the ground as she spoke.

'Yes,' said Miss Briggs; 'do you know that I am Pharaoh's daughter, and this is little Moses whom I drew out of the water?'

'Hold your tongue, Elizabeth Briggs, and come here instantly!' said the dark woman, tapping the ground again with her staff.

Hugh Boy knew the tone. He had heard something like this before.

'Is that your "awfu' woman"?' he said aloud, pointing with his finger at the woman leaning upon the stick.

'Elizabeth Briggs,' she commanded again, pointing at the little girl with her stick, 'come in to your lesson this minute. And you, whatever you may call yourself, take yourself off at once, or I'll get the police to you!'

'Yes, do go away, nice little boy,' said Miss Briggs; 'but when you grow big, come back to the house of Rascarrel and Miss Briggs will marry you. And I will give you another kiss at the garden stile—and so will Peter!' she added. For she felt that some extra kindness and attention was due, to make up for the most unscriptural hardheartedness of her Aunt Robina.

So the children took their way together to the garden stile, and as they went out of sight, Boy Hugh turned round to the dark-browed woman:

'My name is Boy Hugh,' he said, 'but I'm not a beggar, Awfu' Woman!'

The children walked slowly and sorrowfully along a gravel walk thickly overgrown with chickweed and moss. Their feet made no sound upon it. On either side box borders rose nearly three feet high, straggling untended over the walks. Still further over were territories of gooseberry bushes, senile and wellnigh barren, their thin-leaved, thorny branches trailing on the ground and crawling over each other. Beyond these again was a great beech hedge rising up into the sky. Boy Hugh looked at the dark Irish yews standing erect at the corner of every plot. He thought that they presented arms like the sentinels at the gate of Holyrood, at whom he used to gaze as often as he could slip away from the Tinklers' Lands.

Then all suddenly and unexpectedly he began to cry. Miss Briggs stopped aghast. She was, like all womenfolk, well accustomed to her own sex's tears. But a male creature's emotion took her by surprise.

'What is the matter?' she said; 'tell me instantly, nice little boy.'

'This place maun be heaven, after a',' he said, 'an' your awfu' woman winna let Boy Hugh bide.'

Presently they came out upon a circular opening where the bounding beech edge bent into a circle, and the gloomy yew-tree sentinels stood wider about. Overhead all the crisp leafage of the copper beeches clashed and rustled.

Here was a great garden seat of stone, and there at the back rose a fountain with stone nymphs—a fountain long since dry and overgrown with green moss. It seemed to Boy Hugh as if they could never get out of this vast enclosure.

There was also a little stone building at the end

down the vista of the gravel walk. Its door stood open and Boy Hugh looked within. It was empty like a church. The floor was made of unvarnished wood in squares and crosses. There were painted pictures on the walls, and a shining thing with candles standing upon it at the far end. Behind this the sun shone through a window of red, and yellow, and blue.

'Is that God?' asked Hugh Boy, in a hushed voice, after gazing a long time at the glory of the shining crimson and violet panes and the shining gold upon the altar.

But Miss Briggs dragged him away without making him any answer.

Presently they came to half a dozen steps in an angle of the orchard, which led over the outer wall. They had slipped under a mysterious archway of leaves and so through the beech hedge, in order to reach this ladder of stone.

'Good-bye!' said Miss Briggs; 'remember—come back, nice little boy, as soon as you are growed up, and I will marry you. And then we will send Aunt Robina to the poorhouse. Kiss me, nice boy—and now kiss Peter.'

With that Miss Briggs disappeared, running as hard as ever she could, so that she would not need to cry within sight.

But as soon as she got to the great circle of the beeches and yews, she burst out sobbing. 'He was the very nicest boy—the nicest boy. But of course there could be nothing in it. For after all he is only a mere child, you know!'

But Boy Hugh walked stolidly up the steps, and so out of Paradise.

'I am very hungry!' he said.

ADVENTURE XXXIX

THE ADVENTURE OF SNAP'S PORRIDGE

BUT he found Providence just over the wall. For there sat Vara and there was the great stone behind which they had spent the night. All his wanderings had just brought him back to where he started from. But for all that he was exceedingly glad to see Vara.

He called her, standing still on the top of the wall. She started up as if she had heard a voice from the grave. And the face which she turned to him was colourless like chalk.

'Wi' Vara,' said Hugh, 'what's wrang? Your face looks terrible clean?'

'O, Boy Hugh—Boy Hugh,' she cried, bursting into hot relieving tears, 'it's you. What a night you have given me!'

But not a word of reproach came from the lips of Vara Kavannah. She had, indeed, enough to do to keep the babe quiet. For having run hither and thither over the moor looking for her brother, she had not had time to seek for any farmhouse where she could get some milk for Gavin's bottle.

In a little, however, they were again walking hand in hand, and Boy Hugh was pouring out all the story of his adventures in the Paradise of the House of Rascarrel.

Chiefly he dwelt upon the divine beauty and abounding merits of Miss Briggs.

'Dinna you think she was an angel frae heeven?' said Boy Hugh.

'I think she was a nasty, wicked, enticing little monkey!' burst out Vara. For though it is part of womanhood's glorious privilege to put up with the truantry of mankind without complaint, it is too much to expect her to suffer gladly his praises of the Canaanitish women he may have collogued with upon his travels.

And then Vara walked a long way silent and with her head in the air. Hugh Boy kicked all the stones out of his path and was silent also.

Nevertheless, though in this sulky silence, they travelled steadily on and on. Horizon after horizon broke up before them, spread out on either side, streamed dispersedly past them, and recomposed itself again solidly behind them.

'I'm awesome hungry!' at last said Boy Hugh, humbly. Vara became full of compassion in a minute.

'And Vara has nothing to give ye!' she said; 'poor Boy Hugh!'

The baby woke with a faint cry.

They had passed off the moor and were now come among inhabited houses again. They were just opposite a cottage which stood with its end to the road, when a little boy came out of the gate with a great bowl of porridge and milk in his hand.

'Snap! Snap!' he cried, and looked up and down the road. A small terrier pricked its ears briskly over a wall and then leaped down upon the road. 'Here, Snap!' cried the boy.

Snap came slowly walking down the dusty highway. He smelled a little indifferently at the dish of porridge and milk. Then he sniffed loudly upon the nose of contempt. For he had just been dining richly in the outhouse on a rat which he had killed himself.

Vara's eyes blazed at the sight of the porridge and milk.

'O, gie that to the baby!' she cried, her eyes fairly sparkling fire. 'Gie that to wee Gavin. The dog doesna want it!'

The little boy ran back into the house, crying out at the top of his voice, 'O mither, mither, here's a lassie wants to gie our Snap's porridge to a babby!'

A kindly-faced, apple-cheeked country woman came to the door of the cottage. She had been baking cakes, and she dusted the oatmeal off her hands as she stood there.

'Can I get the dog's porridge for the bairns? He doesna want them. 'Deed he doesna!' cried Vara, beseechingly.

'Of course, lassie, ye can hae the porridge and welcome!' said the woman, doubtfully.

'O, thank ye, mem, thank ye!' cried Vara, pouncing instantly on the porridge, lest the permission should be withdrawn. In a minute she had put most of the milk into the babe's bottle and the rest into the hands of Boy Hugh, who fell upon the porridge unceremoniously with his fingers. Vara smiled as she looked. She was certainly hungrier than either—but also happier.

The woman stood with a strange look on her face, watching the wolfish eagerness of the younger children at the sight of food. Her lip tightened and her expression grew sterner. Suddenly Vara glanced up at her with frank blue Irish eyes, brightened by hunger and suffering. They looked through and through the woman at the door.

'Mither,' said the boy, 'they're eatin' up a' our Snap's porridge, and there will no be a drap left——'

The woman turned on him with a kind of gladness.

'Hold your tongue!' she said, with quite unnecessary vehemence. And she slapped her son smartly for no particular reason. The tears were running down her cheeks. She almost dragged the children into the house. Then and there she spread such a breakfast for them as Vara had been seeing in her dreams ever since she grew hungry. It seemed that Gavin grew visibly plumper before her very eyes, with the milk which he absorbed as a sponge takes up water. And there appeared to be no finality to Boy Hugh's appetite. He could always find room for just another scone, spread with fresh butter and overlaid with cool apple-jelly such as Vara had never in her life partaken of.

Vara herself was almost too happy to eat. But the kind woman pressed her and would not let her leave the table.

'But I have naething to pay ye wi'!' said Vara, whose soul was great.

'Hoot, hear to the lassie! I wadna tak' pay frae the Queen hersel', if she caaed in aff the road to drink a dish of tea. My man's the Netherby carrier. But tell me what's brocht ye here, wi' sic a bairn as that?'

And Vara told her as much as was necessary.

'To Liverpool to find your faither,' said the woman. 'Ye dinna stir a fit till the morrow's morn, and then ye can get a ride wi' our John as far as Netherby, at ony rate.'

Vara was more than grateful to her. She was the first person who had taken their quest seriously. So the carrier's wife kept them till night, and helped Vara to give the baby and Hugh a bath. Then she made Vara strip herself, and shut the door upon her till the girl had enjoyed such a tubful of warm water as she had never washed in before. As Vara was finishing rubbing her slender, wearied body and blistered feet with a soft towel, the carrier's wife opened the door. 'Put on these,' she said; 'they were my wee Gracie's, and I canna bear to keep them in the house.' Vara would have protested, but the woman shut the door with a slam.

When Vara came out, Gavin was sitting on the carrier's knees and plucking at his beard. For 'our John' had come in and heard their story. He was a wise carrier, and knew better than to attempt to interfere with his wife's benevolences. Then what was Vara's astonishment to find the babe also clad in a new frock, and giving rustling evidence of fresh underclothing. She could hear Boy Hugh's voice outside. He and Snap's master had made up the peace, and were now out somewhere about the barn, encouraging Snap to possess himself of another dinner of rat.

The woman's wonderful kindness went to Vara's heart.

'Ye shouldna, oh, ye shouldna!' she said, and bowing her head in her hands, she wept as she had never done in the worst of all her sufferings.

'Hoot! can ye no haud your tongue, lassie?' said the carrier's wife. 'So mony bairn's things were just a cumber and a thocht to me in this hoose. Our youngest (Tam there) is ten, an' we hae dune wi' that kind o' nonsense in this hoose. What are ye lauchin' at, guidman?' she cried, suddenly turning on the carrier, who had been quaintly screwing up his face.

'I wasna lauchin',' said 'our John,' his face suddenly falling to a quite preternatural gravity.

'They were juist a cumber and a care,' continued the carrier's wife. 'And they are better being o' some use to somebody.'

'Now ye will lie down and sleep in the back room, till the guidman starts on his round at five i' the mornin'.'

So the wearied children were put to bed in the 'back room,' and they fell asleep to the sound of psalm-singing. For the good carrier and his wife were praising the Lord. It is quite a mistake to suppose that most psalm-singers are hypocrites. Much of the finest good of the world is wrought by those who, being merry of heart, sing psalms.

ADVENTURE XL

A NEW KIND OF HERO

THEN with the morning came the new day. The bitterest of the blast was now over for these small pilgrims. The night's rest, the clean clothes, the goodness of the kind carrier folk brought new life to Vara. There was brighter hope in her heart as the carrier's wife set them under the blue hood of the light cart, for her 'man' did not expect any heavy loads that day. The children, therefore, were to ride in the covered waggon. The good woman wept to let them go, and made Vara promise many a time to be sure and send her a letter. As they went away she slipped half a crown into Vara's hand.

'For the baby!' she whispered, like one who makes a shamefaced excuse. And at that moment the carrier pretended to be specially busy about his harness.

But Hugh Boy had quarrelled again with Snap's master, and that enterprising youth sat on the fence opposite and made faces impartially at the party, till his mother, turning round somewhat quickly, caught him in the act.

'Ye ill-set hyule,' said she, 'wait till I get ye!'

But her first-born did not wait. On the other hand, he betook himself down the meadow with much alacrity. His mother's voice followed him.

'My lad, wait till bedtime. It'll dirl far waur

then. "Warm skins, guid bairns!" I'll learn you to make faces ahint my back.'

And as Snap's master went down the meadow, the parts likely to be nocturnally affected began to burn and tingle.

And the thought of the interview she would have with her son in the evening, did something to console the carrier's wife for the loss of the children to whom she had taken such a sudden liking.

The light cart went jingling on. The Netherby carrier whistled steadily as he sat on the edge of his driving-board, with his feet on the shaft. Every now and then he passed a bag of peppermint drops over to the children.

'Hae!' he said.

The Netherby carrier was a man of few words, and this was his idea of hospitality. Hugh Boy did not remember ever to have been so happy in his life. Kissing was very well in its way, though Vara had not been pleased when she heard of it. But it was nothing to sitting in a blue-hooded cart and hearing the click and jingle of brass-mounted harness. Now and then the carrier stopped at snug farmhouses, and went in to chaffer with the goodwife for her eggs. Then he left the horse in charge of Hugh Boy, and so completely won that small heart. When the carrier came out again, the farmer's wife mostly came too, and the bargaining and bantering were kept up as the wheels receded from the door. Even when the blue-hooded cart was far down the loaning, a belated and forgetful goodwife would oftentimes come running to some knowe-top, and from that eminence she would proceed to give further directions for commissions from the town.

'Mind ye buy the thread at Rob Heslop's—no at that upstart sieffer's at the corner, wi' his wax figgurs an' his adverteesements. I dinna haud wi' them ava'!'

For there are still uncouth and outlandish parts of the country where the medical axiom, that it is wicked and unprofessional to advertise, holds good in practical commerce. Now, the road toward England does not run directly through Netherby, but leaves the town a little to one side, with its many spires and its warring denominations. From the outside Netherby looks like a home of ancient peace. But for all that, there were hardly two neighbour shopkeepers down all its long main street who belonged to the same religious denomination—the only exceptions being Dickson the baker and Henderson the butcher. But even Henderson and Dickson did not speak to one another, having quarrelled anent the singing of paraphrases in the Seceder kirk.

However, the poor benighted Kavannahs did not know one kirk from another. And, what was worse, indeed held almost criminal in Netherby, they did not care.

It was here at the parting of the roads that John the carrier took his leave of them. His farewell was not effusive.

'Weel,' he said, cracking his whip three times over, while he thought of the rest of his speech, 'guidday. Be sure and come back and see us, as the wife bade ye. The sooner the better!'

But he put a shilling into Hugh's hand as they parted.

'For peppermints!' he said.

Vara did not know when she might come to

another town on her way, so she decided to buy a loaf in Netherby before going further. For, though they never asked for food, except when driven by hunger, as in the case of Snap's dinner, yet since the terrible night on the moor she had resolved to ask for shelter if they came to any house at nightfall. So, after the carrier was gone, with many charges Vara left Hugh in care of Gavin and went into the town to make her markets.

Hugh Boy sat a good while by the roadside, till the time began to pass very dully. Then he became interested in the trains which kept shunting and whistling behind him. So he carried Gavin across to the side of the railway line, where he could just see the road by which Vara would return. He was quite sure that he could not be doing any harm. Directly opposite there was a fascinating turn-table, upon which two men stood with iron poles in their hands wheeling round a great engine as if it had been a toy. This was really too much for Boy Hugh. Forgetting all about Vara's warning, he scrambled over the wire paling and staggered across the netted lines in order to get a nearer view of the marvel.

But just at that moment up came the main line express twenty minutes behind time, and the engine-driver in a bad temper. And if Muckle Alick had not opposed the breadth of his beam to the buffer of Geordie Grierson's engine, this tale, so far at least as two of the Kavannahs were concerned, would have ended here. But when Muckle Alick gripped the children in his great arms, and made that spring to the side, the engine caught him so exactly in the right place that it did no more than very considerably accelerate his lateral motion, and project him half-way up the bank. As has been recorded, Muckle Alick's first exclamation (which immediately became proverbial all over the Greenock and South-Eastern) was, 'Is there aught broke, Geordie, think ye?'

They talked of getting up a testimonial to Muckle Alick. But the hero himself strongly discouraged the notion. Indeed, he went so far as to declare that he 'wad gie the fool a ring on the lug that cam' to him wi' ony sic a thing!' This was a somewhat unusual attitude for a hero to assume in the circumstances. But it was quite genuine. And so well known was the horse-power of Alick's buffet, that it would have been considerably easier to recruit a storming party in Netherby than a deputation to present a 'token of esteem' to the head porter at Netherby Junction.

In time, however (though this is somewhat to anticipate the tale), there came from the Royal Humane Society a medal, together with a long paper setting forth the noble deed of the saving of the children. No notice of this ever appeared publicly in the local prints, to which such things are usually a godsend.

For Alick immediately put the medal in the bottom of his trunk, beneath his 'best blacks' which he wore only twice a year, at Sacraments.

He had heard that the editor of the 'Netherby Chronicle and Advertiser' had collogued with the provost of the town to bring about this 'fitting acknowledgment.' Now Muckle Alick could not help the thing itself, but he could help people in Netherby getting to hear about it.

So Muckle Alick called upon the editor of the 'Chronicle.' He found him in, and engaged in the difficult task of penning an editorial which could not possibly alienate the most thin-skinned subscriber, but which would yet be calculated to exasperate the editor of an opposition local paper published in the next county.

'Maister Heron,' said the head-porter, 'I juist looked in to tell ye, that there's nocht to come oot in the "Chronicle" aboot me the morn.'

'But, my dear sir,' said the editor, 'the item has been specially communicated, and is already set up.'

'Then it'll juist hae to be set doon again!' said Muckle Alick, firmly.

'Impossible, impossible, I do assure you, my dear friend,' remonstrated the editor. He was proprietor —editor and proprietor in one. Such editors in agricultural communities are always polite to subscribers.

'But it's no onpossible. It's to be!' said Alick— 'Or there's no a paper will leave the junction the morn —aye, and there'll no be a paper sell't in this toon eyther.'

It was not clear to the editor how Muckle Alick could bring about this result.

'But,' said he, tapping the desk with his pen, 'my dear sir, the station-master—the railway company——'

'Ow aye, I ken,' said Muckle Alick, 'there wad be a wark aboot it after, nae doot. But it's the morn I'm speakin' aboot, Maister Heron. It is possible I micht get the sack ower the head o' it—(though I'm thinkin' no). But that wadna help your papers to sell the morn.' Alick paused to let this sink well in. Then he took his leave.

'Noo mind, I'm tellin' ye. Guid-day, Yedditur!'

That afternoon Alick presided at a gathering of the amalgamated paper boys of the town, being accredited representatives of all the various newsagents. The proceedings were private, and as soon as strangers were observed, the house was counted out (and stones thrown at them). But the general tenour of the resolutions unanimously passed may be gathered from the fact that when Mr. Heron heard of it, he ordered the junior reporter to 'slate a novel' which had just come in—a novel by an eminent hand. 'It's to make three-quarters of a column, less two lines,' he said.

So that we know from this the length of the suppressed article on the presentation of a medal of the Royal Humane Society to 'our noble and esteemed townsman, Mr. Alexander Douglas.' The 'Netherby Chronicle and Advertiser' enjoyed its normal circulation next day. And (after Muckle Alick had carefully searched every column of the paper) the parcels were forwarded from the junction with the usual promptitude and despatch.

But this is telling our tale 'withershins about,' as they say in Netherby. We return to Vara and her bairns.

ADVENTURE XLI

'TWA LADDIES—AND A LASSIE'

MUCKLE ALICK trotted the children soberly down the street, and at the foot he turned his long, lumbering stride up a country road. For Alick had a little wife who was an expert market-gardener and bee-keeper.

Her name was Mirren, and her size, as reported by her husband, was somewhere 'near-aboots as big as twa scrubbers.' It was for her sake and because he could not help himself, that Muckle Alick lived so far from his work.

'D'ye think that because I hae to put up wi' a great hulk like you, comin' hame at nicht smellin' o' cinders and lamp oil, that I'm gaun to leeve in a hut amang the coal waggons? Na, certes, gin ye want to hae Mirren Tereggles to keep ye snug at nicht, ye maun e'en walk a mile or twa extra in the daytime. And it will be the better for keepin' doon that great muckle corporation o' yours!'

And that is the way that Muckle Alick Douglas lived out at Sandyknowes. It was to his small garden-girt house that he took the children.

'What's this ye hae fetched hame in your hand the nicht?' cried the little wife sharply, as she saw her husband come up the loaning. 'It's no every wife that wad be pleased to hae a grown family brocht in on her like this!'

'Hoot, Mirren woman!' was all that Muckle Alick said, as he pushed Vara and Hugh in at the gate before him, Gavin nestling cosily in his arms the while.

'Whaur gat ye them, Alick?' said Mirren, going forward to look at the bairn in his arms. 'They are bonny weans and no that ill put on.'

Little Gavin was so content in the arms of Muckle Alick that he smiled. And his natural sweetness of expression struggling through the pinched look of hunger went right to the heart of Mirren, who, having no bairns of her own—'so far,' as Muckle Alick remarked cautiously—had so much the more love for other people's. She turned on Vara, who stood looking on and smiling also. The little woman was almost fierce.

'What has been done to this bairn that he has never grown?' said Mirren Douglas.

Vara flushed in her slow, still way at the apparent imputation that she had not taken good care enough of her Gavin—to pleasure whom she would have given her life.

'I did the best I could,' she said, 'whiles we had to sleep oot a' nicht, an' whiles I had nae milk to gie him.'

'Lassie! lassie!' cried Mirren Douglas, 'what is this ye are tellin' me?'

'The truth,' said Vara Kavannah, quietly; 'Gavin and Boy Hugh and me hae walked a' the road frae Edinburgh. We hae sleepit in the hills, and——'

'But how cam' the bairn here?' asked Muckle Alick's fiercely tender little wife; 'tell me quick!'

'I hae carried Gavin a' the road!' said Vara, simply.

'You, lassie!' cried Mirren, looking at the slip of pale girlhood before her, 'it's juist fair unpossible!'

'But I did carry him. He's no that heavy when ye get the shawl weel set.'

'O lassie, lassie, ye juist mak' me fair shamed,' cried Mistress Douglas. 'Alick, ye muckle useless bullock; what for are ye standin' there like a cuif? Gang ower to Mistress Fraser's and ask for the lend o' her cradle. Thae bairns are gaun to bide——'

'But, wife, hae ye considered?' Alick began.

'Considered, my fit—did ye no hear me? Dinna stand hingin' there, balancin' on your flat soles like a show elephant lookin' aboot for cookies—gang, will ye!'

The little wife stamped her foot and made a threatening demonstration. Whereupon Muckle Alick betook himself over the way to Mistress Fraser's, and he never smiled till he got past the gate of the front garden, in which Mirren kept her old-fashioned flowers.

'I thocht that's what it wad come to,' said Alick to himself, 'whenever she saw the bairns. I wonder if she means to keep haud o' them a' thegither? She's been wearing her heart on the flooers a lang while, puir lassie. It wad be a farce if three bairns should come hame at once to Sandyknowes after sae lang withoot ony, twa o' them walkin' cantily on their ain feet!'

Thus Alick mused, laughing a little to himself as he went over to borrow Mistress Fraser's cradle. He had an idea.

'There'll be some amusement at ony rate,' he said, 'but I maunna be ower keen. Na, and I maun haud back an' make difficulties. And then the wife will tak' the ither side and be juist daft to get her ain way and keep them.'

Alick was well aware of the domestic value of a certain amount of opposition, judiciously distributed.

He arrived before long at the cottage of Mistress Fraser. It was set like his own in the midst of a garden. But instead of being bosomed in flowers, with beeskeps scattered about, the garden was wholly taken up with potatoes, cabbage, and curly greens. It was a strictly utilitarian garden. As soon as Muckle Alick hove in sight, turning slowly up off the main road like a liner altering her course, a covey of children broke from the door of the house and ran tumultuously towards him. They tripped one another up. They pulled each other back by the hair or caught those in front by the heels or the coat-tails. It was a clean-limbed, coltish lass of thirteen who gained the race and sprang first into the arms of Muckle Alick. Then two boys gripped each a mighty leg, while a whole horde of smaller banditti swarmed up Alick's rearward works and took his broad back by storm. When he got to the potato garden he looked more like the show elephant his wife had called him than ever. For he was fairly loaded with children 'all along the rigging,' as Mistress Fraser said.

She was a buxom, rosy-cheeked woman, gifted upon occasion with an astonishing plainness of speech.

'Guid-nicht to ye, Alick,' she said, 'thae bairns maks as free wi' ye as if they were a' your ain?'

Alick disentangled the hands of one of the rearward harpies from his beard and mouth. Whereupon the offended rascal was not to be appeased. He slid down, caught the giant about the knee, and began to kick an outlying shin with all his might.

'Ye should ken best whether they are or no,' said Alick, 'there's plenty o' them at ony gait!'

'An' what wind has blawn ye frae Sandyknowes this nicht? It taks naething less than an earthquake to shake ye awa' frae Mirren. Ye hae fair forgotten that there's ither folk in the warl.'

'I was wanting the lend o' your cradle, guidwife,' said Alick, looking down with affected shamefacedness, well aware of the astonishment he would occasion by the simple request.

Mistress Fraser had been stooping over a basin in which she was mixing meal and other ingredients, to form the white puddings for which she was famous. She stood up suddenly erect, like a bow straightening itself. Then she looked sternly at Alick.

'Ye are a nice cunning wratch to be an elder— you and Mirren Terregles baith—and at your time o' life. An' hoo is she?'

'Ow, as weel as could hae been expectit,' said Muckle Alick, with just the proper amount of hypocritical resignation demanded by custom on these occasions. Mistress Fraser, whose mind ran naturally on the lines along which Muckle Alick had so wickedly directed it, was completely taken in.

'An' what has Mirren gotten?—a lassie, I'll wager,' said the excited mother of eleven, dusting her hands of the crumblings of the pudding suet, and then beginning breathlessly to smooth her hair and take off her baking apron. So excited was she that she could not find the loop.

'Aye,' said Alick, quietly, 'there's a lassie!'

'I juist kenned it,' said Mistress Fraser, drawing up wisdom from the mysterious wells of her experience; 'muckle men and wee wives aye start aff wi' a lassie— contrarywise they begin wi' a laddie. Noo me and my man——'

What terrible revelation of domestic experience would inevitably have followed, remains unfortunately unknown. For the half dozen words which at that moment Muckle Alick delicately let drop, even as the chemist drops a rare essence into two ounces of distilled water, brought Mistress Fraser to a dead stop in the fulness of her career after the most intimate domestic reminiscences.

'But there's a laddie come too!' said Muckle Alick, and looked becomingly at the ground.

Mistress Fraser held up her hands.

'Of a' the deceitfu', hidin', unneighbourly craiturs,' said Mistress Fraser, 'Mirren Terregles is the warst— an' me to hae drank my tea wi' her only last week. I'll wager, if I live to hae fifty bairns——'

'The Lord forbid,' said her husband, unexpectedly, from the doorway. 'We hae plenty as it is——'

'And wha's faut's that?' retorted his wife over her shoulder. 'O the deceitfu' randy——'

'In fact,' said Muckle Alick, dropping another word in, 'there's twa laddies—*and* a lassie!'

Mistress Fraser sat down quite suddenly.

'Gie me a drink frae the water can, Tam!' she said; 'haste ye fast, Alick's news has gi'en me a turn. Twa laddies and a lassie—I declare it's a Queen's bounty! Preserve me, it's no a cradle ye want, man, but a mill happer! A time or twa like this, and ye'll hae to plant taties in the front yaird—ye will hae to pay soundly for your ploy at this rate, my man. Three at a whup disna gang wi' cancy-lairies in the cabbage plots, my lad.'

'It's a maist notoriously curious thing,' began Tam Fraser, unexpectedly, 'that I saw Mirren carryin' twa cans o' water this very mornin'——'

Muckle Alick gave him a warning look, which made him catch his next unspoken sentence as a wicket-keeper holds the ball before the field has seen it leave the bat.

'But—but she didna look weel——' added Tam.

'I wad think no, juist,' cried Mistress Fraser, who in an inner room was busy putting a selection of small white things into a covered reticule basket. 'An puir Mirren, she'll no be ready for the like. Wha could be prepared for a hale nation like this—I'll tak' her what I hae. O the deceitfu' besom—I declare it wad tak' little to gar me never speak to her again.'

'Dinna do that!' said the hypocritical giant; 'think on her condeetion——'

'"Condeetion, condeetion," quo' he—I wonder ye are no black ashamed, Alick Douglas. And nane o' the twa o' ye ever to say a word to me, that's your nearest neebour——'

'I gie ye my word,' said Muckle Alick, 'I kenned nocht aboot it till an hour or twa afore the bairns cam' hame!'

Mistress Fraser turned fiercely upon him.

'Weel, of a' the leers in this pairish—and there are some rousers—ye beat them clean, Alick Douglas —and you an elder amang the Cameronian kirk! Hoo daur ye face your Maker, to say nocht o' the kirk folk as ye stand at the plate on Sabbaths, wi' siccan lees in your mouth?'

'Come awa, man,' she cried from the door in her haste, 'I hae twa bagfu's o' things here. Tam, gang ower by to the Folds and up to Cowdenslack and borrow their twa cradles. They'll no be needing them for a month or twa—I ken that brawly—na, they are straightforrit women, and never spring the like o' this on puir folk to set them a' in a flutter!'

'I think a single cradle wad do. It was a' that Mirren asked for,' said Alick, demurely; 'but please yoursel', Mistress Fraser, it is you that kens best.'

'Yin,' cried Mistress Fraser, 'the man's gane gyte. Gin ye wull bring a family into the warld by squads o' regiments, ye maun e'en tak' the consequences. Lod, Lod, three cradles a' rockin' at the same time in the same hoose, it will be like a smiddy—or a watchmaker's shop! It'll be fine exerceese for ye, Alick, my man, when ye come hame at nichts—nae mair planting o' nastyhurcheons and pollyanthies. But every foot on a cradle rocker, and the lassie's yin to pu' wi' a string. An' serve ye baith richt. O, the deceitfu' madam; wait till I get ower to the Sandyknowes!'

And Alick had to take his longest strides to keep pace with the anxious mother of eleven—to whom he had told no lie, though, as he afterwards said, he 'had maybes keeped his thumb on some blauds o' the truth.'

'It shows,' said Alick, 'what a differ there is atween the truth and the hale truth—specially when there's a reason annexed in the shape of a woman's imagination, that naturally rins on sic like things.'

But as they neared Sandyknowes it is not to be doubted that Alick grew a little anxious. His position would not be exactly a pleasant one, if, for instance, Mirren should suddenly come out of their little byre with a full luggie of milk. And it was about milking time.

'There doesna appear to be muckle steer aboot the place, for siccan an awfu' thing to hae happened so lately!' said Mistress Fraser.

'Na,' said the arch-deceiver Alick, making a last effort, 'we are tryin' to keep a' thing as quaite as possible.'

'And faith, I dinna wonder. Gin the wives nooadays had ony spunk in them ava', ye wad be mobbed and ridden on the stang, my man!' Then her grievance against Mirren came again upon Mistress Fraser with renewed force, 'O, the randy, the besom,' she cried; 'wait till I get near her!'

By this time they were nearing the door of Sandyknowes.

'I dinna think I'll come ben wi' ye the noo. I'll gang ower by to the barn instead. There's some things to look to there, I misdoubt,' said Alick.

Just then they heard Mirren's voice raised in a merry laugh. It was really at the tale of Boy Hugh and Miss Briggs, which Vara was telling her.

But the sound brought a scared look to the face of Mistress Fraser.

'She's lauchin', I declare!' she cried; 'that's an awesome bad sign. Guid kens hoo mony there may be by this time——'

And she fairly lifted her voluminous petticoats, and, with her bundles under her arm, ran helter-skelter for the door of Sandyknowes, more like a halfling lassie than a douce mother of eleven bairns.

Muckle Alick saw her fairly in at the kitchen door.

'I think I'll gang ower by to the barn,' he said.

But he had not got more than half-way there when both leaves of the kitchen door sprang open, and out flew Mistress Fraser with the large wooden pot-stick or spurtle in her hand. Alick had admired her performance as she ran towards the house. But it was nothing to the speed with which she now bore down upon him.

'It was like the boat train coming doon by the Stroan, ten minutes ahint time, an' a director on board!' he said afterwards, describing it.

At the time Muckle Alick had too many things to think about, to say anything whatever. He ran towards the barn as fast as he could for the choking laughter which convulsed him. And behind him sped the avenger with the uplifted porridge spurtle, crying, 'O ye muckle leein' deevil—ye blackguaird—ye cunnin' hound, let me catch ye——'

And by the cheek of the barn door catch him Mistress Fraser did. And then, immediately after, it was Muckle Alick who received the reward of iniquity. But Mirren stood in the doorway with little Gavin in her arms and Vara and Boy Hugh at either side, and laughed till the tears ran down her cheeks in twin parallel rills.

'Gie him his paiks, and soundly, Mistress Fraser; pink him weel. Hit him on the knuckles or on the elbows. Ye micht as weel hit Ben Gairn as try to hurt him by hitting him on the head!'

Alick was speechless with laughter, but Mistress Fraser exclaimed with each resounding stroke, 'Twa laddies and a lassie! O ye vermin!—And me has sent to the Folds and the Cowdenslacks for twa cradles to mak' up the three. Ye hae made a bonny fule o' me. I'll never hear the last o' it till my dying day in this countryside. But, at ony rate, I'll take my piper's pay in ha'pence out o' your skin, my man Alick!'

ADVENTURE XLII

MUCKLE ALICK CONSIDERS

'Noo that the collyshangie's dune,' quoth Mirren Douglas, 'ye micht gie us a word o' advice what we should do wi' the bairns. But come oot by. They are a' to their beds doon the hoose. And we can be takin' a look at the blossoms as we gang.'

'We are to plant cabbage here next year, Mistress Fraser says!' cried Muckle Alick.

'Havers!' said his wife. But Mistress Fraser gave Alick a look which said as plain as print, 'Have you not had enough?'

'Heard ye what the name o' the puir wandering things might be?' asked Mistress Fraser.

'Aye,' said Mirren, briskly, 'I hae heard a' aboot it. Their name is Kavannah. Their faither gaed awa' to Liverpool a whilie since to look for wark. And the bairns has left their mither in Edinburgh to seek their faither. And I judge their mither is a gye ill yin.'

'Did she tell ye that?' asked Muckle Alick, quickly.

'Na, but I jalloused it!'[1] said his wife.

'And hoo in the world could ye jallouse sic a thing as that?' said he.

'Just the way ye jallouse that the express is comin''

[1] Shrewdly suspected it.

when ye hear the whistle, and the signal draps to "clear," ye muckle nowt!' said his wife, taking what is known as a personal example.

'The lassie didna tell me yae single word, but the boy showed me an *arr*-mark on his temple. "The awfu' woman did that!" says he.'

'" And wha's the awfu' woman, my bonny man?" says I.'

'The lassie tried to turn him, but he oot wi' it. "It's just my mither!" says he. And if ye didna caa that a gye near signal, I ken na what is. It's as plain as findin' bits o' a dog collar in the sausage or a burn troot in the milk!'

But her husband did not laugh, as he usually did at her sayings. His own humour was not of that kind, but slow, ponderous, and deliberate.

'What are ye standin' there gapin' at?' demanded his wife.

Alick held up his hand. His wife knew that this was a signal that he wished to be left to think undisturbed a little longer. So she hurried Mistress Fraser along to look at what she called her 'nastyhurcheons.' Sandy's mental machinery, like his bodily, was slow to set in motion, but it worked with great momentum when once it was set a-going.

Muckle Alick was putting two and two together.

'I ken a' aboot it,' he said at length, when the process was complete. 'We will need to be awesome careful. Thae bairns' faither never got to Liverpool; consequently it's little use them gaun there to seek him. He's either in his grave or the Edinburgh Infirmary. D'ye mind yon tramp man that gat the hurt in his head last spring, by hiding and sleepin' in the cattle waggons when they were shuntin'? His name was James Kavannah. I'se warrant he was the bairns' faither!'

Mirren Douglas gave Muckle Alick a bit clap on the shoulder.

'Whiles ye are nane so stupid, man,' she said, 'I believe ye are richt.'

'And he was on his road to Liverpool, too,' added Alick, 'for when he was oot o' his mind he cried on aboot gettin' there a' the time. And aye the owerword o' his sang was "She'll no catch me in Liverpool!"'

His wife looked at Alick. And Muckle Alick looked at Mirren.

'We'll keep them awhile, onyway, till they can get a better hame. The lassie will soon be braw and handy,' said Mirren.

'I'm thinkin',' said Alick, 'that the flower-beds will hae to come up after a', and we'll plant taties if the porridge pot shows signs o' wearin' empty.'

It was thus that our three wanderers found a place of lodgement in the wilderness in the kindly house of Sandyknowes.

'There's my sister Margaret up at Loch Spellanderie,' said Mistress Fraser; 'she was tellin' me on Monday that she was wantin' a lass. She's no very easy to leeve wi', I ken. But she will gie a guid wage, and the lass would get an insicht into country wark there. It micht be worth while thinkin' aboot.'

'It is kind o' ye to think o't,' said Mirren, doubtfully.

'O,' replied Mistress Fraser, 'I'm nane no sure o' that. As I tell ye, oor Meg is nane o' the easiest to serve. But, as the guid Buik says, it's a good and siccar lesson for the young to bear the yoke in their youth.'

'An' I'm sure thae puir bairns hae had their share o't,' said Muckle Alick.

'I suppose,' said Mistress Fraser, as she prepared to take her leave, 'that ye canna keep your thumb on the joke aboot the twa laddies and a lassie. Na, it's no to be expected o' you, Mirren. It's ower guid a tale to tell, specially on me, that aye prided mysel' on letting naebody draw my leg. But ye did me to richts this time, ye great stirk—to bring me fleein' ower here wi' my coaties kilted a' to see three newly-come-hame bairns, and the auldest o' them near woman muckle. And the loon that gaed me the cheat an elder o' the kirk! Sorrow till ye, Alick, but I could find it in my heart to clour your lugs even yet.'

'Ye hae my richt guidwull,' said Mirren, encouragingly.

But Muckle Alick only laughed. Then Tam Fraser came in seeking his wife.

'I hae been hearin' a' aboot your daft ploy, rinnin' in front o' the engine and gettin' dunted oot o' the road,' said he. 'Some folk was threepin' that it was awesome brave o' ye, but I think it was juist a daft, rackless triflin' wi' Providence. That's my thocht on't.'

'What was that? I hae heard tell o' it for the first time,' said Mirren. 'But that's nae new thing in this hoose. Alick's married wife is aye the last to hear o' his daft-like doin's.'

'O, nocht very special this time,' said Tam Fraser. 'He only threw a hundred and six Irish drovers oot o' a third story window ower the engine o' the Port express, but there's nae mair than ten o' them dead sae far. And then he louped in front on an engine gaun at full speed and to draw some bairns frae below the wheels,' said Tam Fraser, giving the local version, corrected to date.

'Is this true?' said his wife severely, fixing her eyes upon Alick with a curious expression in them.

'There's juist aboot as muckle truth in it as there is in Netherby stories for common, after they hae gotten ten minutes' start,' said Muckle Alick.

'What is your version o't?' said his wife, never taking her eyes off her husband.

'O, it was naething to tell aboot,' said Muckle Alick. 'There was some drovers in a carriage where they had nae business, and they wadna come oot, till I gaed in to them—and then they cam' oot! And the wee laddie an' the bairn were comin' alang the line afore the engine. And Geordie couldna stop. So I gied them a bit yirk oot and gat a dunch in the back wi' the buffer.'

Mirren took her husband by the rough velveteen coat-sleeve.

'My man!' she said, rubbing her cheek against it. 'But what for did ye no tell me?'

'I was gaun to tell ye the morn's mornin',' said Alick. 'There was nae harm dune, ye see, but yin o' my gallus buttons riven off an' the buffer of Geordie's engine smashed. I was gaun to tell ye in the mornin' aboot the button needing sewin' on.'

'Did ye ever see siccan auld fules?' said Tam Fraser, as he and his wife went home, 'rubbin' her cheek again his airm, that's as thick as a pump theekit frae the frost wi' strae rapes?'

'Haud your tongue, Tam,' said his wife, whose temper had suffered; 'if I had a man like that I wad rub my cheek against his trouser leg, gin it pleasured him, the day by the length.'

ADVENTURE XLIII

TOWN KNIGHT AND COUNTRY KNIGHT

Mr. Cleg Kelly awoke early on the day upon which he was to make the bold adventure of getting to Netherby Junction without enriching the railway company by the amount of his fare. But his conscience was clean; he was going to work his passage. It is true that neither the general manager nor yet the traffic inspector had been consulted in the matter. But for the sake of Cleg's friend (to be exact, Cleaver's boy's sweetheart's fellow-servant, cook at Bailie Holden's), Duncan Urquhart was willing to engineer Cleg's passage to Netherby without fee or reward.

Duncan was friendly with the guard of his goods train, which is a thing not too common among those who have to run goods trains together, week in and week out. The shunting at night in particular is wearing to the temper, especially in the winter time, when it is mostly dark in an hour or two whenever your train happens to start.

'Can you stand there and turn a brake?' said Duncan to Cleg, setting him in a small compartment by himself; 'screw her up whenever we are running downhill. Ye will ken when by the gurring and shaking.'

Mr. Duncan Urquhart was a very different man

during the day, from the gay and gallant evening caller who had won the easy-melted heart of the cook at Holden's—which a disappointed suitor once said bitterly was made of dripping. He was very grimy; he spoke but seldom, and then mostly in the highly imaginative and metaphorical language popular on the Greenock and South-Eastern. Duncan Urquhart, as has already been mentioned, was quite a first-class swearer, and had an originality not common among engineers, which he owed to his habit of translating literally from the Gaelic. Also, though he swore incessantly, he never defiled his mouth with profanity, but confined himself assiduously to personal abuse, which, if less sonorous, is infinitely more irritating to the swearee.

So hour after hour Cleg stood in the train and was hurled and shaken southwards towards Netherby. He helped at the shunting, coupling, and uncoupling with the best. For, from his ancient St. Leonard's experience, he could run the coal-waggons to their lies as well as a professional. And though his occupations had hitherto been varied and desultory, Cleg was a born worker. He always saw merely the bit of work before him, and he set his teeth into it (as he said picturesquely) till he had clawed his way through.

Thus it was that Cleg found himself at Netherby Junction one Saturday night at six o'clock. It was the first time he had ever been further than the confines of the Queen's Park. And his vision of the country came to him as it were in one day. He saw teams driving afield. He saw the mowers in the swathes of hay. He watched with keen delight the grass fall cleanly before the scythe, and the point of the blade stand out at each stroke six inches from under the fallen sweep of dewy grass.

'Netherby Junction! Guid-nicht!' said Duncan Urquhart, briefly. He had an appointment to keep with the provost's cook, who was also partial to well-bearded men in blue pilot-cloth jackets. Duncan would not have been in such a hurry, but for the fact that it took him half an hour to clean himself. He knew that half an hour when you go a-courting, and when the other fellow may get there first, is of prime importance.

Now, as Cleg Kelly stepped out upon the cattle-landing bank, he caught a glimpse of the biggest man he had ever seen, walking slowly along the white dusty road which led out of the passenger station. He was swinging his arms wide of his sides, as very big and broad men always do.

Cleg sped after him at top speed and took a tour round him before he spoke. The big man paid no attention, walking with his eyes fixed on the ground.

'Are ye the man that pitched oot the drovers?' said Cleg at last, coming to anchor in front of the giant.

Muckle Alick stopped in the road, as much surprised as if the town clock had spoken to him. For Cleg put a smartness and fire in his question to which the boys about Netherby were strangers.

'Where come ye frae?' he said to Cleg.

'I come from Edinburgh to see Vara Kavannah,' said Cleg. 'Is she biding wi' you?'

'She was, till yestreen,' said Alick.

'And where is she noo?' said Cleg, buckling up his trousers.

'She is gane to serve at Loch Spellanderie by the Water o' Ae!' said Alick.

'And how far micht that be?' asked Cleg, finishing his preparations.

'Three mile and a bittock up that road!' said Muckle Alick, pointing with his finger to a well-made dusty road which went in the direction of the hills.

'Guid-nicht!' cried Cleg, shortly. And was off at racing pace.

Muckle Alick watched him out of sight.

'That cowes a'!' he said, 'to think that I could yince rin like that to see a lass. But the deil's in the loon. He's surely braw an' early begun!'

Then Muckle Alick went round and told his wife.

'It will be the laddie frae Enbra that got them the wark in the mill, and gied up his wood hut to the bairns to leeve in. What for did ye no bring him to see Hugh Boy and the bairn?'

'I dinna ken that he gied me the chance,' said Alick. 'He was aff like a shot to Loch Spellanderie. I wad gie a shilling to hear what Mistress McWalter will say to him when he gets there. I houp that it'll no make her unkind to the lassie! If it does I'll speak to her man. And at the warst she can aye come back to us. At a pinch we could be doing without her wage!'

'Aweel,' said his wife, 'the loon will be near there by this time.'

And the loon was.

Cleg was just turning up over the hill road towards Loch Spellanderie, when he heard that most heartsome sound to the ear of a country boy—the clatter of the pasture bars when the kye are coming home. It is a sound thrilling with reminiscences of dewy eves, of heartsome lowsing times, of forenichts with the lasses, and of all that to a country lad makes life worth living.

But to Cleg the rattle of the bars meant none of these things. Two people were standing by the gate —a boy and a girl. Cleg thought he would ask them if this was the right road to Loch Spellanderie.

But as he came nearer he saw that the girl was Vara herself. She was in close and, apparently, very friendly talk with a stranger—a tall lad with a face like one of the white statues in the museum, at which Cleg had often peeped wonderingly on free days when it was cold or raining outside.

'Vara!' cried Cleg, leaping forward towards his friend.

'Cleg! What are you doing here?' said Vara Kavannah, holding out her hand.

But there was something in her manner that froze Cleg. He had come from far with a glowing heart. He had overcome difficulties. And now she did not seem much more glad to see him than she had been to talk with this young interloper at the gate of the field.

'This is Kit Kennedy,' said Vara, with a feeling that she must by her tactfulness carry off an awkward situation.

'O it is, is it?' said Cleg, ungraciously.

Vara went on hastily to tell Cleg about the children—how well and how happy they were, how Gavin was twice the weight he had been, how Hugh Boy ran down the road each night to meet Muckle Alick, and how she was now able to keep herself, besides helping a little to support Hugh and Gavin also.

Cleg stood sulkily scraping the earth with the toe of his boot. Kit Kennedy left them together, and was on the point of going off with the cows towards the byre. He had seen a tall, gaunt woman, who was not to be trifled with, walking through the courtyard, and he knew it was time to take the kye in.

Vara stopped talking to Cleg somewhat quickly. For she also had seen Mistress McWalter. She walked away towards the farm. Cleg and Kit were left alone.

Quick as lightning Cleg thrust his arm before Kit Kennedy's face.

'Spit ower that!' he said.

Kit hesitated and turned away.

'I dinna want to fecht ye!' he said, for he knew well what was meant.

'Ye are feared!' said Cleg, tauntingly.

Kit Kennedy executed the feat in practical hydraulics required of him.

'After kye time,' said he, 'at the back o' the barn.'

Cleg nodded dourly.

'I'll learn ye to let my lass alane!' said the town boy.

'I dinna gie a button for your lass, or ony ither lass. Forbye, there was nae ticket on her that I could see!' answered he of the country.

'Aweel,' said Cleg; 'then I'll warm ye for sayin' that ye wadna gie a button for her. I'm gaun to lick ye at ony rate.'

'To fecht me, ye mean?' said Kit Kennedy, quietly.

Thus was gage of battle offered and accepted betwixt Cleg Kelly and Kit Kennedy.

ADVENTURE XLIV

CLEG RELAPSES INTO PAGANISM

THE lists of Ashby were closed. The heralds and pursuivants did their devoirs, and the trumpets rang out a haughty peal. Or, at least, to that effect—as followeth :

'Come on !' said Cleg Kelly.

'Come on yoursel' !' said Kit Kennedy.

'Ye're feared,' cried the Knight of the City, making a hideous face.

'Wha's feared?' replied the Knight of the Country, his fists twirling like catherine-wheels. The boys slowly revolved round one another. It was like the solar system, only on a somewhat smaller scale. For first of all their fists revolved separately round each other, then each combatant revolved on his own responsible axis, and lastly, very slowly and in a dignified manner, they revolved round one another.

All this happened in the cool of the evening, at the back of the barn near the farmhouse of Loch Spellanderie. It was after the kye had been milked and Vara Kavannah was at work in the house clearing away the porridge dishes, while the mistress put the fretful children to bed to an accompanying chorus of scoldings, slappings, and wailings of the smitten.

As the lads stood stripped for fight Cleg showed

a little taller than Kit Kennedy, and he had all the experience which comes of many previous combats. But then he was not, like Kit Kennedy, thrice armed in the conscious justice of his quarrel.

'Come on,' cried Cleg again, steadily working up his temperature to flash point, 'come on, ye gawky, ill-jointed, bullock-headed, slack-twisted clod-thumper, ye ! See gin I canna knock the conceit oot o' ye in a hop, skip, and jump ! I hae come frae Edinburgh to do it. I'll learn you to tak' up wi' my lass ! Come on, ye puir Cripple-Dick !'

And at that precise moment Kit Kennedy, after many invitations, very suddenly did come on. Cleg, whose passion blinded him to his own hurt, happened to be leaning rather far forward. It was customary, in the giving of 'dares' round about the Sooth Back, for the threatener to stick his head as far forward as he could and shake it rapidly up and down in a ferocious and menacing manner. This ought to continue, according to the rules, for fully ten minutes, after which proceedings might commence or might not, according to circumstances. But Kit Kennedy, farm assistant to Mistress McWalter of Loch Spellanderie, was an ignorant boy. He had had few advantages. He did not even know the rules appertaining to personal combats, nor when exactly was the correct time to accept such an invitation and 'come on.'

So that was the reason why Cleg Kelly's left eye came unexpectedly into violent contact with Kit's knuckles. These were as hard as a bullock's hind leg with rough labour.

The sudden sting of the pain had the effect of making Cleg still more vehemently angry. 'I'll learn you,' he shouted, 'ye sufferin', shairny blastie o' the byres, to strike afore a man's ready. You fecht! Ye can nae mair fecht than a Portobello bobbie! Wait till I hae dune wi' ye, my man. There'll no be as muckle left o' ye as wad make cat-meat to a week-auld kittlin'. What for can ye no fecht fair?'

Our hero's cause was so bad, and his lapse into heathenism became at this point so pronounced, that for the sake of all that has been we decline to report the remainder of his speech.

But Kit Kennedy did not wait on any further preliminaries.

Ding-dong! went his fists, one on Cleg's other eye and the other squarely on his chest. Cleg was speaking at the time, and the latter blow (as he afterwards said) fairly took the words from him and made him 'roop' exactly like a hen trying to crow like a cock.

At this terrible breach of all laws made and promulgated for the proper conduct of pitched battles, what remained of Cleg's temper suddenly gave way. He rushed at Kit Kennedy, striking at him as hard as he could, without the slightest regard to science. But Kit Kennedy was staunch, and did not yield an inch. Never had the barn end of Loch Spellanderie witnessed such a combat. Cleg, on his part, interpolated constant personal remarks of a disparaging kind, such as 'Tak' that, ye seefer!' 'That'll do for ye!' But Kit Kennedy, on the other hand, fought silently. The most notable thing, however, about the combat was, that in the struggle neither of the knights took the slightest pains to ward off the other's blows. They were too entirely engrossed in getting in their own.

The dust flew bravely from their clothes, until the noise resembled the quick, irregular beating of carpets more than anything else. But, after all, not very much harm was done, and their shirts could hardly have been damaged by half a dozen Waterloos. It was like to prove a drawn battle, for neither combatant would give in. All Cleg's activity and waspishness were met and held by the country boy, with his dogged persistency and massive rustic strength. Cleg was lissom as a willow wand, Kit tough and sturdy as an oak bough. And if Cleg avoided the most blows, he felt more severely those which did get home.

Thus not unequally the battle raged, till the noise of it passed all restraint. John McWalter of Loch Spellanderie was making his evening rounds. As he went into the barn he heard a tremendous disturbance at the back among his last year's corn-stacks. He listened eagerly, standing on one foot to do it. The unwonted riot was exceedingly mysterious. Very cautiously he opened the top half of the barn door and peered through. It might be an ill-set tinker come to steal corn. John McWalter had Tweed and Tyke with him, and they frisked their tails and gave each a little muffled bark, to intimate that they should very much like to join in the fray.

John McWalter was not used to facing difficult positions on his own responsibility, so quite as cautiously he slipped back again through the barn, and crossed the yard to the house.

His wife was actively engaged scolding Vara for wasting too much hot water in cleaning the supper bowls. This happened regularly every evening, and Vara did not greatly mind. It saved her from being faulted for something new.

'Ye lazy guid-for-naething!' Mrs. McWalter was saying, 'I wonder what for my daft sister at

Netherby sent a useless, handless, upsetting monkey like you to a decent house—a besom that will neither work nor yet learn——'

At this moment John McWalter put his head within the door.

'There's twa ill-set loons killin' yin anither ahint the barn!' he said.

'What's that gotten to do wi' it, guidman?' replied his wife. 'Guid life! Ye cry in that sudden I thought it was twa o' the kye hornin' yin anither. But what care I for loons? Juist e'en let them kill yin anither. There's ower great plenty o' them aboot Loch Spellanderic at ony rate! Ill plants o' a graceless stock. Never was a McWalter yet worth his brose!'

'But,' said her husband, 'it's Kit Kennedy fechtin' wi' a stranger loon that I never saw afore! And I dinna believe he has foddered the horse!'

Mistress McWalter snatched up the poker.

'Him,' she cried, 'the idle, regairdless hound, what can the like o' him be thinkin' aboot? I'll learn him. Gin he gets himsel' killed fechting wi' tinklers for his ain pleesure, wha is to look the sheep and bring in the kye in the mornin'? And the morn kirnin' day too!'

So in the interests of the coming hour at which the week's cream was to be churned into butter, and from no regard whatever for her nephew's life or limb, the mistress of Loch Spellanderic hasted out to interfere in the deadly struggle. But Vara Kavannah was before her. She flew out of the kitchen door, and ran round the house. The McWalters followed as best they could, Vara's mistress calling vainly on her to go back and wash the dishes.

When Vara turned the corner, Cleg and Kit were

still pelting at it without the least sign of weariness or abating interest. Cleg was now darting hither and thither, and getting in a blow wherever he could. Kit was standing doggedly firm, only wheeling on his legs as on a pivot, just far enough to meet the town boy's rushes. It was a beautiful combat, and the equality of it had very nearly knocked all the ill-nature out of the boys. Respect for each other was growing up in their several bosoms, and if only they could have stopped simultaneously, they would have been glad enough to shake hands.

So when Vara came flying round the corner and ran between them, the boys were quite willing to be separated—indeed even thankful.

'Run, quick!' she cried to Cleg, 'they are comin'. O haste ye fast!'

But Cleg did not know any respect for the powers that be. He knew that the ordinary 'bobby' of commerce did not dwell in the country. And besides, even if he did, the lad who could race red-headed Finnigan, the champion runner of the Edinburgh force, and who had proved himself without disgrace against the fastest fire-engine in the city, was not likely to be caught—even in spite of the fact that he had run all the way from Netherby Junction that night already.

So Cleg turned a deaf ear to Vara's entreaties, and, very simply and like a hero, wiped his face with the tail of his coat, which he lifted from the ground for the purpose.

Kit Kennedy also kept his place, a fact which deserves recognition. For he, on his part, faced a peril long known and noted. The mystery of unknown and unproven danger did not fascinate him.

In a moment more Mistress McWalter, a tall, masculine woman, with untidy hair of frosty blue-black, came tearing round the corner, while at the same time out of the back barn door issued John McWalter, armed with a pitchfork, and followed by Tweed and Tyke, the clamorous shepherding dogs of Loch Spellanderie.

Cleg found his position completely turned, and he himself beset on all sides. For behind him the Loch lay black and deep. And in front the wall of the barn fairly shut him in between his enemies. Mistress McWalter dealt Kit Kennedy a blow with the poker upon his shoulder as she passed. But this was simply, as it were, a payment on account, for *his* final settlement could be deferred. Then, never pausing once in her stride, she rushed towards Cleg Kelly. But she did not know the manifold wiles of a trained athlete of the Sooth Back. For this kind of irregular guerilla warfare was even more in Cleg's way than a plain, hammer-and-tongs, stand-up and knock-down fight.

As she came with the poker stiffly uplifted against the evening sky, Mistress McWalter looked exceeding martial. But, as Cleg afterwards expressed it, 'a woman shouldna try to fecht. She's far ower flappy aboot the legs wi' goons and petticoats.' Swift as a duck diving, Cleg fell flat before her, and Mistress McWalter suddenly spread all her length and breadth on the ground. Instantly Cleg was on his feet again. Had the prostrate enemy been a man, Cleg would have danced on him. But since (and it was a pity) the foe was a woman Cleg only looked about for an avenue of escape.

Kit Kennedy pointed with his finger an open way round the milk-house. And Cleg knew that the information was a friendly enough lead. He had no doubts as to the good faith of so sturdy a fister as Kit Kennedy. He was obviously not the stuff traitors are made of.

But a sudden thought of inconceivable grandeur flushed Cleg's cheek. Once for all, he would show them what he could do. He would evade his pursuers, make his late adversary burst with envy, and wring the heart of Vara Kavannah, all by one incomparable act of daring. So he stood still till Mistress McWalter rose again to her feet, and charged upon him with a perfect scream of anger. At the same time John McWalter closed in upon the other side with his hay fork and his dogs. Cleg allowed them to approach till they were almost within striking distance of him. Then, without giving himself a moment for reflection, he wheeled about on his heels, balanced a moment on the brink over the deep water, bent his arms with the fingers touching into a beautiful bow, and sprang far out into the black lake.

So suddenly was this done that the good man of Loch Spellanderie, approaching with his hayfork from one direction, ran hastily into the arms of his spouse charging from the other. And from her he received a most unwifely ring on the side of the head with the poker, which loosened every tooth John McWalter still retained in his jawbones.

'Tak' that, ye donnert auld deevil, for lettin' him by!' cried the harridan.

'Ye let him by yoursel', guidwife,' cried her husband, who did not often resent anything which his wife might do, but who felt that he must draw the line at welcoming the poker on the side of his head. 'Dinna come that road again, my woman. I declare to peace, had it no been for the hay-time comin' on, and few hands to win it, I wad hae stuck the fork brave and firmly intil ye, ye randy besom!'

To what lengths this conjugal quarrel would have gone if it had been allowed to proceed will never be known. For just at that moment the head of Cleg emerged far out upon the dark waters of Loch Spellanderie.

Cleg Kelly swam nearly as easily in his clothes as without them. For he had cast his coat at the beginning of the fray, and, as to his trousers, they were loose and especially well ventilated. So that the water gushed in and out of the holes as he swam, much as though they had been the gills of a fish. Indeed, they rather helped his progress than otherwise.

Then from the dusky breadths of the lake arose the voice, mocking and bitter, of the Thersites of the Sooth Back, equally equipped for compliment and deadly in debate.

'Loup in,' he cried, 'try a dook. It is fine and caller in here the nicht. But leave the poker ahint ye. It will tak' ye a' your time to keep your ain thick heid abune the water. Come on, you!' he cried pointedly to Mistress McWalter. ''That face o' yours hasna seen water for a month, I'll wager. A soom will do you a' the guid in the world! And you, ye guano-sack on stilts, come and try a spar oot here. I'll learn ye to stick hay-fows into decent folk!'

But neither John McWalter nor yet his wife had a word to say in answer.

Then began such an exhibition as Loch Spellanderie had never seen. Cleg trod water. He dived. He swam on his back, on his side, on his breast. His arms described dignified alternate circles—half in air and half in water. He pretended to be drowning, and let himself, after a terror-striking outcry, sink slowly down into deep water, from which presently he arose laughing.

And all the time his heart was hot and prideful within him.

'I'll learn her,' he said over and over to himself, 'I'll learn her to tak' up wi' a country Jock.'

And then he would execute another foolhardy prank, dismally rejoicing the while in Vara's manifest terror.

'Cleg, come oot! Ye'll be drooned!' Vara cried, wringing her hands in agony. Simple and innocent herself, she could not understand why her kind good Cleg should suddenly act in this wild manner. She had no conception of the evil spirit of pride and vainglory, which upon occasion rent and tormented that small pagan bosom.

'I'll show her!' remained the refrain of all Cleg's meditations for many a day.

Finally, when this had gone on for a quarter of an hour, Cleg trod water long enough to kiss his hand and cry 'Guid-nicht!' to Mistress McWalter and her husband, who meanwhile stood dumb and astonished on the bank.

Then he turned and swam steadily away across the loch. He did not know in the least how he would get his clothes dried, nor yet where he would have to sleep. But his many adventures that day, and in especial the way he had 'taken the shine oot o'' that loonie wi' the curls,' warmed and comforted him more than a brand-new suit of dry clothes. So long as he could see his enemies, he looked over his shoulder occasionally. And when he noted the four dark figures still standing silent on the bank, Cleg chuckled to himself and his proud heart rejoiced within him.

'I telled ye I wad show her,' he said to himself, 'and I hae shown her!'

ADVENTURE XLV

THE CABIN ON THE SUMMIT

LIKE most Scottish lakes, Loch Spellanderie is not wide, and Cleg manfully ploughed his way across without fear of the result. For he had often swum much further at the piers of Leith and Trinity, as well as much longer in the many lochs which are girt like a girdle of jewels round about his native city. But presently his clothes began to tire him, and long ere the dark line of the trees on the further side approached, he was eager to be on shore again.

Sometimes also he seemed to hear the voices of men before him, though owing to the deep shadow of the trees he could see no one. Cleg's arms began to ache terribly, and his feet to drag lower and lower. The power went out of his strokes. He called lustily upon the unseen men to wait for him. He could hear something like a boat moving along the edge of the reeds, rustling through them with a sough as it went.

Suddenly Cleg saw something dark swimming slowly along the surface of the water. He struck towards it fearlessly. It was a curiously shaped piece of wood, moved, as it seemed, by some mysterious power from the shore. Cleg called out again for the men whose voices he had heard to wait for him. But instead of waiting, they promptly turned and fled.

Cleg could hear them crashing like bullocks through the briers and hazels of the underbush.

However, he was not far from the land now, and in a minute more he felt his feet rest upon the shelving gravel of the lake shore. Instinctively Cleg brought the wedge-shaped piece of wood with him. He found, upon holding it close to his eyes in the dim light, that a double row of hooks was attached to it beneath, and that there were half a dozen good loch trout leaping and squirming upon different sides of it.

Cleg had no notion of the nature of the instrument he had captured. Nor indeed had he the least idea that he had disturbed certain very honest men in a wholly illegal operation.

He only shook himself like a water-dog and proceeded to run through the wood at an easy trot, for the purpose of getting back some heat into his chilled limbs. He carried his trout with him.

As he ran his thoughts returned often to Loch Spellanderie, and each time he cracked his thumbs with glee.

'I showed her, I'm thinkin'!' he said aloud.

Suddenly Cleg found himself out of the wood. He came upon a slight fence of wire hung upon cloven undressed posts, beyond which ran the shallow cutting of the railway to Port Andrew.

Cleg knew himself on sure ground again, so soon as he came to something so familiar as the four-foot way. He felt as if he had a friend in each telegraph post, and that the shining perspective of the parallel metals stretched on and on, into direct connection with Princes Street Station and the North Bridge tram lines, which in their turn ran almost to the Canongate Head. He was, as it were, at home.

The boy hesitated a little which way to turn. But ultimately he decided that he would take the left hand. So Cleg sped along the permanent way towards Port Andrew at the rate of six miles an hour.

Had he known it, he was running as fast as he could out of all civilisation. For at this point the railway passes into a purely pastoral region of sheep and muircocks, where even farms and cot-houses are scarcer than in any other part of the Lowlands of Scotland.

Nevertheless Cleg kept up the steady swinging trot, which had come to him by nature in direct descent from Tim Kelly, the Irish harvestman and burglar, who in his day had trotted so disastrously into Isbel Beattie's life.

But Cleg was not to lie homeless and houseless that night, as Vara and the children had often done. The Arab of the City possessed all a cat's faculty for falling on his feet.

At a lonely place on the side of the line he came upon a little cluster of tanks and offices, which was yet not a station. There was, in fact, no platform at all. It consisted mainly of the little tank for watering the engine, and, set deep under an overhanging snout of heathery moorland, an old narrow-windowed railway carriage raised upon wooden uprights.

Cleg stood petrified with astonishment before this strange encampment. For there were lights in the windows, and the sound of voices came cheerfully from within. Yet here was the dark and lonely moor, with the birds calling weirdly here and there about him, and only the parallel bars of the four-foot way starting out east and west into the darkness, away from the broad stream of comfortable light which fell across them from the windows of the wheelless railway carriage.

Finally Cleg plucked up heart to knock. He had a feeling that nothing far amiss could happen to him, so near a railway which led at long and last to Princes Street, where even at that moment so many of his friends were busily engaged selling the evening papers. Besides which, he was in still nearer connection with his friends Muckle Alick the porter, and Duncan Urquhart, the goods engine-driver at Netherby Junction.

Cleg tapped gently, but there was at first no cessation in the noise. He knocked a second time a little harder; still it was without effect.

A voice within took up a rollicking tune, and the words came rantingly through the wooden framing. Cleg's hand slid down till it rested upon the stirrup-shaped brass handle of a railway carriage. It turned readily in his fingers, and Cleg peered curiously within.

He could now see the singer, who sat on a wooden chair with his stocking-soles cocked up on the little stove which filled all one end of the hut. There came from within a delightful smell of broiling bacon, which hungry Cleg sniffed up with gusto.

The singer was a rough-haired, black-bearded man with a wide chest and mighty shoulders, though he could not be called a giant when compared with Muckle Alick down at Netherby. And this is what he sang:

  Auld Granny Grey Pow,
   Fetch the bairnies in;
  Bring them frae the Scaur Heid,
   Whaur they mak' sic din.
  Chase them frae the washin' pool,
   Thrang at skippin' stanes —

  Auld Granny Grey Pow,
  Gather hame the weans.

The singer's voice sang this verse of the Poet of the Iron Road [1] so gaily that Cleg felt that his quarters for the night were assured. He was about to step within when a new voice spoke.

'Deed and it micht serve ye a deal better, Poet Jock, gin ye wad set doon your feet and lift your Bible to tak' a godly lesson to yoursel', instead o' rantin' there at a gilravage o' vain sangs—aye, even wastin' your precious time in makkin' them, when ye micht be either readin' the Company's rules and regulations or thinkin' aboot the concerns o' your never-dying sowl!'

'You haud your tongue, Auld Chairlie,' cried the singer, pausing a moment, but not turning round; 'gin ye hadna missed thae troots the nicht, and lost your otter to the keepers in Loch Spellanderie, ye wadna hae been sitting there busy wi' Second Chronicles!'

And again the singer took up his ranting melody:

> Bring in Rab to get him washed,
>   Weel I ken the loon,
> Canna do unless he be
>   Dirt frae fit to croon.
> Tam and Wull are juist the same
>   For a' I tak' sic pains—
>
> *Auld Granny Grey Pow,*
> *Gather hame the weans.*

So the singer sang, and ever as he came to the refrain he cuddled an imaginary fiddle under his chin and played it brisk and tauntingly like a dance tune.

> *Auld Granny Grey Pow,*
> *Gather hame the weans.*

---

[1] The brave 'Surfaceman,' Mr. Alexander Anderson of Edinburgh, for a volume of whose collected railway verse many besides Cleg are waiting with eager expectation.

Then, before another word could be spoken, Cleg stepped inside.

'Guid-nicht to ye a'!' he said politely.

The man who had been called Poet Jock took down his feet from the top of the stove so quickly that the legs of the chair slipped from under him, and he came down upon the floor of the carriage with a resounding thump. Auld Chairlie, a white-haired old man who sat under a lamp with a large book on his knee, also stood up so suddenly that the volume slipped to the floor.

'O mercy! Lord, preserve me, what's this?' he cried, his teeth chattering in his head as he spoke.

'Wha may you be and what do ye want?' asked poet Jock, without, however, getting up from the floor.

'I'm juist Cleg Kelly frae the Sooth Back,' said the apparition.

'And whaur got ye that otter and troots?' broke in Auld Chairlie, who could not take his eyes off them.

'I got them in the loch. Did ye think they grew in the field, man?' retorted Cleg, whose natural self was rising within him at the enforced catechism.

'Preserve us a'—I thocht ye had been either the deil or a gamekeeper!' said Auld Chairlie, with intense earnestness; 'weel, I'm awesome glad ye are no a game watcher, at ony rate. We micht maybe hae managed to gie the deil a bit fley, by haudin' the muckle Bible to his e'e. But gamekeepers are juist regairdless heathen loons that care neither for Kirk nor minister—except maybe an orra while at election time.'

'Aye, man, an' ye are Cleg Kelly? Where did

THE CABIN ON THE SUMMIT 307

ye "Cleg" frae?' asked the poet, who contented himself jovially with his position in the corner of the floor, till a few cinders fell from the stove and made him leap to his feet with an alacrity which was quite astounding in so big a man. Then the reason why he had been content to sit still became manifest. For his head struck the roof of the prehistoric little carriage with a bang which made him cower. Whereupon he sat down again, rubbing it ruefully, muttering to himself, 'There maun be the maist part o' a volume o' poems stuck to that roof already, and there gangs anither epic!'

When the Poet and Auld Chairlie had recomposed themselves in the little hut, Cleg proceeded to tell them all his adventures, and especially all those which concerned Mistress McWalter of Loch Spellanderie, and the great swim across the dark water.

ADVENTURE XLVI

A CHILD OF THE DEVIL

'WE'LL e'en hae yon troots to our suppers yet!' said Poet Jock. 'Chairlie, man, pit on the pan. It's wonderfu' the works o' a gracious Providence!'

And so in a trice the noble loch trouts were frying with a pat of butter and some oatmeal in the pan, and sending up a smell which mingled deliciously enough with that of the fried ham which already smoked upon an aschet by the fireside.

The good-hearted surfacemen at the Summit Hut seemed to take it for granted that Cleg was to remain with them. At least neither of them asked him any further questions. This might be because in the course of his story he had mentioned familiarly the well-considered name of Duncan Urquhart, the goods driver, and the still greater one of Muckle Alick, the head porter at Netherby. And these to a railway man on the Port Road were as good as half a dozen certificates of character.

What a night it was in that wild place! The poet chanted his lays between alternate mouthfuls of ham and fried scones of heavenly toothsomeness. Auld Chairlie said quite a lengthy prayer by way of asking a blessing. And the supplication would have continued a longer time still, but for Poet Jock's base trick of rattling a knife and fork on a plate, which caused Auld Chairlie to come to an abrupt stoppage lest any unsportsmanlike march should be stolen upon him.

Finally, however, all started fair.

'I wadna' wonder gin thae troots were poached!' said the poet, winking slyly at Cleg; 'ye wadna' believe what a set o' ill-contrivin' fellows there are in this countryside!'

'As for me,' said Auld Chairlie, 'I can see naething wrang in catchin' the bit things. Ye see it's no only allowed, it's commanded. Did ye never read how the birds in the air and the fishes in the flood were committed to oor faither Aaidam to tell the names o' them? Noo, unless he gruppit them, how could he possibly tell their names? The thing's clean ridiculous!'

'Mony a decent man has gotten sixty days for believin' that!' cried the poet, between the mouthfuls.

In the middle of the meal the poet leaped up suddenly, checking himself, however, in the middle of his spring with a quick remembrance of the roof above him. 'Preserve us, laddie, ye are a' wat!'

'So would you,' quoth Cleg, who in the congenial atmosphere of the cabin had recovered all his natural briskness, 'gin ye had soomed Loch Spellanderie as weel as me! Even a pairish minister wad be sappy then!'

'Aye,' said Auld Chairlie, sententiously, 'that's juist like your poet. He hears ye tell a' aboot soomin' a loch. But he never thinks that ye wad hae to wat your claes when ye did it.'

'But ye didna' speak aboot it ony mair than me, Auld Chairlie!' retorted Poet Jack.

'An' what for should I do that? I thocht the

laddie maybe prefer't to 'bide wat!' said Auld Chairlie, with emphasis.

'Ye are surely growin' doited, Chairles,' said the poet; 'ye took the Netherby clearin' hoose clerk for the General Manager o' the line the day afore yesterday!'

'An' so micht onybody,' replied Auld Chairlie, 'upsetting blastie that he is! Sic a wame as the craitur cairries, wag-waggin' afore him. I declare I thocht he wad be either General Manager o' the line or the Lord Provist o' Glescae!'

'Haud your tongue, man Chairlie, and see if ye can own up, for yince! If we are to judge folk by their wames, gussy pig gruntin' in the trough wad be king o' men. But stop your haverin' and see if ye hae ony dry claes that ye can lend this boy. He'll get his death o' cauld if he lets them dry on him.'

But Auld Chairlie had nothing whatever in the way of change, except a checked red-and-white Sunday handkerchief for the neck.

'And I hae nocht ava' here!' exclaimed the poet. 'Ye maun juist gang to your bed, my man, and I'll feed ye over the edge wi' a fork!'

But Cleg saw in the corner the old flour sack in which the surfaceman had imported his last winter's flour. The bag had long been empty.

'Is this ony use?' said Cleg. 'I could put this on!'

'Use!' cried the poet; 'what use can an auld flour sack be when a man's claes are wat?'

'Aweel,' said Cleg, 'ye'll see, gin ye wait. Railway folk dinna ken everything, though they think they do!'

So with that he cut a couple of holes at the corners,

and made a still larger slit in the middle of the sack bottom. Then he disrobed himself with the utmost gravity, drew the empty sack over his head, and put his arms through the holes in the corner.

'It only needs a sma' alteration at the oxters to fit like your very skin,' he said. Then he took up Auld Chairlie's table-knife and made a couple of incisions beneath the arms, ' and there ye hae a very comfortable suit o' claes.'

The poet burst into a great laugh and smote his thigh. ' I never saw the match o' the loon !' he cried, joyously.

'They are nocht gaudy,' Cleg went on, as he seated himself at the corner of the table, having first spread his wet garments carefully before the stove, ' but it is a fine an' airy suit for summer wear. The surtowt comes below the knee, so it's in the fashion. Langskirted coats are a' the go on Princes Street the noo. A' the lawyers wear them.'

At this point Cleg rose and gave an imitation of the walk and conversation of a gentleman of the long robe, as seen from the standpoint of the Sooth Back.

Once he had looked into Parliament House itself, and managed to walk twice round before 'getting chucked,' as he remarked. So he knew all about it.

He took an oily piece of cotton waste with which Poet Jock cleaned his lamps. He secured it about his head, so that it hung down his back for a wig. He put a penny in his eye, instead of the orthodox legal eyeglass. Then he set his hands in the small of his back, and began to parade up and down the centre of the old railway carriage in a very dignified manner, with the old sack waving behind him after the fashion of a gown.

He pretended to look down with a lofty contempt upon Poet Jock and Auld Chairlie, as they watched him open-mouthed.

'Who the devil are those fellows?' he said; 'lot of asses about surely. Everybody is an ass. Who's sitting to-day? Ha! old Bully-boy—bally old ass he is! Who's speaking? Young Covercase—another bleating ass!'

It is to be feared that Cleg would next have gone on to imitate the clergy of his native city. But he was hampered by the fact that his opportunities for observation had been limited to the street. He had never been within a church door in his life. And that not so much because he would have stood a good chance of being turned out as a mischief-maker, but simply from natural aversion to even an hour's confinement.

Then Cleg wrapped his old sack about him very tightly, and assumed a fixed smile of great suavity. He approached the poet, who was stretching his long limbs in the upper bunk which occupied one side of the hut.

'Ah,' said Cleg, slowly wagging his head from side to side, 'and how do we find ourselves to-day? Better? Let me feel your pulse—Ah, just as I expected. Tongue furry? Have you taken the medicine? What you need is strengthening food, and the treatment as before. See that you get it—blue mange, grouse pie, and the best champagne! And continue the treatment! *Good*-morning!'

Cleg wrapped his sack closer about him as he finished, to express the slim surtout of the healing faculty, and, setting an old tea 'cannie' of tin upon his head to represent a tall hat, he bowed himself out with his best Canongate imitation of a suitable and effective 'bedside manner.'

There was no end to Cleg's entertainment when he felt that he had an appreciative audience. And as the comedy consisted not so much in what he said as in the perfect solemnity of his countenance, the charm of his bare arms meandering irresponsibly through the holes in the corner of the sack, and the bare legs stalking compass-like through its open mouth, Poet Jock laughed till he had to get out of his bunk and lie down upon the floor in the corner. Even Auld Chairlie was compelled perforce to smile, though he often declared his belief that it was all vanity, and that Cleg was certainly a child of the devil.

Chairlie was specially confirmed in this opinion by Cleg's next characterisation.

'Did you ever see the Tract Woman?' said Cleg, dropping for a moment into his own manner. 'I canna' bide her ava. There's them that we like to see comin' into our hooses—folk like Miss Celie, that is veesitor in oor district, or Big Smith the Pleasance Missionary, even though he whiles gies us a lick wi' his knobby stick for cloddin' cats. But the Track Woman I canna bide. This is her!'

And he gathered up his sack very high in front of him, to express the damage which it would receive by contact with the dirt of Poet Jock's abode. Then he threw back his head and stuck out his chin, to convey an impression of extreme condescension.

'Good day, poor people,' he said, 'I have called to leave you a little tract. I don't know how you can live in such a place. Why don't you move away?

And the stair is so dirty and sticky. It is really not fit for a lady to come up. What's this? What's this'—(smelling)—' chops! Chops are far too expensive and wasteful for people in your position. A little nice liver, now, or beef-bone for boiling——What did you say? "Get out of this!" Surely I did not hear you right! Do you know that I came here to do you good, and to leave you a little tract? Now, I pray you, do not let your angry passions rise. I will, however, do my duty, and leave a little tract. Read it carefully; I hope it may do you good. It is fitted to teach you how to be grateful for the interest that is taken in you by your betters!'

As soon as Cleg had finished, he lifted the skirts of his old sack still higher, tilted his nose yet more in the air, and sailed out, sniffing meanwhile from right to left and back again with extreme disfavour.

But as soon as he had reached the door his manner suffered a sea-change. He bounded in with a somersault, leaped to his feet, and pretended to look out of the door after the departing 'Track Woman.'

'O ye besom!' he cried, 'comin' here nosing and advising—as stuffed wi' stinkin' pride as a butcher's shop is wi' bluebottles in the last week o' July! Dook her in the dub! Fling dead cats at her, and clod her wi' cabbages and glaur! Pour dish-washin's on her. Ah, the pridefu' besom!'

And with this dramatic conclusion Cleg sank apparently exhausted into a chair, with the skirts of the sack sticking out in an elegant frill in front of him, and fanned himself gracefully with an iron shovel taken from the stove top, exactly as he had seen the young lady performers at the penny theatres do when they waited in the wings for their 'turn.'

Great was the applause from Poet Jock, who lay almost in a state of collapse on the floor.

'Boys O!' he exclaimed feebly, 'but ye are a lad!'

Auld Chairlie only shook his head, and repeated, 'I misdoot that ye are a verra child o' the deevil!'

ADVENTURE XLVII

THE SLEEP OF JAMES CANNON, SIGNALMAN

On the morrow Cleg was up betimes. But not so early as Poet Jock and Auld Chairlie. His own clothes were now pretty dry, but Cleg had been so pleased with the freedom and airiness of his 'sack suit' as he called it, that, as it was a warm morning and a lonely place, he decided to wear it all day.

Cleg went out, and, starting from the side of the line, he ran light-foot to the top of a little hill, from whence he could look over a vast moorish wilderness—league upon league of purple heather, through which the railway had been cut and levelled with infinite but unremunerative art.

From horizon to horizon not a living thing could Cleg see except the moorbirds and the sheep. But over the woods to the east he could catch one glimpse of Loch Spellanderie very far away, basking blue in the sunlight. He could not, however, see the farmhouse. But he rubbed his hands with satisfaction as he thought of swimming away from them all into the darkness the night before.

'I showed her wha was the man, I'm thinkin'!' he said. And there upon the heather-blooms Cleg Kelly flapped his thin arms against his sack and crowed like a chanticleer. Then in a few moments there came back from over the moor and loch a phantom cock-crow reduced to the airiest diminuendo.

'I'm richt glad I'm no there,' said Cleg, heartily.

Nevertheless he went down the hill again a little sadly, as though he were not quite sure, when he came to think about it, whether he was glad or not.

But on the whole it was perhaps as well that he was where he was, at least in his present costume.

When Cleg got back to the hut, he looked about for something to do till his friends returned. His active frame did not stand idleness well. He grew distracted with the silence and the wide spaces of air and sunshine about him. He longed to hear the thunderous rattle of the coal-carts coming out of the station of St. Leonards. He missed the long wolf's howl of the seasoned South Side coalman. In the morning, indeed, the whaups had done something to cheer him, wailing and crying to the peewits. But as the forenoon advanced even they went off to the loch-side pools, or dropped into the tufts of heather and were mute.

Cleg grew more and more tired of the silence. It deafened him, so that several times he had to go outside and yell at the top of his voice—simply, as it were, to relieve nature.

It happened that on the second occasion, as soon as he had finished yelling—that is, exhausted an entire vocabulary of hideous sounds—a train to Port Andrew broke the monotony. It did not actually stop, because it was a passenger train and had already 'watered up' at Netherby. But Cleg was as pleased as if it had brought him a box of apples. He climbed up and sat cross-legged on the top of the hut in his sack, for all the world like an Indian idol; and the engine-driver was so astonished that he forgot to put the brake on till he was thundering headlong halfway down the incline on the western side of the Summit cabin.

But the stoker, a young man incapable of enthusiasms (as, alas! so many of the very young are), picked up a lump of coal from the tender and threw it at Cleg with excellent aim. However, as the train was going slowly uphill at the time, Cleg caught it and set the piece of coal between his teeth. His aspect on this occasion was such as would fully have warranted Auld Chairlie in setting him down not as a child of the devil, but as the father of all the children of the devil.

The train passed, and Cleg was again in want of something to do. He could not sit there in the sun, and be slowly roasted with a piece of coal between his teeth, all for the benefit of the whaups. He thought with regret how he should like to sit, just as he was, on some towering pinnacle of the Scott Monument, where the police could not get him, and make faces at all the envious 'keelies' in Edinburgh. To do this through all eternity would have afforded him much more pleasure than any realisation of more conventional presentations of the joys of heaven.

He descended and looked about him.

At the end of the little cabin he found a pitcher of tar, but no brush. He searched further, however, till he found it thrown carelessly away among the heather. Whereupon Cleg forthwith appointed himself house-painter-in-ordinary to the Port Andrew Railway Company, and attacked the Summit cabin. He laid the tar on thick and good, so that when the sun beat upon his handiwork, it had the effect of raising a smell which made Cleg's heart beat with the joy of reminiscence. It reminded him of a thousand things—of the brickyard

on blistering afternoons, and also (when the perfume
came most undiluted to his nose) of that district of
Fountainbridge which has the privilege of standing
upon the banks of the Forth and Clyde Canal, and of
containing several highly respectable and well-connected
glue factories. Cleg had once gone there to 'lag for
a boy,' who had offended his dignity by 'trapping' him
at school in the orthography of the word 'coffin.'

Cleg had spelled it, simply and severely, 'kofn.'

The boy from Fountainbridge, however, had spelled
it correctly. Not only so, but he had been elated
about the matter—very foolishly and rashly so, indeed.

'For,' said Cleg, 'it's easy for him. His faither is
a joiner, and makes coffins to his trade. Besides, he
had a half-brither that died last week. He micht easy
be able to spell "coffin"!'

To forestall the pride which so surely comes before
a fall, Cleg waited for the 'coffin' boy and administered
the fall in person—indeed, several of them, mostly in
puddles.

He was therefore agreeably reminded of his visit
to Fountainbridge whenever he stirred up the tar
from the bottom and the smell rose to his nostrils
particularly solid and emulous. He shut his eyes and
coughed. He dreamed that he was back and happily
employed in 'downing' the orthographist of Fountainbridge upon the flowery banks of the Union Canal.

It was after ten o'clock in the evening before Poet
Jock came in sight. He had been on a heavy job
with a break-down gang on the Muckle Fleet incline.
All day long he had been rhyming verses to the rasp
of pick and the scrape of shovel. Sometimes, so busy
was he, that he had barely time to take his mate's
warning and leap to the side, before the engine came

leaping round the curve scarcely a dozen yards away. But Poet Jock was entirely happy. Probably he might have travelled far and never known greater exhilaration than now, when he heard the engine surge along the irons, while he tingled with the thought that it was his strong arms which kept the track by which man was joined to man and city linked to city.

A fine, free, broad-browed, open-eyed man was Poet Jock. And his hand was as heavy as his heart was tender—as, indeed, many a rascal had found to his cost. Those who know railwaymen best are surest that there does not exist in the world so fine a set of workers as the men whose care is the rails and the road, the engines and the guard vans, the platforms, goods sheds, and offices of our common railways.

A railway never sleeps. A thousand watchful eyes are at this moment glancing through the bull's-eyes of the driver's cab. A thousand strong hands are on the driving lever. Aloft, in wind-beaten, rain-battered signal-boxes, stand solitary men who, with every faculty on the alert, keep ten thousand from instant destruction. How tense their muscles, how clear their brains must be, as they pull the signal and open the points! That brown hand gripping lever number seventeen, instead of number eighteen within six inches of it, is all that preserves three hundred people from instant and terrible death. That pound or two of pressure on the signal chain which sent abroad the red flash of danger, stopped the express, in which sat our wives and children, and kept it from dashing at full speed into that over-shunted truck which a minute ago toppled over and lay squarely across the racer's path.

And the surfacemen, of whom are Auld Chairlie and Poet Jock? Have you ever thought of how, night and day, they patrol every rod of iron path—how with clink of hammer and swing of arm they test every length of rail—how they dash the rain out of their eyes that they may discern whether the sidelong pressure of the swift 'express,' or the lumbering thunder of the overladen 'goods,' have not bent outwards the steel rail, forced it from its 'chair,' or broken the rail itself as the sudden weight passed over it?

A few men standing by the line side as the train speeds by. What of them? Heroes? They look by no means like it. Lazy fellows, rather, leaning on their picks and shovels when they should be working. Or this solitary man far up among the hills, idly clinking the metals with his hammer as he saunters along through the stillness.

These are the surfacemen—and that is all most know of them. But wait. When the night is blackest, the storm grimmest, there is a bridge out yonder which has been weakened—a culvert strained where a stream from the hill side has undermined the track. The trains may be passing every quarter of an hour from each direction. Nevertheless, a length of rail must be lifted and laid during that time. A watch must be kept. The destructiveness of Nature must be fought in the face of wetness and weariness. And, in spite of flagmen and fog-signals, the train may come too quick round the curve. Then there follows the usual paragraph in the corner of the local paper if the accident has happened in the country, a bare announcement of the coroner's inquest if it be in the town.

A porter is crushed between the platform and the moving carriages; a goods guard killed at the night shunt in the yard. Careless fellow! Serves him right for his recklessness. Did he not know the risk when he engaged? Of course he did—none better. But then he got twenty-two shillings a week to feed wife and bairns with for taking that risk. And if he did not take it, are there not plenty who would be glad of the chance of his empty berth?

And what then? Why, just this: there is one added to the thousands killed upon the railways of our lands—one stroke, a little figure *1* made at the foot of the unfinished column, a grave, a family in black, a widow with six children moved out of the company's house on which grow the roses which he planted about the door that first year, when all the world was young and a pound a week spelled Paradise. The six children have gone into a single room, and she takes in washing, and is hoping by-and-by to get the cleaning of a board school, if she be very fortunate.

To blame? Who said that any one was to blame? Of course not. Are we not all shareholders in the railways, and do we not grumble vastly when our half-yearly dividend is low? So lengthen the hours of these over-paid, lazy fellows in corduroys—lengthen that column over which the Board of Trade's clerk lingers a moment ere he adds a unit. What matter? They are only statistics filed for reference in a Government office.

But while Cleg waited for Poet Jock something else was happening at Netherby.

It was a bitter night there, with a westerly wind sweeping up torrents of slanting rain through the pitchy dark. Netherby Junction was asleep, but it was the sleep which draws near the resurrection. The station-master was enjoying his short after-supper nap in the armchair by the fire. For the 'up' boat train from Port Andrew and Duncan Urquhart's goods train would pass each other at Netherby Junction at 10.5 P.M.

The signal-box up yonder in the breast of the storm was almost carried away. So tall it rose that the whole fabric bent and shivered in each fierce gust which came hurtling in from the Atlantic. James Cannon, the signalman of Netherby West, was not asleep. His mate was ill, but not ill enough to be quite off duty. James Cannon had applied for a substitute, but headquarters were overtaxed for spare men, and had not responded. Netherby was considered a light station to work, and the duty would no doubt be done somehow.

James Cannon had been on duty since six in the morning—sixteen hours already at the levers. Then he had also been up nearly all the night before with a weakly and fretful child. But the company's regulations could not be expected to provide for that.

James Cannon, however, was not asleep. He had his eyes fixed on the home signal on the high bank, as he caught the gleam of it wavering through the storm. That was the way the boat express would have to come in a few minutes more. The electric needle quivered and clicked behind him. The signal-man thought of the light upon the Little Ross, which he used to see from the green Borgue shore when he was a boy. He had always looked out at it every night before he went to sleep. The signal on the high bank seemed now to flash and turn like a lighthouse. Was that the Little Ross he was looking at? Surely he could hear the chafing of the Solway tides. Was that not rather his mother bidding him lie down and sleep? James Cannon saw the home signal no more. The lights of other days beckoned him, and he attended to their signal.

Below in the left-luggage office stood Muckle Alick. He also was taking his mate's place at that night's express. He had asked away in order to visit his sweetheart, Alick knew, though certainly his mate had not mentioned it in his application to the station master. Many a time had he done the same himself for the sake of Mirren Terreggles.

Muckle Alick was arranging the parcels—which were to be forwarded, and which were to be delivered on the morrow. He laid them out neatly on long high benches at opposite sides of the room, with the larger ones below on the floor. There was no work of Muckle Alick's doing which was not perfectly done, and as featly and daintily as a girl twitches her crotchet needles among the cotton.

So engrossed was Alick in this work that it was five minutes past ten before he even looked up at the clock—a cheap one which he had bought from a Jew pedlar, and fixed upon the wall himself—'to see the time to go home by,' his mates said. The clock told him it was time to go home already.

Muckle Alick had heard Duncan Urquhart's train come grumbling and snorting by, but it was more indistinctly than usual, for the wind was blowing great guns from the north-west and roared about the junction as though to blow its wide-spanned sheds and light-roofed outbuildings bodily over the moors. After a little, as he continued to arrange his parcels, his ear caught the bump and rumble of the shunting beginning across in the goods yard.

'Duncan is hurrying up with getting his stuff out!' muttered Alick to himself.

He knew that in a few minutes the express would flash past, with the wind on her flank to drive her down the hill, and he was glad because then he would be able to lock up and go straight home to Mirren. He smiled a little also, for he pitied Duncan Urquhart, who had no Mirren to greet him when he had his last waggon shunted and his engine safe housed in the shed.

But outside, on the sidings of the goods yard, Duncan was hurriedly enough disposing of his charge. The wind was simply fiendish, and roared through the opening between the great goods engine and the tender, with a yell which almost drowned the steam whistle itself. It happened that Duncan had to 'fly shunt' a waggon too highly loaded with light goods, one at which he had more than once shaken his head earlier in the evening as he passed it. But now in the darkness he had forgotten what a surface it spread for the wind; and so, being anxious to get home to his lodging and his supper, he caused his engine to 'kick off' rather sharply, and the top-heavy waggon ran back into its siding with much greater force than he had intended, while Duncan had promptly puffed out again with his remaining trucks.

But the waggon thus started did not so easily stop, for upon reaching the guarding buffers at the end of the siding, the crashing blow of the stoppage, and the overpowering force of a furious gust of wind delivered simultaneously, jerked the high-loaded waggon off the rails, and in a moment more caused it to tilt over and lie foul of the up main line, upon which the boat express was due at any moment.

ADVENTURE XLVIII

MUCKLE ALICK SEES THE DISTANT SIGNAL STAND AT 'CLEAR'

WITHIN, Muckle Alick's ear noted instinctively a strange sound, which did not appear to be part of the routine of Duncan Urquhart's shunting. He looked at the clock above his head. The express was already two minutes overdue. Alick seized his cap and rushed out. He glanced up first of all at the signal-box. It seemed strangely dim and dusky.

'James Cannon has surely let his lamp go low!' muttered Alick to himself.

The Junction itself was dark, for the sudden gusts had snatched out most of the lamps, and those that remained flickered uncertainly. Alick glanced up and down the line, shading his eyes from the plashing, gusty rain with his hand.

All at once, just outside the circle of feeble illumination spread by the remaining lights of the 'passenger side,' Alick saw a dark unaccountable bulk lying upon the metals of the 'up' line. Without a moment's delay he ran along the platform so far as it extended, and then leaped between the metals of the down line. But when he reached the dark bulk, Alick's heart nearly stopped. For he found the corner of the derailed truck extending over the metals along which the

THE SIGNAL STANDS AT 'CLEAR' 327

boat train would in a few moments more come flying eastwards. Above, the signal cabin was dark. The signals were all clear for the express. Obviously, James Cannon could not have seen the accident to the waggon, though it had happened within a short distance of the window of his signal-box, and it was his duty to keep an eye on the shunting.

Just then the rending shriek of the express pierced to his heart. Alick shouted with all his might, but the wind whirled away his cries as if they had been those of little Gavin.

Muckle Alick had no time left him for thought, but, running back a few steps, he snatched up a heavy bar of metal, which was used for turning round the engine on the table by the engine-house.

With this ponderous tool in his hand, Muckle Alick rushed to the overturned waggon. It was, of course, impossible for him to lift the truck itself, but, clearing the *débris* of the load and inserting his bar beneath the waggon frame, he found that it lay so poised that he might just manage to 'slew' it round clear of the metals. With the strength of Samson Alick bent himself to his task. Slowly and unwillingly, inch by inch the truck swung clear.

'God help me just a minute more—for the sake o' thae hundred folk and their wives and bairns!' prayed Muckle Alick, his whole soul in the muscles which gripped the iron.

With a hoarse roar and a leaping volcano of fire-lighted smoke the express leaped by, the glow from the engine illuminating for a moment the strong man bending with tense arms and set face over the bar beneath the overturned waggon.

'Thank God! Thank God! Thank God!'

muttered Muckle Alick between his set teeth as each winking carriageful tore past, the travellers within reading their papers or settling themselves to sleep, alike unconscious of their deadly peril and their brave deliverer.

The way of the express was clear.

But something, it was thought the iron framework of the catcher on the postal car next the guard's van, suddenly caught Muckle Alick and jerked him thirty feet from where he had been standing. And then, without so much as a quiver, the express flew past the Junction and out again into the darkness, the black tempest hurtling behind her and the engine whistle screaming a true man's death-knell.

None had seen Muckle Alick. None had noted his deed of heroism, save only Duncan Urquhart, who, unconscious of danger, had cried cheerfully as he passed, 'What are ye hanging on to a post there for, Alick?'

It was fully a quarter of an hour later that Urquhart went to look for Muckle Alick. He thought he would walk the first part of his way home with him. It was always wholesome and always cheerful to walk with Muckle Alick, even when he was going home from a long spell of overtime.

At that moment the station-master woke up with a start. *It was twenty minutes past ten. The express——!*

He rushed out. The signal-box was quite dark. Duncan Urquhart was coming up the platform alone with his coat over his arm. He called out to the station-master:

'Is your signal-man dead, or only sleepin'?'

A few moments after James Cannon was rudely awakened from a pleasant dream of the Ross Lighthouse.

'Get up, man!' cried the station-master, standing

over him with a lantern; 'God kens how many lives ye hae lost through your ill deeds!'

Dazed and bewildered, James Cannon arose to the damning fact that the boat train was past, and he knew well that he had never watched the shunting or seen that the metals were clear for its passage.

Five minutes later Duncan Urquhart found Muckle Alick. He was lying half on and half over the embankment of the cattle shipping bank, where the express had tossed him like a feather.

'Oh, what's wrang, what's wrang, Alick!' cried Duncan Urquhart in terror.

'It's a' richt, Duncan,' said Muckle Alick, slowly but very distinctly. 'I slewed the waggon and held it till the express won by!'

'Can ye bide a minute, Alick?' said Duncan tenderly.

'Ow aye,' said the wounded man, 'dinna fash yoursel'. There's nae hurry.—Mirren wasna' expectin' me!'

Faster far than his own train had passed the points, Duncan Urquhart sped back to the station.

'Alick's lying killed doon on the cattle bank!' he cried. 'Help us wi' that board!'

And, rushing into the empty waiting-room, he laid hold of a newly erected partition which with unwonted consideration had been set up to keep draughts from the waiting passengers.

It resisted his single strength, but with the stationmaster to help him, and a 'One, Two, Three,' it yielded, and the men tore down the platform with it.

With the help of poor dazed James Cannon and another, they laid the giant tenderly upon it. But they had to wait for other two, hastily summoned from the nearest railway houses, before they dared try to lift Muckle Alick.

'Does it hurt, Alick?' asked Duncan of Inverness gently, like the kindly Highland man he was.

'It's no that sair,' said Alick, as quietly, 'but juist try no to be ower lang wi' me!'

They carried him to the left-luggage office, into which a few weeks before he had taken the children whom, at the peril of his life, he had saved from death. They were going to lay down the partition with its load upon the table on which he had been arranging the insured parcels half an hour before.

'Put me on the bench,' said Alick, calmly, 'dinna meddle the parcels. They are a' ready to gang oot wi' the first delivery the morn.'

So, even as he bade them, on the wide bench they laid Alick down. What like he was I know, but I am not going to tell. His wife, Mirren, might even now chance to read it.

There were tears trickling down Duncan Urquhart's face. The station-master had already run for a doctor.

'Dinna greet, Duncan,' said Alick. 'The boat train won by a' richt, and I manned to haud the waggon for them.'

But Duncan Urquhart could answer him no word. In the corner sat James Cannon with his head on his hands, rocking himself to and fro in speechless agony of soul.

'Oh, I wuss it had been me!' he wailed. 'I wuss it had been me!'

'Hoot na, James,' said Alick. 'It's better as it is —ye hae a young family.'

Then, as if he had been thinking it over—

'Duncan,' he said, 'Duncan, promise me this—ye'll no let Mirren see me. Mind ye, Mirren is no to see me. I dinna want her to think o' me like this.'

'She was aye sae taen up aboot me, ye see,' he added apologetically, after a little pause.

The doctor came. He bent over Alick. He moved him tenderly, this way and that. Then he ordered all out of the left-luggage office, except Duncan Urquhart and the station-master's wife, a quiet motherly woman.

Then, while the doctor did his duty, Alick sank into a kind of stupor. Presently he woke from it with a little start.

'Doctor, is this you?' he said; 'this is terrible kind o' ye. But it's a cauld nicht for you to be oot o' your bed so late—and you wi' a sair hoast!'

'Wheesht, Alick!' said the doctor. And said no more for a little. For, like every one else, he loved the soft-hearted giant.

Then Alick beckoned the station-master to him from the door of the left-luggage office, where he stood nervously clasping and unclasping his hands. The station-master came and bent his head.

'The boat train,' whispered Muckle Alick, 'ye'll hae to enter her in the schedule five meenites late. But ye can say that she passed Netherby all well—and the signals standing at clear.'

He was silent a moment. Then he looked up again.

'Mind ye, there's to be nocht said aboot it in the papers. Doctor, you'll see to that, will ye no? It's my wish. But if the company likes to do aught, it'll aye be a help to Mirren.'

There was a sound of stifled sobbing at the door, and the station-master suddenly shoved the youngest porter out on the platform with his foot.

'Has—ony—body gaen to tell Mirren?' asked Alick in a little.

The doctor nodded. He had, in fact, sent his own coachman over to Sandyknowes with a gig.

'Puir Mirren,' said Alick again, 'I'm some dootsome that she'll tak' this hard. She wasna expectin' it, like.'

He looked about him apologetically again.

'She was aye that sair set on me, ye see—maybe wi' us haein' nae bairns, ye ken.'

He was quiet a little while after this, and then he said, more brightly, 'There's three comed noo, though. Maybe they'll be a blessin' to her. The Lord sent them to her, I'm thinkin'. He wad ken o' this aforehand, nae doot!'

Suddenly Alick held up his hand, and there was a light shining like a lamp in his eyes.

'Hearken! that's the whistle!' he cried. 'Are the signals clear?'

There was no train in the station nor yet near it.

Muckle Alick went on. He lifted his head and looked through the open door out upon the dark platform, as one looks ahead under his hand when the sun is strong.

'I can see the distant signal. It is standing at clear!' he cried, and sank back.

And thus the soul of Muckle Alick passed out of the station—with the distant signal standing at clear.

They brought the little wife in to him a quarter of an hour after. Already her face seemed to have shrunk to half its size and was paler than Alick's own.

The doctor had him wrapt delicately and reverently in the station-master's wife's fairest linen. The face was untouched and beautiful, and as composed as it was wont to be on Sacrament Sabbaths when he carried in the elements at the head of the session, as it is the custom for the elders to do in the Cameronian Kirk.

His wife went up to him quietly and laid her hand on his broad white brow. 'My man—my ain man!' she said. And she bent down and touched it, not with her lips but with her cheek.

She looked up at the station-master's wife.

'He aye liked me to do that!' she said, smiling a little, as it were, bashfully.

And in all the room, where now stood ministers and doctors, men and women that had loved him well, hers were the only dry eyes that dark midnight.

'I wad like to get him hame the nicht, if it's nae great trouble till ye,' she said; 'I think I wad be mair composed gin I had him hame to me the nicht!'

So they took her dead home to her at quiet Sandyknowes. They carried him in between the beds of dusky flowers and laid him in his own chamber. Then they left her quite alone. For so she desired it. The wandering children, Hugh and Gavin, were asleep in the next room. So Mirren watched her man all that night, and never took her eyes off the broad and noble brow, save once when little Gavin woke and cried. Then she rose calmly and prepared him a bottle of milk, mixing it with especial care. As she did so, she raised her eyes and looked out into the dissolving dark. And there on the brae face was the light of the distant signal still shining like a star in the midst of the brightening sky of morn.

ADVENTURE XLIX

CLEG COLLECTS TICKETS

CLEG KELLY had long finished the tarring of the hut at the Summit. Poet Jock had not come home, though it was after ten at night. Auld Chairlie wandered to and fro in front of the house and out on the muir at the back, waiting upon him and complaining that the supper would be spoilt. Cleg busied himself with 'reddin' up' till it grew too dark to see. That is, he carried all the old mouldy boots to a mosshole and sank them out of sight. Then he arranged the useful articles each upon its own shelf round the walls, and the bunks were never so well made before nor was the stove ever so bright.

But not that night, nor yet for three nights, did Poet Jock return. It was seven o'clock on the evening of the third day when he arrived. He came walking up the Big Cutting with his head sunk on his breast, and he did not even look up when Cleg called to him. He came in slowly, and instead of explaining, inquiring heartily for supper, or sniffing as usual at the fragrant steam of the frying-pan, he threw himself sullenly down on the wooden shelf which constituted his bed.

'What has happened to ye, Poet Jock? Where

hae ye been? Ye'll be reported, as sure as daith,' said Auld Chairlie, after silent contemplation of this marvel for full five minutes. 'Hae ye been fu' or as she gi'en you up at last?'

The last was a question prompted by the fleeting nature of Poet Jock's loves, and the ever-recurring crisis through which his muse had to pass before he could settle upon a worthy successor to the latest faithless fair.

But Poet Jock lay still and made no answer.

'Are ye no for ony supper?' said Cleg, practically. He was now as familiar and free of the little cabin of the Summit as if he had been the poet's twin brother—a little more so, in fact, for Jock was not on speaking terms with his brother. To tell the truth, his brother and he had had a fight on Monday fortnight at the level crossing—the subject of contention being the minister's sermon the Sabbath before. The theology of Poet Jock prevailed. His dogmatic was most convincing. He 'downed' his brother three times. But though his brother owned that he had had enough of theology, he had not since visited at the hut on the Summit. But for all that they continued to sit side by side on Sabbath in the kirk, and to 'look on' the family psalm-book, taking it as usual in turns to find the places and shutting the book unanimously when a paraphrase was given out.

It was now the fourth day of Cleg's sojourn at the hut. Every day he had gone up to the top of the craigs that looked towards Lock Spellanderie. And each day his resolve never to go near the place again because of the faithlessness of woman sensibly weakened.

But he had something else to think about now.

For since he came into the domains of the kindly surfacemen, Cleg had seen nothing so mysterious as the obstinate refusal of the Poet to take any supper.

Auld Chairlie tried again.

'Look you here,' he said, 'either you tell's what is the maitter wi' ye, or I'll send doon wi' the late passenger for the doctor to come up the first thing the morn's mornin!'

Poet Jock groaned, but said nothing for some minutes.

'Chaps,' he said at last, 'I may as weel tell ye. Muckle Alick at Netherby was killed shiftin' a waggon to let by the boat train. And his wee bit wife's a widow the nicht! I hae been at Netherby lettin' a man off to fill his place.'

Auld Chairlie dropped the tin platter which was in his hand.

'O Lord,' he said, 'could ye no hae ta'en ony o' the lave o' us? It wadna hae made so verra muckle differ. But Alick——'

He stood still contemplating the gap that there was in the world.

'That's what they hae been crying at me off the engine the last twa days, but I'm gettin' that deaf I couldna hear!'

But Cleg was prompt in action as ever.

'Guid nicht, lads,' he said, 'I'm gaun doon to Netherby to see gin I can be ony use.'

Poet Jock started up from his bunk, instinctively guarding his head from the roof even in the midst of his distress of mind.

'What hae ye to do wi' it?' he cried, his voice sounding angrily, though he was not angry.

'The twa bairns I telled ye aboot are in Muckle

Alick's hoose. He saved their lives, and I'm gaun doon to see what I can do for them.'

'Ye canna gang that gate, man. Ye hae nae claes fittin' for a funeral!' said Chairlie. 'Ye hae nocht on but that auld sack!'

'I'm no carin',' stoutly asserted Cleg; 'I'm gaun doon to see if I can help. It's no the funeral I'm carin' for, it's what's to come after.'

Poet Jock got up and began cautiously to forage on all the shelves.

'A' my things are awesome big across,' he said, 'but maybe there will be eneuch amang us to fit ye oot.'

Cleg's wardrobe had dwindled to a shirt and a pair of trousers. He had lost his cap in Loch Spellanderie.

But Auld Chairlie, in spite of his previous want of success, found him a pair of socks and a pair of boots— which, though they were not 'marrows' or neighbours, were yet wearable enough. Cleg treated himself to a velveteen sleeved waistcoat, which, by merely shifting the buttons, became a highly useful garment. It had been exposed for some time to the weather, and when Cleg saw it, it was mounted upon two sticks, out in the little patch of cornland which Poet Jock had sown at the back of the cabin, upon a quarter acre of ground which the company had included within its wire fence with some idea of constructing a siding some day, when the traffic increased.

'Where gat ye that braw waistcoat?' queried Poet Jock when he came in, looking admiringly at the remarkable change in Cleg's appearance.

'O I just changed claes wi' the craw-bogle!' replied Cleg with a certain quiet complacency, which became him like his new garment.

'Dod,' said Auld Chairlie, 'it's a maist remarkable improvement, I declare.'

Poet Jock gave Cleg a grey woollen shirt with a collar attached which had washed too small for him, but which still reached nearly to Cleg's feet. He added a red-and-green tie of striking beauty (guaranteed to kill up to sixty yards), and an old railway cap, which had been a castaway of some former occupant of the cabin.

'There noo,' he said, when Cleg was finally arrayed. 'Ye are nane so ill put on! Ye micht e'en gang to the funeral. I hae seen mair unfaceable folk mony a time. I'll get ye doon on the late express, that is, if it is no Sulky Jamie that's in chairge o' her.'

Sulky Jamie was the name of a guard who withheld his hand from any work of mercy, if it involved the least official irregularity. He was an incomparably faithful servant to the railway company of Port Andrew. But he could not be said to be very popular among his fellow-servants along the line.

So Poet Jock, seeing that Cleg was bent upon his quest, withstood him no more. But, instead, he walked all the long way down the incline with him to Dunnure station, and there waited to pick up a 'chance of a ride' on the night passenger. For no one in the cabin had a farthing of money. Poet Jock, indeed, never had any four days after pay day, and Auld Chairlie always sent his down to be banked, saving only what had to be paid monthly to Sanders Bee, the shopkeeper at the Dunnure huts, for his share of their provisions.

'I canna trust mysel' when there's siller in the hoose!' said Auld Chairlie, who knew himself to be a brand plucked from the burning, and who still felt the embers glowing a little below the surface.

But it was with great good hope that Poet Jock walked with Cleg to Dunnure, in order to arrange a free passage for him down to Netherby.

The last 'stopping' passenger before the boat train was late, and they had a good while to wait in the ill-lighted station.

But it came at last, and lo! Sulky Jamie was in charge.

Poet Jock went boldly up to his van and tackled him. He stated the case with eloquence and lucidity. He argued with him, as Sulky Jamie moved to and fro, swinging his lantern and never looking at the orator.

But the guard was incorruptible, as indeed he ought to have been. No tramp should come on his train so long as he was the guard of it.

Whereupon Poet Jock, stung to the quick, told Sulky Jamie his opinion of him. He said that when it came his time to leave the line, there would be a hurrah which would run along the metals all the way from Port Andrew to Netherby. He further informed him that there was one testimonial which would be subscribed with enthusiasm among his mates—a coffin for Sulky Jamie. But even that only on condition that he would promptly engage to occupy it. Poet Jock ended by offering to prepare him for burial on the spot, and was in the act of declaring that he would put all these things into rhyme when the guard blew his whistle.

Cleg was nowhere to be seen, but Sulky Jamie had kept his eyes wide open while he listened to the poet. He blew his whistle again, waved the lamp, and stopped the train as it was moving out of the station. Then he plunged into the forward van, which was sacred to the 'through' luggage. In a moment

Cleg came out with a fling which sent him head first upon the platform. A white-haired military-looking man looking out of the next carriage laughed loudly, and clapped his hands with glee.

This act of Sulky Jamie's aroused Poet Jock to fury.

'Wait,' he cried, 'wait till the Netherby fast day an' I'll settle wi' ye, ye muckle swine, pitchin' oot the bit boy like that.'

But Sulky Jamie was unmoved.

'I'll be pleased to see ye on the fast day or ony ither day. But I'll hae nae tramps on my train!' said he, as he swung himself on board.

Yet, had he known it, he was carrying one at that moment. For it so happened that a Pullman carriage had been invalided from the morning boat train owing to a heated axle and an injury to the grease box. Now the resources of the Port Andrew fitting shop, though adequate for all ordinary purposes, were not sufficient to deal with the constitution of such a delicate and high-bred work of art as a bogie Pullman.

So Cleg waited till he saw the guard at Dunnure station raise his hand to blow his whistle. Then he darted sideways, in and out among the carriages, and before the train was properly in motion he was lying at full length on the framework of the bogie part of the Pullman.

With a growl and a roar the train started. Cleg's heart beat quickly. He was jolted this way and that. The dust and small stones swept up by the draught under the train nearly blinded him. But Cleg hung on desperately. He had determined at all hazards to travel upon Sulky Jamie's train. So the boy clutched the bars tighter and twined his feet more firmly round the bogie, determined to win his passage to Netherby in spite of all the ill-natured guards in the world.

Indeed, the jarring laugh of the man with the white moustache when he was thrown out at Dunnure station, rankled much more in his small heathen heart than all the hard blows of Sulky Jamie.

'What was his business wi' it?' Cleg demanded of himself half a dozen times, during that interminable period before they came to the next station.

The train stopped at last, and Cleg dashed the wet locks off his brow and cuddled his beam closer. He could stand it out now, he thought. He was congratulating himself on being in Netherby in a few minutes, when he heard the military voice above him.

'Guard,' it said, 'the boy you threw out of the train at Dunnure got in below the empty Pullman. I think he is in there now.'

Then Sulky Jamie swore loudly and emphatically. Cleg could hear him swinging himself down from the platform upon the line.

The light of the lantern would show him the bars and wheels of the forward bogie.

But Cleg did not wait for the arrival of Sulky Jamie. He dropped down and sped out at the dark side of the station, with bitter anger in his heart against the interfering military man. As he looked down from the wire paling he saw the deserted platform of Newton Edward, and a vengeful thought struck him. He ran quickly round the stern lights of the train and climbed upon the platform. A lantern was sitting on a barrow. The station-master was talking to the engine-driver far away at the front, for the late boat train was always long. The guard was routing out tramps beneath the Pullman.

With sudden determination Cleg pulled the stem of his cap over his eyes, and buttoned the sleeved waistcoat of railway velveteen closer about him. Then he took the lantern in hand. He was going to pay his debt to that evil-conditioned military man with the white moustache.

He could see him now, sitting at his ease, and trying to read his paper by the light of the miserable oil lamp, fed with scanty drains of dirty, half-melted oil, which to this day is all that is supplied as an illuminant by the Port Andrew Railway Company.

Cleg opened the door smartly.

'Ticket, sir!' he said briskly.

The military man put his hand in his side pocket, and handed out his ticket without looking up, with the ease and freedom of a well-seasoned traveller. He never took his eyes off his paper.

'Netherby—right, sir!' said Cleg Kelly, ticket collector.

Then Cleg went to the nearest compartment and promptly jumped in. It was half full of sleepy commercial travellers, who took little notice of the curiously attired boy.

Cleg could hear the tramp of his enemy as he came up from routing below the Pullman. It sounded sulkier than ever upon the platform.

'Did you not nab him?' cried the voice of the military man from his carriage window.

'None of your gammon!' replied the other voice. And the whistle sounded promptly.

The temper of Sulky Jamie was distinctly ruffled.

The train ran on down to Netherby. There the tickets were taken at the little platform to which Muckle Alick had so often run, late and early, with lamp in hand. It was a sleepy emergency man from the head offices who took the tickets in Cleg's compartment. He lumped them all together, and paid no attention whatever to the yellow first-class through ticket among its green brethren, which Cleg handed to him with such a natural air of loafish awkwardness.

Clang went the door. But the window was down for air, and Cleg could hear the angry accents of Sulky Jamie further down the train.

'Nonsense! Your ticket took at the last station! More o' your gammon, like enough. Find that ticket or pay for the journey from Port Andrew—seven-and-nine! And look something slippy, that's more! I can't keep my train waiting all day on the like of you, and the express due in twenty minutes.'

Cleg could not catch the answer of the military man. But the guard's reply was clear.

'I don't care if ye were the Prince of Wales. Pay up or I'll give ye in charge!'

The train started down to the main platform. And Cleg had the door open before the commercials in the corner were more than half awake. He slipped out, and ran back down the platform instead of up. At the corner stood James Cannon's signal-box, by the side of a white bridge. Cleg swarmed up the pole at the corner, set a foot lightly on the white painted palings, and dropped like a cat upon the road.

He was a modest boy, and did not desire to give any further trouble.

But he thought of the military man with joy in his heart.

'Now I guess we're about quits!' he said.

ADVENTURE L

GENERAL THEOPHILUS RUFF

CLEG slept that night in a hay-shed half a mile out of the town. He did not mean to go to Sandyknowes till the morrow. And even then it was not quite clear to him what he could do to help the widow. But as usual he would think it out during the night.

The morning came, fiery with lamb's wool in fluffy wisps all about the sky. Cleg shook himself, yawned, and elaborately dusted off the hay from his garments.

Then he stepped over the edge of the stack and put his foot to the road. He was very hungry and he had nothing upon which to break his fast, except only the water of the brook. He stooped at the first burn which crossed the road, and drank his fill. Presently he met a man who came walking smartly down the brae. He carried a cow switch in his hand and chewed a straw.

'Can you tell me the road to Sandyknowes, if you please?' said Cleg politely.

The rustic with the straw in his mouth looked Cleg carefully all over. Then he roared with laughter, while Cleg flushed angrily.

'Your boots are no marrows!'[1] he cried. 'O Lord, a stemmed bonnet and his grandfather's waistcoat!'

[1] Not neighbours.

And he went off again into such a fit of laughter that he let the straw slip out of his mouth. But he perceived his loss, and lifted it from the dust, wiping it carefully upon the dirtiest part of his trousers before restoring it to the corner of his mouth.

'Can ye tell me the road to Sandyknowes, man?' said Cleg again, with a little more sharpness and a little less politeness.

'I can, but I'll no!' gaped the rustic. And he went into another prolonged fit of merriment, fairly hugging himself and squirming in his enjoyment. It was the best jest he had made for a month. And he rather fancied he landed some good ones.

Cleg Kelly's hand dropped upon a stone. The stone whizzed through the air and took effect on the third button of the man of straw's new waistcoat.

The laugh ended in a gasp. The gasp was succeeded by a bad word, and then the young man gave chase. Cleg pretended to run slowly —'to encourage him,' as he said afterwards. The yokel thought all the time that he was just about to catch Cleg, but always just at the critical moment that slippery youth darted a dozen yards ahead and again avoided him.

At last the young man gave up the chase. He had suffered indignities enough. He had lost his straw. But he had an appointment to keep with a farmer three miles further on to whom he was offering his valuable services. So he had perforce to turn away and content himself with promising what he would do to Cleg when he caught him.

What Cleg did was simpler. He patrolled the heights above, keeping exact pace, step for step, with his enemy below. And with the aid of the pebbles which plentifully strewed the brae face, he afforded the young man of straw some of the finest and most interesting active exercise in getting out of the way he had had for many years. Indeed, his whole line of march for more than a mile was completely enfiladed by the artillery of the enemy.

'Will ye tell me the road to Sandyknowes noo?' cried Cleg, jubilantly, as he kept the youth skipping from side to side of the highway.

At last he bade his adversary farewell, with a double machine-gun fire of words and still heavier ammunition.

'This will maybe learn ye, country,' he cried, 'after this to gie a civil answer to a civil question.'

'Wait till I catch you!' the young man shouted, stung to desperation.

Whereupon, just for luck, Cleg ran in and delivered a volley at point-blank range, which sent the man of straw clattering up the road. It was certainly not wise to dally with the prize marksman of the Sooth Back, who on his good days could break any particular pane in a fifth-story window that you liked to specify, nine times out of ten.

After this Cleg Kelly returned along the heights to find out the way to Sandyknowes for himself. More than a mile back, a girl driving cows pointed out to him the little path which led to Mirren's door. But Cleg did not go up directly. He played idly about, whittling sticks and poking in hedge roots in his assumed character of vagrant boy. Yet all the time he kept a bright look-out upon the door of the little house among the flowerbeds. The window blinds were drawn down, and stared white like empty eye-sockets of bone. The thought of the brave, strong

man who lay dead within oppressed Cleg's heart.
Presently he saw a woman come to the door, and go
after the cow over the little meadow pasture. Muckle
Alick's wife, he thought. But he was wrong. It was
her warm-hearted neighbour, Mistress Fraser. Then
presently his heart melted within him when he saw Boy
Hugh come running round the back of the house.

Cleg had arrived in time for Muckle Alick's
funeral day. The large company of mourners began
to gather very early. All the town of Netherby was
there. Even the District Superintendent of the railway, who happened to be in the neighbourhood on a
tour, had telegraphed for his 'best blacks' from his
wife in Greenock. And there he was, standing outside
the house, waiting for the minister to finish the service,
for all the world like any common man.

Poor James Cannon was also there, the tears
coursing steadily down his cheeks. The provost
and magistrates were there. Every member of the
School Board was there, all agreed for once. Such a
funeral had never been seen in Netherby 'within the
memory of man.' That was the exact phrase used
(it is believed not for the first time) in describing the
occasion in the 'Netherby Chronicle and Advertiser.'
But otherwise Alick's dying request for silence was
scrupulously regarded.

When the hearse moved away from the door, and
the sombre congregation fell in behind it, Mirren
Douglas came to the door and watched it out of sight.
The good women who abode in the house to company
with her in her bereavement, begged her to go in and
compose herself. But she would not.

'I am in no ways discomposed,' she said, 'but I
will watch him oot o' sicht for the last time. I did it

every mornin', ye ken,' she explained to them. 'Let me bide!'

The black procession went serpentining down the road from Sandyknowes, the men pacing slowly and gravely after the horses between the summer hedges and under the green beech leaves.

Soon it approached the turn which would hide the hearse from those standing at the door of the house. But a little hillock rose, grassy to the top, at the gable end. It was the place to which she was used to run out to watch for Muckle Alick's return, in order to 'mask' the tea in time for his supper, that all might be ready for him when he came home wearied.

Mirren Douglas ran out thither, and, standing on the top of the hillock, she waved her hand to that which was going out of sight. She did not care who saw her.

'Fare ye weel, Alick,' she cried, 'fair ye weel that ever wast o' men the kindest. Few are the choice hearts that will match thine—aye, even up there, where thou art gane. And nane like to thysel' hast thou left amang us. Fare ye weel, my ain man, Alick! Naebody's man but mine!'

And with that she turned and walked in quite quietly.

As the funeral passed the end of the road Cleg withdrew behind the hedge, because, though his heart was full of love for the strong man whom he had seen but once, he did not wish to disgrace that solemn procession with his sleeved waistcoat and unpaired boots. As the hearse passed him Cleg took off his railway cap and stood bareheaded behind the hedge. So intent was he on the procession, that he did not see a tall tightly-coated man of military carriage who had stepped over the field towards him, and now stood silently by his side. The old officer also took off his hat, and stood reverently enough till the last of the mourners had passed by.

Then he laid his hand upon Cleg's shoulder.

'I'll trouble you for the price of my railway ticket!' he said. Cleg turned. It was the man who had laughed when he was pitched out of the carriage at Dunnure by Sulky Jamie!

For a moment all his usual readiness forsook Cleg. He stood silent and gazed dumbly at the tall figure before him, and at the right hand which pulled grimly at the drooping moustache.

'You had better come away to the police station!' said the gentleman.

'Ye'll hae to catch me first, then!' cried Cleg, suddenly twisting himself free and springing over the hedge into the highway. The old soldier made no attempt to follow, but continued to gaze fixedly at Cleg.

'What is your name, boy?' he said, still keeping his eyes upon the lad.

'Slim Jim Snipe o' Slippery Lane!' replied Cleg promptly, 'and muckle obleeged to ye for speerin'!'

'You young imp!' cried the old man, advancing to the fence with his cane uplifted threateningly, 'would you dare to insult me?'

Cleg retreated.

'That's a guid enough name to gie to the poliss,' he said. 'If ye ask me ceevilly, I'll tell you. Nae thanks to you that I got here ava!'

'I beg your pardon,' said the old soldier, lifting his hat as to an equal, with a certain punctilious restraint. 'I have the honour to inform you that my name is Major-General Theophilus Ruff, of Barnbogle and Trostan.'

'And mine,' said Cleg Kelly, taking off his stemmed bonnet as politely, 'is Cleg Kelly o' the Sooth Back o' the Canongate, and late o' Callendar's Yaird!'

The General bowed ceremoniously.

'And now,' he said, 'what do you propose to do about my railway ticket?'

'I'll work it out!' said Cleg quickly.

There was something in 'the looks of the starchy old geeser' (as Cleg remarked to himself) which the boy rather liked, though without doubt he was as mad as a hatter.

'Work it out,' cried the General; 'what can you do?'

'Anything!' said Cleg. (It was his one touch of his father's dialect that he still said 'annything.')

'That's nothing!' said the General.

'Wait till you see,' retorted Cleg. 'You try me. I'm nae country gawk, but reared in the heart o' the toon. I can rin errands. I can howk[1] yairds for taties—or,' he added, thinking of his flower-garden round the old construction hut, 'for flooers. And if I dinna ken the way to do onything, I can find oot.'

The General appeared to consider.

'Do you see that house over there among the trees—across the railway?'

'Aye,' said Cleg, 'I canna help seein' it! It's big eneuch and ugly eneuch to be a jail!'

'Do you think that you could keep that house in order?'

'Me?' said Cleg, 'me keep yon hoose—it's as big as the Infirmary.'

[1] Dig.

'I live there all by myself,' said the General. 'I cannot have women about my place. The sight of them kills me. And I cannot trust a grown man not to bring a woman about the house. I might try a lad.'

Cleg looked carefully from the General to the house and back again. He was not sure that it might not be a joke.

'Have you a character?' asked the old man.

'Aye,' said Cleg, 'Miss Celie wad gie me yin.'

The General turned pale and stamped with his foot.

'A woman,' he said, 'I could not apply to a woman. There is always something odious about a woman's letter. I actually do not recover from the shock of handling the writing of one of these creatures for days. Do you not know any one else?'

'There's Maister Donald Iverach,' said Cleg. 'He wad gie me a character if I got Miss Celie to ask him,' answered Cleg.

'My nephew in Edinburgh, that smug young three-legged stool! You'll do nothing of the kind,' cried the General. 'I would not give a brass button for his own character. And besides, from the tone in which you speak, I have little doubt that the two persons you mention are contemplating matrimony. I do not wish any communication with anything so disgusting —much less when one of the parties is an ungrateful and grasping relative of my own.'

By this time Cleg had had enough of the General's catechism.

'I'll be requiring a reference mysel',' he said, in the tone which he had heard Mistress Roy of the paper-shop adopt when a new customer asked for a week's credit.

'A what?' said the General, astonished.

'A reference as to your moral character, if I am to serve in your house!' replied Cleg, unabashed.

The General clapped his hands with unfeigned pleasure.

'Bless you, my boy, you please me immensely!' he said, chuckling; 'do you know that it is more than fifty years since General Theophilus Ruff had such a thing?'

'All right,' said Cleg, 'suppose we baith chance the moral characters.'

'Done!' said the old soldier, offering Cleg his hand.

Cleg took it and wrung it hard.

'I think we'll agree very well,' the General said. 'I may be Ruff by name, but I am Theophilus by nature. That's Greek, my boy—all I can remember, indeed. The folk about here will tell you that I am crazy. They are no judges. And my nephew wishes I were. Once his father tried to prove it. But when the judge had looked inside my account books, and examined my system of book-keeping, he said that, mad as I might be, it was a kind of madness which was very well able to take care of itself.'

Cleg accompanied the General over the fields to his house. The walks and drives were completely overgrown with mossy grass and tangled ferns. The gates were all padlocked and spiked. Whenever the General came to one, he unlocked it with a brightly polished steel master-key which he took from his pocket. Then, as soon as they had passed through, he locked it behind him again as securely as before. 'Spiked on the top,' he said to Cleg, with a cunning look, 'keeps out the women, you see. They don't like having their frills and furbelows torn.'

Cleg nodded as though he understood. He was not particular either way.

'By-the-by, you don't mind coffins and things?' said the old soldier, glancing swiftly under his brows at Cleg.

'I don't think so if they are empty. I yince slept in a coffin shop for three months!' said Cleg.

'Have you anything you want to settle before you engage with me?' asked the General.

'Yes,' said Cleg. 'There's a wife over the hedge yonder that has lost her man. And I maun hae either the afternoons or the forenichts to help her.'

'Take any part of the day you like; only, change your clothes when you come back,' said the General testily. 'But mind, if you bring any woman inside the policies, I shall certainly give you up to the police for obtaining railway tickets under false pretences.'

ADVENTURE LI

THE GENERAL'S ESTABLISHMENT

THEY were now standing at the front door. Cleg had never seen such a house as this in his life. It was barred and defended like the Calton Jail, but no glass was to be seen in any of the windows. Indeed, through some of the openings which served for lighting, one could see straight through to the barred windows on the further side.

Barnbogle House had in time past been an ancient fortalice. But both the former and the present lairds had spent large sums upon alterations and repairs. The latest of these, General Theophilus Ruff, had a vast and far-reaching local fame. Gamesome lasses skirled at his name, and refused to keep their trysts for the terror of meeting him, wrapped in his blue military cloak, stalking lonely by the light of the moon. The very poachers would not fish in his streams or shoot in his coverts. He had at once the repute of a wizard and the fame of a miser—rich beyond calculation, but seeing things unseen to mortals. 'He wasna canny!' summed up the collective verdict of the countryside.

Theophilus Ruff had been an Indian officer at the time of the Mutiny. And those terrible days of midsummer, when the sun dried up the blood even as it was spilt, had changed the gay casual young officer into the man whom all the country knew as the 'daft general.'

His father had been first a spendthrift and then a 'neegar'—that is, one who had become as great a screw as he had formerly been a mighty and lavish spender.

The popular report of the contents of Barnbogle House told of chests of gold and silver, cases of the most precious jewels, the spoil of captured Indian cities—all watched over by the General himself with an armoury of deadly weapons. For it was not the least of his terrors that he dwelt all alone in that huge hundred-barred castle.

Yet there had been a time when Theophilus Ruff drove coach and six, and when he saw only the gayest of gallant company. Among themselves the chin-shaking elders would tell, with many cross-shoulder glances, of the bold wanton eyes of ladies with once famous names, who had sat beside Theophilus Ruff when he drove that coach and six, and of the golden candlesticks which had sparkled on the board, wide-branching, holding aloft many lights. Then Barnbogle was a gay place indeed, alive with brilliant company, humming with raffish mirth. For General Theophilus Ruff had 'used the company of the singing woman,' and, as the Writ sayeth, he had certainly been taken in her attempts.

'He's garrin' the Indian yellow boys spin!' the Netherby people said of him at this time. Yet they said it with a kind of pride, that such imperial wickedness should have happened in their parish.

But suddenly one morning, just when the repair to his house was greatest, when gold tresses shone most aureate, when bright eyes were most winsome and sparkling, Theophilus Ruff came downstairs and gave every soul within his house an hour's notice to quit. Great was the consternation, mighty the upheaval. Ladies, lately so *débonnaire*, left by carriagefuls, wrangling fiercely as they went. Their gay companions took horse and rode silently and wrathfully away. Theophilus Ruff stood on the step of Barnbogle House and grimly watched them go. Then he went upstairs, called his servants into the drawing-room, and dismissed them, paying them their wages and board for six months in full. He kept on a stableman or two till he could sell his horses, a manservant till he had disposed of his cattle. Then he let his more distant grass parks, and dwelt all alone in the great house with barred and defended policies. After this Day of Judgment workmen from Glasgow were quartered at Barnbogle for nearly a year. With them there came a man-cook to prepare their food, and rough masons' labourers were lodged in the dainty, dismantled bedrooms where last had dwelt delicate ladies of the blonde allures.

Now and then, on Sundays, one of these Glasgow callants would steal out, at the risk of discovery and dismissal, to see the Netherby lasses. Or, mayhap an elder smith or joiner would escape to the public-house of a dark evening. But it was at the peril of their places and their excellent wages.

To them chiefly could be traced the tales of mighty strong-rooms, of triple-barred gratings, of wondrously fitting doors, with bolts which at the click of a key worn on the watch-chain locked so firmly that none could open again without secret passwords.

During this period General Theophilus Ruff had become an extremely pious person. Every Sunday he

THE GENERAL'S ESTABLISHMENT 357

conducted service with his workmen in person. One day he would read the prayers and Litany of the Church of England with such a grace of intonation and dignity, that it caused the douce Glasgow Presbyterians to fear that even double wages would hardly make up to them for their souls' peril in thus sacrificing to idols.

But by the succeeding Sunday the General had discarded the service book, and he would lead them in prayer with all the interjectional fervour of a ' ranter ' —which at that date was the name by which revival preachers were called.

Every church in the neighbourhood benefited by by the benefactions of the General. And there was not a division of the Derbyites, Close, Open, or Original, which did not receive a visit from him, and which had not good cause to believe that the Brethren had secured the richest convert the sect had ever made. But the General contented himself with making the most liberal contributions, and with listening to the brothers' mourning for each other's backslidings, and to their equally sincere rejoicing that they alone of all mankind could escape hell-fire. Then he would return home, and the very next day proceed to give another denomination the benefit of the doubt.

But, nevertheless, while the fit lasted, the General was ready to assist all and sundry to erect suitable places of worship. His purse was long and deep. So it happens the district of Netherby is distinguished among its neighbours for the number of its spires and for the surpassing whiteness of the outside of its cup and platter.

The only stipulation which the General made was that he, and he only, should have the right to prescribe the plan of the building, and the time at which it was to be finished. This is the reason why the ' Englishy ' kirk worships in a tabernacle erected in miniature of Mr. Spurgeon's. So that the heart of the incumbent (who left the Church of England in England to secure greater liberty of ritual) is daily broken by the impossibility of having a procession within it, other than one briefly semicircular ; and also by the fact that he has to read his purple-clad sermon behind a table, fitted only for holding the glass of water and Bible which equip the popular tribune.

Similarly the Kirk of Scotland by law established in Netherby presents all the characteristics of a Little Bethel meeting-house. And a new minister of æsthetic tastes has to wrestle with the fact that there is no place in which to bestow an organ except in the coal-cellar from which the heating apparatus is worked.

But both the Auld Lichts and the Baptists are housed in haughty fanes—not large, indeed, but built on the most approved cathedral principles. The meeting-house of the Baptists, indeed, has no less than two spires and the beginnings of another, after the fashion of Lichfield. The whole front of the Free Kirk is a-glitter with quartz-faced rock. For during the time of its erection Theophilus Ruff would arrive each day with his pockets full of stones with this shell-white glance upon them. He even marked spots upon the moor, and sent out masons to bring in the larger pieces which took his fancy. And one by one these all found their way into the frontage of the Free Kirk.

The most curious point about all this building of religious edifices was, that Theophilus Ruff never allowed one of them to be finished. When the last turret of the spire was on the point of being finished, Theophilus would dismiss all the men, order the unfinished pinnacle to be covered with lead to preserve it from the weather, and so leave the church with an ugly hooded hump upon its back.

Or he would permit a rough stone dyke and a dozen old sand-pits and lime-heaps to remain lying for years about the gate, just as they had been thrown down at the time when the building was begun. He preferred to see one gate-post up and the other down. He had been known to build a mill and fit it with expensive machinery, to construct a mill dam with the most approved modern sluices, and to import the most advanced American 'notions' in the way of farm implements. Then one fine morning he would arrive, and when everything was almost complete he would pay the labourers their wages, discharge the engineers in the midst of fixing a steam boiler or laying hot-water pipes for the most improved method of preparing food for cattle. Thereafter he would write their masters a cheque, and there was an end. Not an ounce of water would ever run out of that granite-embanked mill dam. Not a wheel of that beautiful machinery would so much as turn round. No horse wearing shoe-iron would ever tread the asphalted floor of these sanitary stables. Year after year the whole premises would stand empty. The glass would early disappear from the windows under a galling cross fire from the catapults of all the boys in the neighbourhood, with whom it was a point of honour to break everything breakable about the various 'follies' of General Theophilus Ruff. Never did houses get the reputation of being haunted so quickly as those buildings erected by him in all manner of unlikely places. Even during the very week after the workmen had been unceremoniously dismissed, and while the new gloss was yet on the handles of the doors and the shop polish upon the machinery, the place and neighbourhood would begin to be deserted after dusk by every man, woman, and child in the neighbourhood.

Nay, more than this, the same mysterious blight was instantly communicated to any property acquired by the General. For at this time it was his habit to buy all that came into the market, without any discrimination whatever. He had been known to buy the middle house of a row of respectable tenements, turn out the occupants, look through the windows one by one to see if they were all gone, then he would lock the door, and stalk solemnly away with the key in his pocket.

That very night the premises were haunted. The next day the boys began to break the windows from a safe distance with their catapults, frightening each other the while with the cry that the General was coming. In six months the house was a mere melancholy wreck, in which tramps camped at nights, and (if the police did not occasionally interfere) pulled out the frames of the windows and the fittings of the kitchen to burn upon their fires.

It was no wonder that Cleg Kelly looked with much interest upon Barnbogle House. And had he known its sinister repute, and the character of his new master, he might never have set foot within its doors. But he had never so much as heard of Theophilus, as the General was familiarly called by all the neighbourhood—behind his back. The minister of the U.P. denomination (the only one in the town which had not been fostered by the General's money) explained on a sacramental occasion that Theophilus meant a friend of God, but hastened to add that this might be taken ironically, and that even the devil sometimes appeared in the guise of an angel of light.

THE GENERAL'S ESTABLISHMENT 361

Nevertheless, it was at the time thought a strange thing that the U.P. cow died on the U.P. pasture, soon after the close of the service at which this explanation was delivered from the U.P. pulpit.

This induced a carefulness of speech with regard to the General in the pulpits of other denominations —except, perhaps, when the ministers had probationers supplying for them. For probationers never have any cows.

When Cleg and he arrived at the house, the General bowed a moment, with his back to his visitor, over the handle of the front door, whirled a manylettered combination, clicked a key, touched a knob, and lo! the massive door swung noiselessly back.

When he invited Cleg to enter, Cleg put his foot over the threshold as if he had been entering the Calton Jail. But he had pledged himself, and could not in honour draw back. Besides, Cleg had in him, as we have seen, the spirit of the natural adventurer. He constantly did a thing for the sake of seeing what would come of it, and embarked upon perilous adventures only to see how the problem would work itself out.

The hall in which he found himself was of old panelled oak, with lights which came from very high above. Oak furniture stood sparsely here and there. The only remarkable things were a couple of plain white tablets let into the wall at either side, like marble memorials in a church.

Through many passages and past the doors of innumerable rooms Theophilus Ruff led our young hero. Bookcases filled with solemn-looking books stood along the corridors. Marble timepieces squatted silently on the ledges. White statues held out cold glimmering arms from dusky recesses. Here and there, on little round tables by oriel windows, large-type family Bibles lay open, many of them having bookmarks inserted here and there—some of discoloured ribbon, but many of common pink and white string such as is used by country grocers to tie up parcels of sugar.

They went next through a great echoing kitchen, with all manner of rusted machinery for roasting and turning, cobwebbing the walls; by the side of vast black cooking-ranges, past a glimmering and diminishing array of brass pans and silver dish-covers upon the walls, Cleg followed the General like his shadow.

'We shall have some dinner presently,' said Theophilus Ruff. 'I always dine in the middle of the day ever since I began to keep house for myself.'

He spun another combination lock, clicked a key, and Cleg found himself in a little brick addition, plastered like a swallow's nest against the rear wall of Barnbogle House.

Here were a little table of scoured woodwork and a cheap cooking-range with a paraffin stove, which, like all its kind, leaked a little and smelled a good deal. Upon a shelf under the window were tumbled roughly a cooking pot, a frying-pan, a skillet, a brander, two tin plates, and half a dozen cheap knives and forks, all of the poorest and most ordinary description, and most of them dirty in the extreme.

The General ushered Cleg into this place with some ceremony and condescension, like a superior initiating a new and able, but untried assistant into the work of his department.

'I will show you how to light the stove,' he said; 'it is an exceedingly convenient invention. I wish we had had them in the army in my time. I will do the cooking myself on this occasion, in order that you may see in what manner you may best assist me in the future.'

'There are herring here,' he said, waving his hand to a barrel which showed through a sparred locker, 'and a ham there beyond. Butter you will find in that firkin on your left. It is the best Danish from Kiel. The tinned beef on the shelves is to be kept for emergencies. It is not to be touched. The butter I import myself, and dispose of what I do not use to an Italian warehouseman in Netherby. I find that it can be made to take the place of lard also. Here is flour for sauces, and I always bring home a four-pound loaf every second day, which I find to be amply sufficient. I propose to continue the duty, and shall bring two in future. If there is anything necessary for your health which you do not find, I shall be happy to supply it. I think I have a suit of clothes—not my own, but which I happen to possess. They can easily be adapted for your use.'

ADVENTURE LII

THE THREE COFFINS IN THE STRONG ROOM

WHILE the General was in the act of explaining all these things, he was at the same time deftly handling the gridiron upon which he was cooking the four red herrings which he had laid out. These, with bread and the aforesaid best specially-imported Danish butter, dug out of the keg with a scoop, furnished their simple meal. General Theophilus made tea in a black kettle, by the simple process of putting in a soup ladle filled with tea and allowing the water in the kettle to come to the boil.

'The tea is of the best quality,' he said, 'though I am somewhat prodigal of it, as you see. But a man must have some luxuries.'

Yet all the time, while Cleg was partaking of the herrings, cutting the bread, and drinking the tea, he was oppressed by the dark overwhelming bulk of the house behind him, through which he had been led. He instinctively felt it to be full of secrets, of unknown echoing passages, of doors that clicked and sprang, and of all untold and unutterable mysteries.

All through their dinner time the General was most courteously polite, handing the salt and helping the herrings with infinite address. And when Cleg in his ignorance or his awkwardness committed a solecism, the General only in the slightest degree emphasised the correctness of his own demeanour, so that Cleg, if he chose, might benefit by the lesson in deportment. Not that Cleg needed many, for had he not often taken tea with Miss Celie Tennant, which in itself was a charmingly liberal education?

When the meal was finished, Theophilus Ruff took Cleg into a little room adjoining. Here there was a fixed washtub and a tiny boiler.

'I do my own washing, you see. Cleanliness is most important!' the General explained. 'I learned the art while campaigning in Afghanistan. For the present, therefore, I shall continue to do the washing, though I shall be glad of your assistance in the matter of drying and ironing!'

Cleg could hardly credit his ears—a General and the owner of all this wealth talking freely of doing his own washing. Cleg looked at the beautiful linen sheets on the bed and marvelled still more. Then he remembered what Theophilus had said about the presence of women.

'This is your bedroom,' said the General, opening a still smaller room, which contained nothing but a washstand and a small 'scissors' camp-bed. Upon a nail behind the doors hung a couple of suits of clothes.

'These are yours,' explained the General; 'this room also is yours. I shall not again enter it. I beg of you, therefore, that when you have been visiting your friend the widow you will wear one of these suits, either as it pleases you. But when you come into the rooms which I share with you, or undertake any of the duties connected with your position, you will be good enough to take the trouble to change into the other.'

Cleg touched the nearer suit of clothes gently with his hand. It was of fine texture, though of a fashion somewhat antique, with wide lapels to the coat and the vest cut very long. The General opened a drawer.

'Here,' he said, 'you will find collars, shirts, and stockings, which, though a little large for you, are such as you will rapidly grow into. Consider them as your own. Assure yourself completely that the owner of these has no further need for them.'

Cleg thanked his benefactor frankly, but without subservience or profusion.

'Now,' said the General, turning rapidly upon Cleg, 'I should like to come to financial terms with you. I am willing to give you one pound sterling or twenty shillings a week and your food. At the present rate of the rupee in India, from which much of my income is derived, I am not desirous of making it more. But in the event of any decided appreciation in the price of silver, I should be willing to consider your claims to a supplement.'

'It's far ower muckle as it is,' cried honest Cleg. 'Man, I wad be glad o' the half o't!'

The General waved his hand.

'My dear sir,' he said, 'you are as yet unaware of the intensely peculiar services which your position here will require of you. You may have to see strange things sometimes, and to learn to say nothing. I desire, therefore, to remunerate you suitably in advance. What I must reveal to you is perfectly harmless, as I shall show you. But still I am aware that there is a not unnatural prejudice against such experiences, especially among the young. We will call it, therefore, for the present a pound a week.'

Cleg nodded. He was willing to sleep in a vault amongst skulls and crossbones, with a reliable up-to-time ghost thrown in, for a pound a week.

'I will now show you my own bedroom,' said his new master.

The General opened the locks of the doors leading into the house with the same precise caution, and with some additional secrecy as well. But even in this the General behaved with a gentlemanly reticence.

'You will observe,' he said, 'that I do not for the present make you free of the passwords of the fortress. That in time will doubtless come. But in the meantime you will consider me as the governor of the castle, with discipline to maintain and my own secrets to keep.'

'Your nerves are strong, I trust?' he added, as they went along gloomy passages through which the draughts blew gustily as in some cave of the winds.

'I'm no feared, gin that's what ye mean. I dinna ken aught aboot nerves,' said Cleg.

The General led him sideways down a flight of steps like one that goes stealthily into a cellar.

They stopped before a door of massive iron, painted red as a ship is before she is launched, and with the boltheads neatly picked out in white.

'You observe,' said the General, 'this door is entirely of my own construction—aided, that is, by the most skilled smiths and mechanicians. You notice that the rock upon which the house is built is above our heads, and also that the door is really excavated in the stone itself. The iron frame upon which the door closes is mortised so deeply and completely into the solid rock all round, that to all intents and purposes it is practically one piece with it.'

The General pointed upwards to where a pale yellow gleam on the wall showed through a range of open and glassless, but triply barred windows.

'That,' he said, 'is *Cheiranthus Cheiri*, the common, yellow, or wild wallflower—of a different species from that of the garden, and, in my opinion, a much finer plant. It is growing up there on the natural rock. So that I sleep, as sayeth the Scripture, " within the living stone ! " '

Cleg looked at the General. His eyes seemed to grow darker, his figure became more erect. He continued every few minutes to refer to his watch.

'This lock,' he said, patting the keyhole, 'is a highly ingenious union of a time-lock and the commoner letter combination lock. This morning I set the wards to open at two in the afternoon. So that it is now almost the time when we shall be able by the application of the key-word to open the door.'

He waited till the hands of the watch were opposite the hour.

'Now ! ' he said, and stepped forward with some show of eagerness.

The son of the burglar looked on with an interest which was almost painful.

The General twirled the lock till he had brought five letters into line upon the dial. Then he inserted a little key which hung at his watch-chain. The massive red iron door, with its white-studded nails, swung back softly of its own accord.

'A simple application of the principle of the water balance,' he said, 'thus—I open the lock, the water runs out and the door opens. In another five minutes the small cistern will fill of its own accord, and its weight will automatically close the door.'

Cleg hung back. He was not at all afraid, as he had said. But it seemed an uncanny place to be shut up in with only a madman for company. For Cleg had no doubt whatever that the General was out of his mind.

General Theophilus Ruff noticed his hesitancy.

'Do not be afraid. I have the combinations all in the inside of my watch scales, so that even if I were suddenly to die here, you would still be able to make your way out.'

The two stepped within, Cleg being ashamed to show any further feelings of reluctance to trust his benefactor.

The General touched a match to a large lamp which stood on a pedestal. The whole room, which had been pitchy dark a moment before, seemed now fairly bursting with light.

'My bedroom!' said the General, circling the place with his hand, with the air of one who makes an important introduction.

The walls were of red-painted iron throughout, the red of farm carts in the district, and the bolts were again picked out with white. But the furniture was the strange thing. There was nothing whatever in the room save three coffins, each arranged squarely upon its own table.

The lids of the two at either side were hinged and closed. The centre one stood open. The coffins were not large or fine ones, but, on the contrary, common and covered with black cloth. The lid of the centre one was off, and stood leaning against the wall at the coffin head. Cleg could easily read the inscription, which was in white letters upon a black-painted plate :—

>MAJOR-GENERAL THEOPHILUS RUFF,
>E.I.C. BENGAL ARMY.
>BORN JULY 21ST, 18—.
>DECEIVED JULY 21ST, 18—.
>UNDECEIVED JULY 21ST, 18—.
>DIED —— ———— .

'It cannot be long now,' he said, pointing to the last line. 'I have not added the year, you observe. But it was revealed that all my days of fate should culminate on the 21st of July. And so hitherto they have. I do not think I shall see more than other four.'

Then a new thought seemed to strike him. He turned to Cleg Kelly sharply.

'Note the lettering on the coffin,' he said; 'I did it all with an ordinary sharpened knitting-needle. I bought a plain black tin plate from the carpenter of the village, and he showed me how the paint scrapes off. It is quite easy. But I have done it much more neatly than could the carpenter himself. I have since attended quite a number of male funerals in order to observe the quality of the lettering upon the coffin. I do assure you it is, in general, disgracefully slipshod. The man does not appear to take the least pains to improve. I have even thought of offering to do the job for him for nothing.'

Cleg was continuing to look about him, when a sudden noise behind him caused him to leap to the side. The great red iron door had swung to with a little well-oiled click.

The General smiled indulgently and reassuringly.

'It is only the water balance I told you of. It is

THE COFFINS IN THE STRONG ROOM 371

now full; the little wet-bob rises to the top, and the door swings to of its own accord.'

Cleg continued to look about him. The room was about thirty feet square and half as high. But there was no bedstead or any other furniture to be seen.

The General noticed his perplexity.

'I observe,' he said, smiling, 'that you are looking for my bed. Here it is,' laying his hand on the central coffin. 'Oblige me with your hand. I usually depend upon a stick, but your shoulder is better.'

The General balanced himself for a moment upon the edge of the coffin, and let his head drop back upon the little white pad. Then he arranged his shoulders into the fiddle-shaped swell, and deftly drew in his feet after him.

'Now,' he said, 'damp the herbs in that pipe. Light a ribbon of the prepared paper at the lamp, and put it in the bowl to smoulder.'

Cleg hastened to obey. It was a large-headed Indian pipe with a flexible handle, and a mouthpiece of fine pale amber.

'You observe,' said the General, as he calmly and carefully adjusted his pipe-stem over the edge of the coffin, 'I do not use ordinary tobacco, but a mixture of Indian hemp and *Datura stramonium*, or thornapple, a common dunghill plant. With ordinary people the smoking of these would produce madness. But in my case they only induce a peculiar exaltation, and then a kind of ethereal coma, without at all being followed by the evil effects of opium.'

He beckoned Cleg to come nearer. Cleg did so, and took up his position at the foot of the coffin with some reluctance.

'Now,' he said, 'I am about to take my siesta. Do you set the time arrangement by carefully turning the hands of the small clock to seven—the lower dial, if you please. Thank you. Now bring the letters of the word FALSE to the face of the lock attachment, and you will be able to open it by the use of this duplicate key. The same word will (for this day only) enable you to open the outer door—from the inside, that is, not again from the outside. The password is changed every day. I always write it on a paper inside my watch every morning.'

As Cleg was leaving the room the face and neck of the General were suddenly jerked up, so that he rose almost to a sitting position. Cleg's muscles twitched, and with a sharp cry he leaped into the air.

The General waved the hand which was not employed in managing the pipe-stem, upon which his eyes remained steadily fixed.

'I beg your pardon most heartily,' he said; 'I should have warned you of this before. The fact is, I have an automatic attachment, which I have applied beneath the pillow, by which at certain intervals my head is raised. For though so remarkably spare of person, I have several times in the East been threatened with apoplexy; and, indeed, I suffer constantly from asthma, for which I find the *Datura stramonium* most useful.'

And as Cleg whirled the combination circles in imitation of the General, he prayed that he might never again have to enter that ghastly chamber. Yet it was his fortune to abide with the General four years as his body servant, and to enter the strong-room of Barnbogle nearly every day.

ADVENTURE LIII

A STORMY MORNING AT LOCH SPELLANDERIE

IT had been a stormy morning at Loch Spellanderie. It was not wholly that the winds howled gustily up the loch, or that the tiny breakers lashed the shore in mimic fury. Mistress McWalter had ofttimes been a deceived woman, but never before had she taken to her bosom so complete a viper as Vara Kavannah. She had, indeed, been telling her so for wellnigh four years. Even Kit Kennedy had become for once almost an angel of light when compared with her. The reason of the sudden riot was that Cleg Kelly had been discovered talking to Vara by the orchard dyke the night before.

'Ye brazen-faced besom—ye toon's madam,' cried Mrs. McWalter; 'I'll learn you to bring your ragged, unkempt, stravagin followers here. Guidman, gin ye were worth your salt, as ye are not, ye wad tak' speech in hand, and order sic a randy instantly frae 'boot the hoose!'

It was early in the morning. Mrs. McWalter was still in bed, and her husband was pretending to be asleep. But she was well acquainted with his guile.

'Ye needna pretend ye are sleepin', John, for brawly do I ken that ye hear every word.'

Vara, grown by this time into a tall, handsome girl,

was already brushing out the kitchen and lighting the fire. Kit Kennedy was whistling cheerfully about the stables. Mistress McWalter always assisted at reveille in the house of Loch Spellanderie. Her voice was so sharp and shrill that it could easily reach every corner of the house from her bed. And upon occasion, when she felt generally that she was doing herself justice, it had been known to sweep the cart-shed, and even beat upon the walls of the barn with considerable effect. But that was, of course, when the front door of the dwelling-house was open.

While thus lying comfortably upon her back, Mistress McWalter could keep up, in a high-pitched falsetto, a steady and destructive criticism of life, as it was represented below in the sweeps of Vara's brush and the patter of Kit Kennedy's clogs upon the stone floor.

'What are ye doin' near the dresser, ye sly ill-contrivin' limmer,' she cried; 'hae I no telled ye a thousand times, that if I catch ye takkin' as muckle as a sup o' the milk, that was skimmed yestreen for the bairns' breakfast this mornin', I will hae the polissman at ye? But the jail wad be no surprise to the likes o' you. Na, I'm guessin' ye hae been weel acquaint wi' the poliss a' your days. Tak' up the water-cans and gang your ways to the well for water. Then haste ye fast back and put on the muckle pot and the porridge pot, baith o' them. Or, my certes, I'll come at ye wi' a stick, ye careless, trapesin' slut, ye!'

Vara was not slow in obeying this command. To go to the well meant at the least to be for five minutes out of the hearing of the all-compassing tongue of Mistress McWalter, and out of the shrill ding-dong of her vocabulary. It was not much, still but it was something.

The girl took the blue cans readily, and went towards the door.

'Gang some deal quaiter,' cried Mistress McWalter, 'or, by my faith, I'll thresh ye like a sheaf o' corn when I rise to ye, ye misleared gamester frae the streets! Dinna wauken a' the puir tired bairns, for they were honestly gotten and weel brocht up. And shut the door after ye, when ye gang oot. Ye want us a' to get our deaths o' cauld, nae doot!'

The anger that burned in Vara's breast was healthy and natural, and it would have done her a world of good if she had been able to allow herself occasionally the safety valve of intemperate speech. But she only said to herself, 'I'll thole awhile yet for Boy Hugh's and wee Gavin's sake, till they can fend for themselves. They need the siller she pays me.'

Kit Kennedy met Vara as she crossed the yard. Now in order to reach the well, it was necessary to go through the gate at the far angle of the enclosure, and to walk some distance along the grassy road which led to the next farm. The gusts blew off the lake and twirled Vara's hair becomingly about her face. She was certainly growing a tall, shapely, personable lass. And so thought Kit Kennedy, and indeed frequently said so, at least with his eyes.

Kit also was tall and strong. There was nothing rustic about his appearance. He had the profile and pose of head of the young Apollo of the Bow. He did not, indeed, possess the sinewy, gipsy alertness of Cleg Kelly, nor yet the devil's grit, turned, on the whole, to good intents, which drove that youth safely through so many adventures. Kit Kennedy was slower, more thoughtful, more meditative. Cleg never by any chance wasted a moment in meditation, so long as there was an opportunity of doing anything. And when he did, it was only that he might again dash the more determinedly and certainly into the arena of action.

But Kit Kennedy could call friends out of the visionary air to sit with him in the 'sessions of sweet silent thought.' Often he walked day after day in a world all his own. And the most stinging words of Mistress McWalter did not affect him one whit more than the gusts of wind-born rain, which dashed at him across the lake as he tended the sheep and cut the turnips.

In the same circumstances Cleg would simply have smitten Mistress McWalter with a stone, or, if more convenient, with a poker, and so departed well content. But Kit Kennedy forbore, and made nothing of her persecution. He could dodge her blows by watching her hand. And he could go on calmly rehearsing the adventures of Sir Aylmer de Vallance, while the abuse of his aunt provided a ready-made background of storm and fret, which gave a delicious relish to a victorious single combat in Kit's imagination.

When Kit met Vara on the well road he took the cans naturally out of her hands, as if he had been well accustomed to doing it. He had been waiting for her. In his heart he always called her his Lady Gloriana, and it was only with difficulty that he could remember to call her Vara. Kit had been much happier during the years since Vara came. He had now a heroine for his romances, as well as a companion for his hours of ease. For Kit went about acting another life all day long. He fed the bullocks to the clatter of cavalry hoofs. He shepherded the sheep towards pastures new, to the blast of trumpet and the beat of drum. Or, as a great general, he stood gloomily apart upon a knoll, with his staff around him, and sent a barking aide-de-camp here and another there, to direct the woolly battalions how to make their attack upon the bridge. He always thrust one hand into his breast, in order to represent the correct attitude of a great general on such occasions. He was compelled to unloose the third button of his waistcoat in order to do it. This seemed strange. He had never read that this was necessary. He wondered what heroes did in such cases. But it struck him afterwards that very likely they had their waistcoats made specially open on purpose.

Again, in his books of chivalry there was always a lady to be the guiding star of every life of well-regulated and moral adventure. Each knight, if he was of any respectability at all, provided himself at least with one. Even the great Don Quixote had done that. For the Knight Dolorous was, in the opinion of Kit Kennedy (as indeed in that of all fair-minded people), a most high-minded and ill-used man.

Kit had tried in various directions to find a lady of his vows before Vara came. For lack of better, he had even tried to imagine his aunt as a divinity, beautiful and cruel. But something was always happening to destroy this illusion. Nothing is more fatal to exalted sentiment than a box on the ear, adminis tered unexpectedly from behind. So after a fair trial Kit was compelled definitely to give his aunt up, at least as a possible queen of love and courtesy. It could not be done, even with all Kit's very generous goodwill. So, instead, he called her the False Duessa, the black hag Sycorax, and especially and generally Beelzebubba, for the last name pleased him greatly. And whenever she mocked him with her bitter tongue, Kit hugged himself, saying, 'Ah! if only I were to call her

Beelzebubba! Little knows she that in the history of my mighty and knightly deeds she is condemned to go down to posterity yet unborn, under the name of the Loathly Beelzebubba!'

So Kit carried the Lady Gloriana's silver vessels to the fountain of the Elixir of Life, swinging them lightly and talking briskly all the way.

Vara looked often at Kit, with his free breezy ways and erect carriage. Indeed, she looked so often, that if Cleg had been within sight there would certainly have been another fight.

But Vara was constantly mindful of Cleg. She prayed for him night and morning. She remembered all his goodness, and she wished that he could oftener come to see her. But in the meantime it was undoubtedly pleasant to have some one at hand, so ready to help with sympathy for herself and abuse of the enemy as Kit Kennedy.

The lad and the girl stood awhile at the well, leaning elbows upon the dyke, while Vara confided to Kit all the morning enormities of Mistress McWalter, and Kit bade her be of good cheer, for there was a good time coming for them both. And also, doubtless, a very bad time for Beelzebubba. It always was so in the story books.

'How splendid,' said Kit, 'if the devil were just to come for her as he did for poor Faust! He *will* some day, you may depend. Beelzebubba would be coming stealthily after me with a stick. She would run on and on, getting nearer and nearer to the barn end. I should first show the devil exactly where to wait for her. Then I should put my hat on a stick and watch her coming, crawling, crawling slowly—to get a whack at me. By-and-by she would get to the corner, and then—

pouch! the devil would jump at her and catch her, the earth would fly open, and nothing be left of Beelzebubba but a smell of sulphur like there is after a bee-killing.'

The vision was monstrously comfortable as Kit painted it. But Vara did not laugh.

'I think it's wicked to speak that gate,' she said.

'What?' said Kit, hardly able to believe his ears, yet scenting a new and unsuspected perfection in his Lady Gloriana; 'it is only my aunt. It is just Beelzebubba.'

Vara shook her head. She could not give reasons, but she did not think such talk could be right even to imagine.

'She is no that ill after a', if you consider that she keeps us,' she said.

Kit did not know that Vara had known intimately a far worse woman than Mistress McWalter.

At the door Kit gave the cans of water to Vara, brimming full as he had carried them, but silently, lest his aunt should hear from her bed above. He touched Vara's hand lightly for reward. For he was a boy as full of sentiment as his romance books were primed with it. He had brought a dozen of his father's volumes with him, and though his aunt daily prophesied their destruction by fire, Kit thought that she knew better than to do that.

But, while Vara had been gone to the well for the water, momentous things had been happening in the privacy of the chamber shared by Mistress McWalter and her husband. The worm had turned. But, alas! even when worms turn, they do not gain much by it. Except that perhaps they may assist the early bird to wriggle down its breakfast a little more easily.

Mistress McWalter had gone storming along her devious way of abuse after Vara's departure.

'I wish ye wad let that lassie alane!' suddenly broke in John McWalter, awaking out of his deep silence at the thirtieth repetition of the phrase 'impident madam of the street.' 'The lassie's weel eneuch so far as I see, gin ye wad only let her alane!'

For a long minute Mistress McWalter lay petrified with astonishment. The like of this had not happened since six months after their marriage. But the checked tide of her speech was not long in overflowing the barrier like a bursting flood.

'Is't come to this between you an' me, John McWalter, that I may rise and pack, and tak' awa me and my bairns, puir harmless bits o' things? For it comes to that! After a' my thirty years aboot the hoose o' Loch Spellanderie, that ye should tak' the pairt o' a reckless randy gang-the-road trollop, against your ain married wife! Have I watched and tended ye for this, when ye had the trouble in your inside, and could get rest neither day nor nicht, you wantin' aye fresh mustard plaisters? Is it to be lichtlied for a lichtfit rantipole limmer that I hae fed ye and clad ye—aye, and tended your bairns, washing them back and front ilka Saturday nicht wi' a bit o' flannel and guid yellow soap, forbye drying them after that wi' a rough towel? And noo since I am to hae a besom like this preferred before me—I'll rise and be gaun. I'll bide nae mair about this hoose. Guid be thanked there's them in the warld that thinks mair o' me than John McWalter, my ain marriet man!'

'Aye, juist na,' said John McWalter, roused at last. 'E'en gang your ways, Mistress, if ye think ye can make a better o't. Ye're braw and welcome to tramp it as far as this hoose is concerned. I'm thinkin' that your new freends will be brave and sune tired o' ye!'

Mistress McWalter bounced out of bed and began hurriedly to gather her apparel, as though she meditated leaving the house just as she was. She would have given a considerable sum of money if at that moment she could have wept real wet tears. However, she did her best with a dry towel.

'To think,' sobbed she, bouncing from chair to chair, 'that ye prefer a wandering gipsy's brat o' a hizzie to me! O what for did I ever leave my mither, and the bonny hoose o' Knockshin, where I was so muckle thocht on? Waes me, for I am but a puir heart-broken deceivit woman!'

At this very moment Vara came in bearing her cans, with a lightened heart after her journey to the well with Kit Kennedy. With a louder voice and more abounding thankfulness, Mistress McWalter took up the burden of her tale.

'Aye, here comes your base limmer. Ye had better be awa doon to her, John McWalter,' cried the Mistress of Loch Spellanderie, 'or she may tak' the country again, after the thief-like loon wha cam' seekin' her on Monday nicht, nae farther gane.'

Then Mistress McWalter went down stairs and opened more direct fire. It was certainly a stormy day at Loch Spellanderie, little doubt could there be of that. For the winds roared about the farm on the hill above the water. And within Mistress McWalter's tongue thundered like great guns in a naval engagement. Vara went about her work with the tear on her pale cheek all that day, and a wonder in her heart what she had done to deserve such misery.

ADVENTURE LIV

KIT KENNEDY'S FAREWELL

IT was about half-past four in the afternoon that Vara was coming round the corner of the barn carrying an armful of hay. She was undisguisedly sobbing now. For though she did not cry in the house where Mistress McWalter could see her, it was too much for her to restrain herself when she was alone out of doors.

John McWalter met her and stopped, with his usual elaborate pretence of being in a hurry and not having a moment to spare. He had really been doing nothing all the afternoon, but looking for a chance of speaking to her.

'Vara, dinna greet, my lassie,' he said, 'ye maunna heed the mistress' tongue. We a' get oor share o't! Can ye no bide for a day or twa what I had tane to bed wi' me every nicht for thirty year?'

'Thank you,' said Vara, 'I am gaun awa' the nicht.'

'Where are ye gaun, my lassie?' asked John McWalter kindly.

'To see Hugh and Gavin, my twa wee brithers at Sandyknowes,' said Vara, and maybe I'll be some use there. An' if not, we will just hae to gang farther on, and look for my faither again.'

'Weel,' said John McWalter, 'Guid kens I dinna

blame ye. Maybe after a' it wad be as weel. I can see plainly there is gaun to be nae peace here, and it was a' my blame no haudin' my tongue this mornin'. But here's something that will help ye on your road wherever ye gang, my lassie, near or far. There's nae better friend in the world that I ken o' than just a pound note.'

And he slipped into Vara's hand a dirty little square of paper folded hard.

'I canna tak' it,' said Vara protestingly, with the paper in her fingers.

'Hoots,' said John McWalter, 'I'm no needin' it. I hae plenty. And I canna let ye gang oot o' my hoose unplenished and unprovided, ony mair than if ye were my ain dochter. Tak' the pickle siller, lassie, and welcome. And hark ye, mind and crave the mistress for your full wage forbye. She'll think a heap mair o' ye for doin' that. And forbye, she'll no jallouse[1] me so readily.'

And that honest man John McWalter slipped like a thief of the night in at the back door of the barn.

Vara promptly announced her intention of going away that very evening. 'Aye and welcome,' said Mistress McWalter, 'the like o' you should never hae entered my door.'

'I shall want my wages,' said Vara, plucking up courage and remembering her master's words.

'Wages, ye randy,' cried the goodwife of Loch Spellanderie; 'wages! Set ye up, indeed, ye crawlin' blastie! Think ye that honest folk's wages are for the like o' you, that canna bide awa' frae your deboshed paramours, and that lies in wait to entrap decent folk's men, silly craiturs that they are?'

[1] Suspect.

'I am but a young lassie,' said Vara, calmly, 'and think on nane o' thae things. Neither will ony body believe them but yoursel'. But I'm gaun to hae my wages, or I'll gang to the kirk yett next Sabbath, and tell a' the neebours how ye treat your servants, starvin' them on scraps like dogs, making their lives a burden to them to get them no to bide aboot the hoose, and then at the hinder end threatening them to gie them nae wages.'

This threat, which would have feared no one who was conscious of good intent, somewhat stilled Mistress McWalter's fury. For she knew that anything of the kind would be greedily listened to, and retailed at all the tea drinkings in the neighbourhood. And she felt, also, that she had not quite the character in the countryside upon which such accusations would fall harmless.

She went to a locked drawer.

'Here's your wages,' she said, 'and an ill wish gang wi' them. Glad am I to be rid of you!' Even thus Vara took her departure from the house of Loch Spellanderic. John McWalter covertly watched her carrying her bundle out of the yard. He was looking round the corner of a corn stack. He dared not come out and bid the girl farewell because of his wife. But the tear was now in his own eye.

'It micht hae been my ain lassie leavin' anither man's hoose. I am heart wae for her,' he said. 'But I'm glad it was a ten pund note that I slippit her. And whatna state wad the wife no be in, gin she kenned!'

And there came a faint pleasure into his grieved heart as he watched Vara out of sight.

Meanwhile Mistress McWalter stood at the door with victory in the very poise of her ungainly figure.

She had disdained to utter a word as Vara went past her and quietly bade her 'Good-night!' But now she cried, 'Kit Kennedy! Kit Kennedy! Kit Kennedy!' with all the penetrative power of her voice.

But there was no answer. Kit was not to be found.

For Kit Kennedy was in a better place. He was bidding his Lady Gloriana adieu. He had, indeed, never let Vara know that he had distinguished her by that name—nor, indeed, save by his kindness and help, that he thought of her at all.

But now she was going away for ever. Her little bundle was in her hand. Her all was in it, and what Loch Spellanderie would be without her, Kit did not like to think just yet.

It was under the orchard apple trees, at the place where they overhang the wall, that Kit was waiting.

'I'm vexed, Vara, I'm sair vexed that ye are gaun awa' to leave us!' said Kit Kennedy, hanging his head. 'I do not ken what we will do without you. It will no be the same place ava!'

'Fare ye weel, lad,' Vara said, holding out her hand; 'ye hae been kind to me. Aye, just past speakin' o'!'

'I'll carry your bundle as far as the march dyke, gin ye'll let me,' said Kit, for once bashfully. 'I canna bear to think on ye gangin' like this!'

'Ye had better no,' said Vara, 'she micht see ye!'

'Her!' said Kit, with a scornful look over his shoulder, 'I wadna care a buckie gin she was walkin' up the loan ahint us!'

Yet, in spite of this gallant defiance, Vara turned round to make sure that the goodwife of Loch Spellanderie was not in the place designated.

They walked a long while in silence. It was Kit who spoke first.

'Vara,' he said, 'will ye whiles think on me?'

'Of course I will that,' said Vara readily; 'ye hae been verra kind to me here!'

'I'm but a laddie, I ken,' said Kit, 'but ye micht no a'thegither forget me. I'll never forget you, lassie!'

There fell another silence between them.

'Ye'll be gaun back to be near *him*?' said Kit, a little sullenly.

'Aye,' replied Vara, in a voice that was almost a whisper, 'maybe! Ye see we hae kenned yin anither a' oor lives. And he kens hoo I was brocht up—and a' aboot my folk! And I ken his.'

'I'm jaloosin' ye'll be desperate fond o' him?' said Kit, in the same hang-dog way, as if he were taking pleasure in his own pain.

'He fed the bairns wi' milk and bread,' replied Vara softly; 'aye, and gied us a' that he had when we were starvin'! He gied up the very roof abune his head, to shelter us when we were turned oot on the street. I canna help bein' fond o' him, Kit. 'Deed I canna.'

Kit Kennedy thought a long time, till, indeed, they had walked quite across a field. Then he spoke.

'I canna feed ye, nor yet look after the bairns for ye. I hae nae hoose to put ye in, Vara. But O, I am *that* fond of ye. It's like to break my heart.'

Vara stretched out her hand.

'An' I'm fond o' you too, laddie!' she said.

'Aye, but no the way I mean!' said Kit sadly, with a sob in his voice.

'I'll be aye thinkin' on ye,' said Vara. 'I wish ye war awa' frae this place.'

'Dinna gie that a thocht!' said Kit bravely; 'I'm no mindin' a hair for my auntie—at least, I wadna if ye had only bided, so that whiles I could hae looked at ye, Vara!'

They had been walking hand in hand for some time. Kit Kennedy was tingling with a great desire. His heart was beating violently as he nerved himself for the plunge.

They were at the march dyke, just where it plunged into the wood of birches and alders. The path went down close along the lake shore from that point. The trees made a green haze of dusk there, with airs blowing cool from off the lake.

'Gloriana,' said Kit suddenly, 'will ye gie me a bit kiss to mind ye by?'

Vara looked at the lad with eyes of shy terror. This was indeed something new. Even Cleg, who would readily have died for her, or given her his coat or his house if he had one, had never offered to kiss her. So at the sound of Kit's voice her heart drummed in her ears emptily, as if her head were deep under water.

She stood still, looking away from him, but not turning her head down. Kit bent his head and kissed her fairly.

A strange pang ran responsively to Vara's heart— a flash of rapture to Kit's. They parted without a word, the girl walking sedately out of the shadows in one direction, and the lad running with all his might back to the farm in the other.

Each had their own several communings.

Vara said to herself, 'Why does not Cleg think to speak to me like that?'

It was a great blunder on Cleg's part certainly,

and, if heartaches were to be spared, one he should speedily set himself to repair.

And as Kit Kennedy went home he said, over and over, 'I hae kissed her. I hae kissed her. Naething and naebody can take that from me, at least.'

But with the stilling of his leaping and rejoicing heart came the thought—' But had I the right ? He fed them and clothed them, and never asked as much. He is better than I. I will not trouble her any more. For he is better and worthier than I.'

So Kit's dreams and imaginings helped him to something more knightly in his renunciation than even in the brief rapturous flash of possession under the trees by the march dyke.

ADVENTURE LV

A YOUNG MAN'S FANCY

MEANWHILE Cleg was looking after the General's interests when, had he known it, he ought rather to have been looking after his own. He closed the doors of the great house that afternoon, as he had done for many months, and left his master in his strange bed. He was not afraid now, any more. For, in spite of his madness, there was something engaging about the General, something at once childlike and ingenuous, which came out in the close intercourse of two people living altogether alone.

Cleg went into the little brick addition at the back, and the barred doors of the great house shut mechanically behind him.

Cleg was making up his mind to ask the General to let him live out of the house. Cleg was thinking, also, of speaking to Vara. But then Vara might not agree. Had he ever asked her? Of course he had not. It was 'soft'—so he had held (up to this point) to talk to a girl about such things. But yet the idea had its pleasures, and some day he would speak to her about it. Had he been hidden that day in the little copse by the march dyke, on the road from Loch Spellanderie, he might have heard something very much to his advantage, which might have spurred him on to speak for himself, even at the risk of being considered exceedingly 'soft.'

But the mere fact that he thought of it at all, argued a mighty change in this Cleg of ours. He was no more only an Arab of the city after all these years. He had given Mirren half his wages and saved the rest, so that, with the Christmas presents the General had given him, he had nearly a hundred pounds in the bank.

Cleg pushed his way through the thickly matted copses of spurge laurel and wet-shot alder. He was going to Sandyknowes. The lush green Solomon's seal was growing all around, with its broad-veined green leaves. A little farther on he came on the pure white blossoms of bog trefoil, with its flossy, delicate petals, lace-edged like feminine frilleries.

A thought came into Cleg's mind at the time which bore fruit afterwards. He thought that, if at any time he should lose his position with the General, he knew what he should do. For Cleg was an optimist, and a working, scheming optimist as well. The man who succeeds in this world is doubtless the man who, according to the copybook maxim, gives his undivided attention to the matter in hand. But he is also the man who has always a scheme or two in reserve. He is the man who is ready, if need be, to 'fight it out on this line all summer,' but who has also at the same time other equally strong fighting lines in reserve for the autumn and winter campaigns.

So Cleg, with his ready brain, turned the wild flowers into a means of getting the little house in the background for Vara and himself, even if the General's kindness should vanish away as quickly and unexpectedly as it had come.

The house of Sandyknowes was very quiet. Mirren Douglas had put away vain regrets even as she had laid away Muckle Alick's things—and that was as neatly as if he was to need them next Sabbath when he made ready for the kirk. She had reviewed her position. And for four years, with Vara's and Cleg's help, she had owed no man anything, and had brought up Hugh and Gavin as if they were her own. But she never thought of herself as Alick's widow. She was his wife still.

Alick and she had been saving people. Also he had been, as was said, 'a weel-likit man aboot the station,' and he had left her nearly four hundred pounds in the bank. But this Mirren, like a prudent woman, had resolved not to touch if she could help it. She had still six years to run of the nineteen years' lease of Sandyknowes—its grass parks and its gardens, its beeskeps and little office houses. But she was often a little wearied at night, cumbered with much service. She felt that now she sorely needed help.

Her thoughts fell on Vara. Should she not bring her home? But yet how could she take her away till the term from Mistress McWalter of Loch Spellanderie?

At that very moment Vara herself opened the door and walked in.

'Wi' lassie!' cried the astonished Mirren Douglas, 'what for hae ye left your place? Hae ye gotten leave to bide away a' nicht?'

'I hae gotten my fee an' my leave, like the brownie Kit Kennedy sings aboot!' said Vara pleasantly.

'And what's the reason o' that?' said Mirren, with great anxiety in her motherly face.

'The master and the mistress fell oot aboot me,' said Vara simply.

'Then I needna ask what yin o' them was in your favour,' said Mirren sharply.

'I must look out for a place,' said Vara. 'O Mirren Douglas, ye hae been kind to me. But I couldna think o' pittin' you to fash and trouble ony longer, noo that I'm woman muckle, and able to be doin' for mysel'.'

'Lassie,' said little Mistress Mirren Douglas of Sandyknowes, 'will ye hae this place here? I was gaun awa' to look for a lass this very minute. Will ye bide at Sandyknowes, at least till ye will be wantin' to leave us o' your ain accord some day?'

'Aye, that I will, and heartily!' cried Vara, smiling gladly.

And the tender-hearted little woman in black fairly took Vara in her arms and wept over her.

'I canna think what's come ower me thae days,' she said; 'I greet that easy. And everything that I tak' in my fingers breaks. Since Alick gaed awa' I think whiles that my fingers hae a' grown to be thumbs!'

There was a rap at the door. Vara rose naturally and went to it as if she had never been away. It was Cleg Kelly.

All his greeting was just 'Weel, Vara!' He did not so much as offer to take her hand. Clever as he thought himself, Cleg Kelly had a great deal to learn. Yet at that very moment he had been dreaming of the little house which was to grow out of the General's bounty, and perhaps also out of the trefoil and forget-me-not in the bog. Yet, when he found his sweetheart at the back of the door, he could only mutter 'Weel Vara!' Nothing more.

Cleg and Vara went in together, without speaking.

Mirren rose to shake hands. But Little Hugh was before her. He distinguished himself by summarily tumbling Gavin heels over head and scrambling towards the visitor.

'Cleg Kelly! Cleg Kelly!' he cried. 'I want ye to fecht the Drabble and gar him gie me back my pistol. I'm big enough noo to keep one! There's an awesome heap o' wild beasts here to shoot if only I had a pistol. In the wood at the back there's lots o' elephants, and leepards, and—and teegars,' he added, when he found that Cleg looked sufficiently credulous.

'And how do ye get on with the daft General?' asked Mirren, with great interest in her tone.

Cleg was amused at her question. He had become quite accustomed to the wonder on people's faces, usually shading into awe, when they asked him concerning his position in the household of the redoubtable General Theophilus Ruff.

'Fine,' said Cleg. 'Him and me 'grees fine. I hae nae faut to the General.'

'Preserve us,' said Mirren, 'I never heard the like. The auld wizard hadna had a leevin' soul aboot him before you came, since his Indian servant Copper-Blackie died. And that's ten year since. And to think that ye hae nae faut to him!'

She looked at Cleg again.

'Noo, come,' she said, 'sit doon and tell us a' aboot what's inside the hoose.'

But Cleg remained uninterestingly discreet. He said nothing about the General's bedroom; but he filled up the tale with the most minute details concerning the vaulted passages, the iron-barred casements in the hall, and the camp-like conveniences of the little brick building at the back.

Vara and Mirren Douglas listened with close attention. Hugh stopped teasing the cat with a feather, as it was trying to go to sleep on the hearthrug. Gavin was already asleep, with a brass door-knob and a whip clutched in his hands.

'Aweel,' said Mirren, when Cleg had finished, 'I thocht it was a deal waur than that. But he maun be a fearsome creature to leeve wi', the General. Yet he has been nane so ill a neebour to me.'

Cleg uncrossed his legs and became instantly at ease. Mirren looked affectionately at Vara.

'Heard ye,' she said, 'that I hae gotten a new servant lass? I am able to do withoot her wage. And it is worth far mair for the company,' she added.

'I wish I could bide and help ye too—for Alick's sake,' said Cleg, shyly.

Mirren rose and ran to the boy. Hastily Cleg held out his hand, and Mirren Douglas clasped it. He was afraid that she was going to kiss him, and though he admitted the thing as an abstract possibility of the future, it had not quite come to that with him yet.

'Cleg,' she said, 'ye are a kind, good lad.'

'Aye, that he is,' chimed in Vara; 'and ye wad say so if ye kenned him as I do.'

Cleg began to expand in this atmosphere of appreciation. He decided to wait for tea. The hours sped all too swiftly, and the appointed time arrived before he knew it, when he must return to the great barred prison with the little brick martin's nest attached to the back of it.

But before Cleg went away, he brought in the water for the night, filling all the cans. He scoured the milk pails ready for the milking of Mirren

Douglas's three cows. He split abundance of kindling
wood. He brought in the peats off the stack—enough
to do for all the following day. He swept the yard
clean as a hearth, with a worn stable brush. He
promised to come back on the morrow and sweep the
chimney, when Mirren puffed her cheeks at the smoke
which blew down it occasionally. Then he brought
home the cows, assisted by Hugh, Vara watching
meanwhile a little wistfully from the gate. She felt
sure that if it had been Kit Kennedy, he would not
have chosen Hugh to help him. Mirren glanced at
the girl with sharp, kindly eyes, but she said nothing.

When Cleg had done everything that he could
think of for Vara and her mistress, he tied a new whip-
lash on Gavin's driving stick, tossed Hugh up to the
ceiling, and departed.

Vara came with him to the door. Cleg did not
even attempt to shake hands. On the contrary, he
edged cautiously away lest Vara should offer to do it.
'A chap looks that saft aye shakin' hands,' was how he
explained the matter to himself. So when Vara stood
a moment at the doorstep, with her hands wrapped
tightly in her white apron and her eyes upon the beehives, Cleg looked at her a long time. It was exceedingly good to look upon her, and he had a little
heartache all to himself as he thought of Theophilus
Ruff in his terrible bedroom. Vara seemed all sunshine
and pleasantness. But still he could think of nothing
to say, till he was about ten yards down the walk.
Then at last he spoke.

'Ye are takkin' your meat weel to a' appearance,'
he said.

Vara understood his meaning and was pleased. It
was more to her from Cleg than all Kit Kennedy's

sweet speeches. Her mind was mightily relieved. Cleg would learn yet.

But Vara only replied, 'Do you think so, Cleg?'

'Guidnicht, Vara,' said Cleg very soberly. He had committed himself enough for that time.

And with that he took his way sedately over the fields and disappeared into the coppice towards the house of Barnbogle. Vara watched him out of sight; but now not so wistfully. There was a proud little expression in her face. She looked almost conscious of her growing beauty.

'He maun think an awfu' deal o' me to say that!' she told herself.

When she went back into the house Mirren Douglas was just putting on her milking apron. She pretended to busy herself with the strings.

'Cleg doesna improve muckle in looks,' she said; 'he's no great beauty, is he noo?'

She spoke with intent to see what Vara would reply. For, after her sorrow, the old Mirren was blossoming out again like roses in an Indian summer.

'I never think muckle aboot his looks when I see him,' said Vara quickly. 'If he had looked like an angel, he couldna hae been kinder to me.'

'Hoots, lassie,' said Mirren hastily, 'I was only jokin' ye. He is growin' a fine personable lad, and when he has some flesh on his banes and a wee tait o' mair growth aboot his face, he'll do verra weel.'

'He does very weel as he is, I think,' said the loyal Vara, who was not yet appeased. 'He has chappit the firewood, fetched the water, brocht in the peats and stalled the kye, soopit the yaird—and he is coming back the morn to clean the lum.'

'And to see somebody else, Vara,' said Mirren

Douglas, with wicked meaning in her tone. 'What said he at the door when he cannily bade ye " Guidnicht," Vara ?'

'He said I was lookin' like takkin' my meat weel,' said Vara, demurely pulling at the corner of her apron, where a knot of the lace was coming loose. At least Vara was rapidly loosening it.

'Let your apron be, lassie ; what ill-will hae ye at it ?' cried Mirren from the doorstep.

Vara dropped the loop as if it had been white-hot iron. And as Mirren Douglas carried her milking stool to the byre, she let fall a few unobtrusive tears. 'I mind sae weel,' she said to herself, 'the time when Alick was a lad and coming aboot the place, I used to like naething better than for folk to be aye botherin' me aboot him !'

And if 'bothering' be a provocative to love, Mirren resolved that neither Vara nor Cleg should lack the amatorious irritant.

ADVENTURE LVI

THE VOICES IN THE MARSH

DURING the days that followed her home-coming Vara was happier than she had ever been. In the warm sunshine of family love and physical well-being the curves of her figure filled out. She seemed to shoot up all at once from the child into the woman. Her eyes lost their old frightened look. Her arms and shoulders hid their angles and became curved and dimpled. On the other hand, Cleg waxed ever more shy and awkward. But, nevertheless, he came every day, and if there was anything to be done about the house or in the little grass parks Cleg Kelly was there to do it. It was Cleg, for instance, who started the wonderful wild-flower industry. This was the secret which he had kept in store against the day when he should fall out with the General.

It was Cleg's idea that if only he could send large enough quantities of the commoner wild flowers to the market, there would soon be a trade in them which might, with proper attention, grow to very considerable dimensions.

Not that Cleg contemplated any great extensions at present. But he desired to make a beginning, so that he might not have to build up from the foundations if anything were suddenly to happen which might cast him again upon the world.

So Cleg advertised in the Scottish city papers, that he was prepared to supply both blooms and entire plants of such ferns and wild flowers as grew in the neighbourhood of Netherby. He got Vara also to send similar advertisements to the *Exchange and Mart* and other papers. And so in a little time he had developed as large a trade as could be carried on directly by parcel and limited orders. He found, for instance, a hill not far off which was entirely overgrown with the parsley-fern. And with this he made great deals in the fern market. For he was able to supply a dozen or a hundred plants for a very modest remittance, and that with merely the trouble of walking to the hill for them.

But he saw that the undertaking must have a surer basis than this haphazard ingathering of chance growths. And so Cleg set himself to plant out and cultivate certain favourite wild flowers in ground naturally suited to their growth. He had the wet morass at hand for the water plants, the burnside for those which loved to be near, but not in, running water. There were shy nooks about the linn for ferns, and for the rest the fine light soil of Sandyknowes. He utilised ground which was not in use for any other purposes, fencing it round with wire, and setting Vara and Hugh to do the watering and caring for the plants, as they had done long ago around the old construction hut in Callendar's yard.

Hugh Boy went to school during the day at Netherby Academy, and was proving a great success. Cleg Kelly taught him how to box, and warned him at the same time not to fight. But Cleg added that if he needed to do it, it was better to do it once for all and be done with it. So these advantages assured Hugh an easy life of it at school.

Cleg had also been thinking much lately of developing the wild-flower business by means of his former friends. He meant to establish an agency in each of the larger towns, and he had already written a letter to Cleaver's Boy offering him terms as his agent and advising him to look out for openings. For Cleg was proving himself above all things practical, and seemed destined to turn out as prosperous a business man as Bailie Holden.

The General often laughed at Cleg's devotion to his flowers and his children. Yet he liked to hear tidings of them. Sometimes, indeed, he reproved Cleg for bringing back with him a floating atmosphere and suggestion of womankind. But Cleg always assured him that he had been careful to change his clothes.

Life at Barnbogle went on uneventfully. Daily the time locks clicked. Daily the General retired to his strange bedroom, coming forth again with the pupils of his eyes dilated and his face drawn with the drugs which he had inhaled and swallowed. Cleg cooked the bacon, brewed the tea, and made a couple of daily pilgrimages to the room of the three coffins. Then he came out again and shut the doors carefully behind him, and slept soundly at nights. Cleg had no spiritual fears and had outgrown his illusions—at least such of them as interfered with a pound a week and all found.

But whenever he went into Netherby he found himself an object of great interest. For not even the peccadilloes of the ministers of Netherby, nor yet the unbecoming gaiety of their wives' attire, supplied so favourite a subject for gossip to the good folk of the town as the madness and the miserliness of General Theophilus Ruff.

The old men would tell over again those tales of the General driving his coach and six, with the lady

by his side who was arrayed like the Queen of Sheba.
Netherby had never had any doubt as to the fascinating
moral character of this personage. And so Theophilus
Ruff still carried the glory of his former sins about
with him, even though he had dwelt for twenty years
a hermit and a madman in his own house of Barnbogle.

His fabulous wealth was everywhere a common
topic. He received his rent in person, but none of
it, so far as was known, was placed in the banks of the
neighbourhood. The builders, the engineers, and the
locksmiths from the city had, as we have seen, all told
tales of the strong rooms they had been erecting and
of the secret arrangements which had been made
with a great firm in London for yet more complete
safety.

'It's a perfect Guid's wonder that ye are no a'
murdered in your beds, wi' thae millions of siller lyin'
in the hoose,' said one of Cleg's most persistent inquisi-
tors, after vainly trying to extract from Cleg whether
he had ever seen the treasure with his own eyes.

'I wadna be in your shoon for a hundred pounds a
week—na, no for a' the gowd in Barnbogle Hoose,'
the respectable shopkeeper told him each time he came
in. 'The General's servants never leave him. Na,
they a' dee—and generally michty suddenly at the tail
o' the day. And naebody kens in what mainner they
come by their ends. I'm thinking that when he gets
tired o' them, he juist locks them up in yin o' his iron
rooms and then—lets them bide there!'

But Cleg was not frightened, as the good grocer
had hoped he would be. He bought his red herrings,
his bacon, and his eggs; and he carried them peacefully
back to the brick building in the rear of the vast blind

wall of Barnbogle House, to be ready when the General should come again from his room.

'A pound a week was never easier earned,' said practical and unimaginative Cleg.

Vara felt that this time of bliss was too sweet to last. Yet, with the fatalism of those bred up in the midst of misery, she was content to bask carelessly in the sunshine of present prosperity. She was like a bird taking its fill of the warmth and delight of summer, without a thought of blusterous winter winds and the shrewd pinch of nipping skies.

But one night, when the year was already drawing to its end, and November expiring in a clear silver-grey rime of frost, Vara was locking up the outhouses at Sandyknowes in the gloaming. She had already been at the byre, and had given the cows their last bits of fodder, and a pat each on the flank as she passed—a pat so remote from the meditative and operative end of the animal, that the action seemed almost as ridiculous as caressing the porch of a church in order to please the parson.

Nevertheless, Vara never omitted the ceremony on any consideration. Yet on this particular evening, all the time she was foddering the cattle, Vara had a strange consciousness that she heard voices somewhere over towards the marsh. The crisp air of coming frost sharpened her hearing, and as the stars pricked themselves out, the whole night rang like a bell with unknown and far-away sounds.

Voices Vara certainly did hear. But she thought that it might be only a lad and lass on their way to the dancing-school, or a herd talking aloud to his dog for company as he went homeward. Yet the sounds did not resemble any of those with which Vara had recently been acquainted. A certain awful paralysing dread, inherited from a former and a more terrible existence, returned upon her.

Her breath came hard and quick. She grew first hot and then cold, as she stole down by the barn-end to listen. She seemed nearer to the voices there. The murmur of them came more instant and terrible up from the swamp above which Sandyknowes sat on its hill. Vara stole on tiptoe nearer and nearer. The old hut in the hollow was a deserted cot-house of the General's—a mere but-and-ben—which Muckle Alick had been accustomed to use for storing old railway sleepers in. For these are the winter fuel of men who work upon the metals of the four-foot way.

Presently Vara saw its white gable-end staring out at her through the bare branches of the underbrush. The angry voices became louder and more threatening. A ray of light stole through a chink in the boarded-up window. Stealthily Vara went on tiptoe round the gable till she could put her eye to the chink. A cloth had been hung up over the window, past one corner of which Vara could just see a fire flickering in the grateless fireplace of the deserted cottage.

But her heart sank within her at the words she heard, which rang like the very trump of doom in her ears: 'Timothy Kelly,' cried a voice which Vara well knew—even that of her mother—'I tell ye I will have no murder done! And on your own son! Shame on ye! It is enough to bring a judgment on us all just to talk about it. I tell ye we can get the stuff out of the house o' the looney General without the like of that.'

Then the piping voice of the weasel-faced Tim Kelly answered, "Tis little that ye know, Sal Kavannah, you that never were at the taking of a farthing's worth in your life, except off boosy softies in the street. I tell ye, woman, that if Cleg Kelly were to come in my road when I am getting out the cargo, I'd spit him like a rat!'

'But, maybes,' said the other voice, which thrilled Vara the most, 'maybes, if ye was to speak peaceable-like to the lad ye might get him to stand in with us.'

'Sorra a fear of him,' replied Tim; 'Clig Kelly might have been a lump of paving-stone, for all the kindness he ever showed to his kin. Aye, and after all that I have done for the boy!'

'Childer! poison them!' cried Sal Kavannah, ''tis little you have had to suffer with your childer, Timothy Kelly! It's me that knows to the roots of my heart. But wait till we have this stuff lifted and safe in Mistress Roy's tea-kettle. Then we'll bring sweating sorrow on them that's the proud ones this day.'

'Set a match to the house this very night, and burn it about their ears,' said Tim Kelly. 'Say the word and I'll do the job for you, and that willin', Sal.'

'I declare my heart's broke entirely with ungrateful children,' said Sal Kavannah; 'but when once we get clear away with the old General's jewels, we will have time and to spare to bring them to their senses.'

Vara listened, now with fire glowing hot in her heart, and the next moment she was again cold as a stone. She had her ear close down against the bottom of the window-sill, and thus for a time she stood, the thought that her enemy had found her out once more overwhelming all other thoughts.

But presently the knowledge of Cleg Kelly's instant and terrible danger came to her. Cleg was in sole charge of the great house of Barnbogle with all its wonderful treasures. The master of it was reported to be away. But, so strange and unaccountable were his comings and goings, that no one knew whether General Theophilus Ruff was really in the neighbourhood or not.

At all events, however Vara thought about it, there could be little doubt that Cleg was in imminent peril of his life. For if he refused to give up the treasures of the General, his father would certainly kill him. And if he should be frightened or tortured into telling, then no one would believe anything else but that he had been sent by his father, to worm himself into the confidence of the mad General and so open the house to the robbers.

Vara meditated what she should do. Could she get to the house of Barnbogle before Tim Kelly, she might be able to put Cleg on his guard. But a curious something, more disabling than fear, kept her chained to the spot.

'The thing is easy as throat-slitting,' said Tim emphatically. 'I tell you the lad has the keys. For I know he can let himself out and in at his pleasure. Now, he shall give up the keys willingly, or I know a way to make him. If the mad ould General comes in the road, I have that in my pocket which will settle him dead for life. But I hear he's off again on his thundering rounds, restless devil that he is!'

'But how,' said Sal Kavannah, 'is the like o' me to hold the boy? He will be as strong as a young bullock by now.'

'He'll be wake—wake as pump-water—when I get him in them hands,' whispered Timothy Kelly, so that the listener barely heard him.

But Vara could see his narrow, weasel face thrust

forward and hear the hateful jar in his voice. 'God's truth!' he said, 'do I not owe him wan? See them holes?' he cried more loudly, his hate mastering him, 'pockmarks ye could lose sixpence in. 'Twas the devil's whelp did that to me! Ah! a fine man was Tim Kelly before that sorra came into the world.'

'Vara, Vara!' cried suddenly a shrill voice behind the listening girl, as she stood with her brow down on the window-sill. Her heart leaped with wild terror. For it was the voice of little Gavin, come out to seek her. And she feared that he would suddenly appear at the door of the house on the bog. He had always a curious faculty for following his sister and finding her. Ever since she came back from Loch Spellanderie he had not cared to let her out of his sight.

'Vara! Vara!' the shrill childish voice came again. She could hear Gavin coming nearer, pushing his way through the crackling copsewood. The wrangling voices within stilled themselves. The telltale light went out at the crack in the board, and Vara knew that the wild beasts inside would be after her in a moment.

If she could only silence Gavin, she thought. She rose to her feet and dashed towards him.

'Vara, Vara!' rose the child's voice, clear on the frostbitten air; 'where are ye, Vara?'

She could hear him beating gleefully with a stick on a wire fence which ran down into the marsh, so that the very hills gave back the clear humming sound. The wire was Gavin's telegraph, and he pleased himself with the thought that he could always communicate with Vara by means of it. The girl ran towards him, leaping over the frozen ditches, and speeding through the briers, heedless of how she might hurt herself. She came on Gavin at the edge of the wood, beating on the wire with his stick and shouting boldly, 'Vara, Vara, come forth!' as he had heard the Netherby minister do in church.

'Hush, hush, Gavin!' she cried anxiously, holding out her arms to him, 'for God's sake, hush!'

And, in an agony of apprehension, she lifted him and strained him to her breast. There came the sound of footsteps running towards them through the wood, and Vara dragged Gavin back into the shelter of the alders which grew thick and rank in the marsh at the end of the fence. She covered Gavin's mouth with her shawl as the flying footsteps clattered nearer.

Presently the dark figure of Tim Kelly ran past them, with his head set very far forward, scenting from side to side like a beast of prey hunting upon a hot trail. He held a shining knife point downwards in his hand. Vara stood still while the terrifying vision passed. Tim Kelly was running towards the house of Barnbogle. She could hear another—and heavier—foot following. And before she had time to move, lo! Sal Kavannah moved into the grey-litten space, and stood still within ten yards of her children.

'The Awfu' Woman!' came from Gavin's lips, even through the folds of the shawl. All terrifying things were summed up for him in that phrase he had learned from his brother Hugh. Something seemed to tell Sal Kavannah that she was near her children. She stood for what seemed an eternity, stark and staring, rooted to the spot, only turning her head slowly from side to side and straining her ears to hear the crack of a twig or the rustle of a leaf.

Vara prayed as she had never done before. Gavin's eyes were fixed in his head with terror. The end of the world had indeed come. 'The Awfu' Woman' was back again, and in a moment the quiet and safety of Sandyknowes had ended for them.

But Vara stood the test. And Gavin had no words which were not shut within him by the soul-terrifying proximity of Boy Hugh's 'Awfu' Woman.' So silently did they stand that Sal Kavannah heard nothing. And with her ears still on the stretch she moved slowly away, following Tim Kelly in the direction of Barnbogle.

Then was Vara's heart fairly torn in twain. Should she go first to Mirren Douglas and Boy Hugh? Or should she strike across through the dark woods towards Barnbogle? Then, like sweet music, there fell on her ears the loud hearty accents of the voice of Mistress Fraser.

'Weel, Mirren, an' hoo's a' wi' ye the nicht? Hearty, thank ye! I hae brocht my guidman an' Gibby, oor auldest callant, ower by to hearten ye up. Gibby is a brave bullock-baned hullion, no bonny ony mair than the daddy o' him—but that like Tam Fraser, that he couldna' deny him even if he was willin'. And that is a guid thing for a decent woman's reputation!'

Vara could not catch Mirren Douglas's reply, but she could hear Mistress Fraser's next words. For that voluble lady always spoke as if it were all-important that the next two parishes should have a chance of benefiting by her wisdom.

'Hoots, no! Gie yoursel' nae thocht aboot the lassie. She has Gavin wi' her, and I'se warrant she'll be keepin' her bit trysts, just as you and me did in the days that's lang bygane. Come your ways in, Gibby. Dinna stand hingin' a leg there!'

Sandyknowes was therefore safe so long as the Frasers remained. The way was clear for Vara to run through the woods to warn Cleg. So, plucking Gavin more closely to her, she lifted him in her arms and ran towards Barnbogle as hard as she could. But the wild beast and the 'Awfu' Woman' had a long start of her.

ADVENTURE LVII

FIGHTING THE BEASTS

GENERAL THEOPHILUS RUFF was at home. He had, in fact, never been away. That very morning his lawyer had visited Barnbogle, and had stayed all day in the little brick addition, with two of his clerks within call in the kitchen behind, writing and witnessing deeds. The General sent Cleg into Netherby in the forenoon upon half a dozen errands, and in the afternoon he told him that he was free to do what he wished with his time. Whereupon Cleg had gone and got a pail of whitewash to brighten up the byre and stables of Sandyknowes, a job which he had been promising himself as a treat for a long time.

After the General had dismissed the solicitor and his two clerks to go back to the town of Drumnith, he withdrew himself into his room and occupied himself with the arrangement and docketing of multitudinous papers. When Cleg came back he made his supper by himself in the brick addition, and was just sitting down with the paper-covered threepenny novel which represented literature to him, when the door opened and the General came in with a roll of papers in his hand. His hair stood nearly straight up, and his eyes were bloodshot and starting from his head. A great change had come over him since the morning.

'Cleg,' he said abruptly, 'you are going to lose your place.'

Cleg stood on his feet respectfully. He was not much astonished. He had been waiting for an announcement like this, ever since he found what manner of man his impulsive master was. His first thought was that he would be able largely to increase the flower business.

'Verra weel, sir,' said Cleg, glancing straight at the General, who stood commandingly in the doorway, looking, in spite of his disarray, imposing enough in his undress uniform; 'verra weel, sir. Ye hae been kind to me.'

'Ah,' said the General, 'I mean ye are going to lose your master, not that he wishes you to leave your place. I have a long journey to depart upon. I am going upon active service in another world. Three times yestreen I heard the black dog summon me below the window.'

'That maun hae been Tam Fraser's collie,' said Cleg promptly, 'nesty brute that he is. I'll put a chairge o' number five in his tail the next time he comes yowlin' and stravagin' aboot here!'

'No,' said the General, without paying much attention, 'it was the Death Dog, which only appears when one of my race is about to die. My hours of life are numbered, or at least I believe they are, which is exactly the same thing. You will find that you are not left with the empty hand, Cleg, my man. See that ye use it as wisely as ye have used my money. For I have proved you an honest lad, and that to the hilt—never roguing your master of a pennyworth, high or low, indoor or out, and saving of the Danish butter when you fried the fish.'

'Thank ye,' said Cleg, 'I am no o' high family, ye see. Nae dowgs come aboot the hoose when the Kellys dee that I ken o', but if your yin bothers ye I'll shoot him. Gin Rab Wullson the polissman hears tell o' it, he'll be at us to tak' oot a dog leesence for him.'

The General held out his hand.

'Good-bye,' he said, 'it is likely that I'll be waiting for you on the waterside when you land. I have a tryst to-day with the old Ferryman. The Black Dog has looked my way. I hear the lapping of the water against the boat's sides, and I have coined my gold for drachmas to pay my passage.'

'Guid-nicht, sir,' answered Cleg briskly. 'Will ye hae herrin' or bacon to your breakfast the morn's mornin'?'

Cleg was accustomed to the General's megrims, and did not anticipate anything special from this solemn harangue.

'Nae fears, sir,' he said, encouragingly, 'you tak' your comfortable sleep, the black collie will never trouble ye. I'll leave the outer door on the jar, an' faith! I'll hae a shot at him if he come youchin' and gallivantin' aboot this hoose.'

'Come up, Cleg,' said Theophilus Ruff, as he stood by the door, 'come up in a quarter of an hour, and I'll take my pipe as usual.'

'Aye, General,' said Cleg, 'I'll be up. Did ye say herrin'?'

The General went out without answering, and Cleg turned unconcernedly to his immediate business of scouring the pans and setting the kitchen to rights. He was naturally neat-handed, and by this time no work, indoors or out, came wrong to him.

He was whistling cheerily and burnishing a tin

skillet when a slight noise at the outer door startled him. He dropped the can, and it rolled with a clatter under the dresser.

'That stravagin' collie o' Fraser's!' he said to himself. 'I'll "Black Dog" him!'

But before he could rise he felt his arms pinioned from behind, and ere he could make any effective resistance he was thrown upon his back on the floor. Cleg struggled gallantly, and it might have proved successfully. But the face which looked hatefully into his, took from him in a moment all power of resistance.

It was his father's face, livid with hate and vile determination. Tim Kelly coolly directed Sal Kavannah to sit upon the lad's feet, while he himself trussed up his hands and arms as if he had been a fowl ready for the market. Cleg suffered all this without showing the least concern. He had no hope of pity. But he steeled himself to be silent and faithful to his benefactor.

His father shut the kitchen door. Then he looked carefully round the brick house, and seemed infinitely relieved to find the door into the house unlocked, as the General had left it when he went out, for Cleg to follow after him.

Presently Tim Kelly came back and kneeled by his son's side.

'Now, young serpent,' he said, 'the reckoning day has come at long and last 'twixt you and me! You have got to tell me where the old chap keeps his keys, and that mighty sharp—or I will see the colour of your blood, sorrowful son o' mine though you be!'

But Cleg maintained a steady silence. Whereupon his father set his fingers to his throat.

'I know a way to make you speak,' he said. 'Sal, take him by the feet and throw him over that bed.'

Sal Kavannah did as she was bid, and between them they threw Cleg across his own bed with his head hanging down on the other side.

'Don't ye be thinking,' said his father, bending over him, 'that because I had the ill luck to be father to the likes o' you, that will do ye any good.'

Cleg still held his peace, biting speech down with a proud masterful heart. He was resolved that, even if he killed him, his father should not draw a single word out of him.

At that moment a loud clang sounded through the archway which led into the dark house of Barnbogle. Cleg's eyes went in spite of him toward the door. He knew that in a moment more the General would appear in the doorway. And he feared that his father would kill him with the revolver which, when on business errands, he always carried attached to his waist by a leather strap.

Cleg started up as far as he could for his bonds and his father's fierce clutch upon his throat.

'General,' he cried, 'run back to the strong room —back as fast as you can to the strong room!'

Then Cleg heard with gratitude the sound of retreating footsteps outside in the passage.

Timothy Kelly rose from his knees with an oath. He felt that he had been tricked. His revolver was in his hand, and he pointed it at his son's forehead. His forefinger hooked itself on the trigger. Cleg Kelly instinctively shut his eyes not to see the flash. But Sal Kavannah jerked up her companion's arm.

'You waste time, man,' she said; 'through the door after the old fellow!'

Tim Kelly lifted the slant-headed bar of iron which he had brought with him to be inserted, if need were, under the sashes of the windows. And as he ran out of the kitchen he struck his son heavily over the head with this, leaving him lying senseless upon the bed.

Through the long, vaulted passages the villain ran, with his accomplice in crime close upon his heels. The door which divided the little brick building from the main house of Barnbogle closed after them. Something like a tall flitting white-robed figure seemed to keep a little way before them. They followed till it vanished through the open door of the strong room. In a moment both Tim Kelly and Sal Kavannah darted in after it, and immediately, with a clang which resounded through the whole house, the door closed upon pursuers and pursued. Then, through the silence which ensued, piercing even the thick walls of the old mansion, ringing all over the countryside, came three loud screams of heart-sickening terror. And after that for a space again there fell silence upon the strange house of Barnbogle, with its mad master and its devilish visitants like wild predatory beasts of the night. But in the brick kitchen Cleg Kelly heard nothing. For the blow from his father's arm had left him, as it proved, wounded and nigh unto death.

. . . . . .

Vara we last saw panting along the road upon her quest of mercy, listening fearfully for the feet of the pursuer. She dared not leave Gavin behind her, but toiled under his load all the way—now stumbling in the darkness and now falling headlong. The lad cried bitterly, but Vara persevered, for she had the vision of Cleg before her, helpless in the hands of the cruel enemies, who were also hers.

When she came to the main door of the house of Barnbogle she found it barred and locked, while the gloomy front loomed above her, with the windows showing like still blacker gashes on its front. However, she remembered Cleg's description, and, taking Gavin by the hand, she ran as swiftly as she could through the dense coppice round to the little brick addition.

She had just reached the closed door when the three shrieks of terrible distress pealed out upon the night silences.

But Vara nerved herself, and, lifting the latch, she pushed the kitchen door open. There across the bed, within three feet of her, lay Cleg, bound, bleeding, and insensible. Vara set down Gavin, sprang towards Cleg, and took him up in her arms. Hastily she unloosed him from his bonds, and dashed water upon his face. But his head fell heavily and loosely forward, and it was with a terrible sinking of the heart that the thought flashed upon her that her friend was already dead. The house continued to resound with cries of fear, demoniac laughter, screams of ultimate agony. At any moment the fiends who made them might burst upon her. Yet she could not leave Cleg to the mercy of the merciless.

With eager hands she tore the sheet from the bed, and, wrapping him in it, she lifted him in her arms and staggered forth into the night. Gavin came after her, speechless with fear, clutching tightly the skirts of her dress.

So, fainting and staggering, and with many halts, Vara bore Cleg across the marsh and up to the little house of Sandyknowes. She was just able to put Cleg Kelly into the arms of Mirren Douglas and sink fainting on the floor.

When she came to herself Tam Fraser and the doctor from Netherby were bending over her.

'What was the maitter—wha hurt the laddie?' asked Tam Fraser.

'The House! The terrible House!' was all that Vara could say.

Cleg Kelly was not dead. The doctor, who arrived some hours after, reported him to be suffering from a severe concussion of the brain, which might probably prevent a return to consciousness for some days.

A band of men hastily equipped themselves and set out for the house of Barnbogle. They stole up to the door of the kitchen. It stood open, as Vara had left it. The light streamed out upon the green foliage and the trampled grass. But inside there was only silence, and all around a wild scene of confusion. The skillet which Cleg had been burnishing lay upon the hearthstone. There was blood upon the stones of the floor where he had been thrown down, and again on the bed from which Vara had lifted him. But about all the house there was only silence.

The blacksmith of the nearest village brought a forehammer, and with great difficulty he and his apprentice broke a way into the gloomy house itself through one of the barred upper windows. But the whole mansion within was entirely in order. The iron fronts of the safes in the hall had not been tampered with. The red iron door of the strong room mortised in the rock underground was close and firm—far beyond the art of Netherby smiths to burst open.

It was considered, therefore, that the General must be from home, on one of his ever-recurring journeys, and that his servant Cleg had been attacked by the ruffians, who had run off at the sound of the alarm raised by Vara.

Yet it was thought somewhat strange that, as the men came back through the empty house, they should find an iron crowbar, stained with blood, lying at the top of the steps which led to the strong room.

ADVENTURE LVIII

WITHIN THE RED DOOR

CLEG hovered long between life and death. The Netherby doctor made his rounds twice a day in the direction of Sandyknowes in order to watch the case. Vara and Mirren Douglas meanwhile waited unweariedly upon him. It seemed so strange a thing to them to see their lightsome, alert Cleg thus lie senseless, speechless, turning his head only a little from side to side occasionally, and keeping his eyes fixed steadfastly upon the ceiling.

After the first night of stupor Cleg slept heavily and constantly for nearly ten days, without being able either to speak or so much as tell his own name.

The Netherby doctor raised each of the patient's eyelids when he came in, but the pupil remained dull. Every day the doctor would say, 'Do not be alarmed. This is a well-marked stage of the trouble, though no doubt it is in this case somewhat unduly prolonged.'

And so it proved, for Cleg did not come to himself until twelve days after the night when Vara found him lying in the brick addition, with the lamp lighted and signs of hideous outrage all about him on the floor. A watch had been kept all the time by the county authorities upon Barnbogle House, and every possible attempt had been made to communicate with the owner. All places which he was known to visit had been watched.

The steamers on the Caledonian Canal, the ferries to the Island of Arran, the passenger boats to Orkney and Shetland had been carefully examined. But so far it had all been in vain. No one answering to the description of General Theophilus Ruff could anywhere be found. Yet there was nothing remarkable in this. For the mad General had been in the habit of going off suddenly on tours by himself, by rail and steamboat, without consulting anyone. Upon his travels by sea he had been distinguished by his habit of taking the officers under his protection, and offering them advice upon the subject of their profession, especially as to the proper way to handle a ship—advice which, strangely enough, was not always received in good part.

But the mad soldier could nowhere be found. His lawyers continued the search in other directions. They came to Netherby, and made very particular inquiries as to the doings of Cleg during the day which had ended so disastrously. Now it chanced that even while Cleg himself lay unconscious upon the bed at Sandyknowes, every hour of his day could be accounted for ; that is, up to the moment when he had gone home to prepare supper for his master. The General had ordered a new fence of barbed wire to be erected by the side of the railway, and Cleg had been out all the forenoon superintending its erection, after having been sent to Netherby by the General. He had been engaged in white-washing the office-houses at Sandyknowes in the afternoon.

So close was the inquiry that the chief of the Netherby police asked more than once of the detective employed by General Ruff's lawyers if he had any cause for suspicion against the young man Kelly.

'None whatever,' said the detective, 'so far as I know. But I understand that there are important testamentary dispositions which will affect the young man—that is, if he gets better and the General does not turn up.'

Cleg did get better, but not suddenly nor indeed speedily.

One morning, when the doctor came from Netherby, Cleg of his own accord twitched an eyelid up and glanced at him.

'Doctor Sidey!' he said feebly, 'have I been ill?'

Without answering, the doctor took his hand and bent over him.

His breathing was weak and irregular, but still perceptibly stronger.

'He'll do!' said Doctor Sidey of Netherby to Mirren Douglas; 'but, mind you, he is to be asked no questions till I can ask them myself.'

So for nearly a week more Cleg lay in the dusky room, with the hens clucking drowsily outside the wall on the sunny winter days, and the sounds of the little farmyard of Sandyknowes coming to him, softened by distance. Vara looked in many times a day, as she passed the window to bring home the cows, or in going with a can to the well. And always at sight of her Cleg smiled contentedly.

Or Mirren came in from the kitchen, drying her hands on her apron, and Cleg smiled again. Then Vara brought him his low diet of milk and cornflour. But she was not allowed to speak to him. He looked at her in a manner so pathetic in its weakness that Mirren

Douglas had often, perforce, to go into a corner and dry her eyes with her apron.

'He used to be so strong and cheery!' she said, explaining the matter to the world in general.

Then Vara would briskly leave the room to bid Boy Hugh hush his noisy calls to the chickens outside. Whereat Cleg Kelly would shake his head; but whether because Vara had left the room, or because he liked the simple, cheerful sounds of the yard coming into his chamber, Mirren Douglas did not know.

It was a clear morning, about seven o'clock, when Cleg came fully to himself. The trees upon the slope opposite stood black and hard against a pale green mid-winter sky. Cleg watched the light grow clearer behind them as a chill wind from the south swayed the branches away from him. He had a delicious sense of reposefulness and physical well-being. But this was suddenly crossed and obliterated by the thought which came to him—that he had lost his place. How long had he been lying here? He could not remember. His master—where was he? That hideous vision of his old life which swept over him like a very eruption of devildom—was it a dream or a reality?

'The doctor! the doctor!' cried Cleg, 'send for him quickly. I have something I must tell him.'

And Vara sped obediently away, putting forth all the strength in her lithe young limbs in order to bring Doctor Sidey to Cleg as quickly as possible.

When he came in he looked at Cleg quickly.

'Worse?' he queried, half to the patient and half to Mirren Douglas, who stood by with folded hands.

'No,' said Cleg, 'not worse, doctor. But I have something to tell you which cannot wait.'

The doctor motioned Vara and Mirren out of the

room. And then, in hurried, breathless sentences, Cleg told the doctor of all that had taken place on the night of the attack. He still thought that it had been just the night before, and the doctor did not immediately undeceive him.

'And the robbers are still in the house wi' my maister,' Cleg asserted. 'I think he is shut up in the strong room. If he doesna come out soon the room must be forced. But he never stays in it more than a night at a time, so he is sure to come out in the mornin'.'

'What did you say?' cried the doctor, surprised out of his reserve. 'General Ruff in the strong room —two robbers with him in the house! Why, it is plainly impossible—it is three weeks on Tuesday since you were hurt.'

'The General was most certainly in the house when I was attacked,' repeated Cleg. 'I heard him go into the strong room and shut the door.'

The doctor went directly into Netherby and telegraphed to the General's lawyers, who lived in the larger town of Drumnith. The two heads of the firm arrived by the next train, and, as the result of a conference with the doctor and Cleg, an urgent message was sent to the great firm of safe and strong-room makers who had engineered the safety appliances, to come and open the room in which lay the most hidden treasures of General Theophilus Ruff.

In response to this urgent application three skilled mechanicians came down that same night, and by five in the morning they stood ready to break in the door. The foreman of Messrs. Cox and Roskell's declared that no power existed by which, in the absence of the keys and the knowledge of the time and word combinations, the lock could be opened without violence.

But the lawyers promptly decided that at all hazards the room must be reached. So, very philosophically, the foreman proceeded to demolish the work of his own hands and brain—the preparation and fitting of which had cost him so many weeks.

He inserted two dynamite cartridges on either side of the red iron door, boring holes for their reception in the rock itself, so that the massive frame might be started bodily from its bed. Then he placed other two under the step which led to the room. There were present only the three artisans, the two lawyers from Drumnith of the firm of Hewitson and Graham, together with Doctor Sidey, who had constituted himself Cleg's representative, and had insisted either on having the regular police called in or upon being present himself.

The six men stood far back from the house while the dynamite was exploded. The foreman timed the fuse with his watch. Presently there came a little jar of the earth, as if a railway train were passing underneath. But the great bulk of the building stood firm. The lawyers and the doctor were eager to run forward. But the foreman held them back till the fumes had had time to clear out of the narrow stone passages and to dissipate themselves through the glassless windows.

Then they went below, each carrying a lantern. The doctor had in his pocket also a case of surgical instruments and the strongest restoratives known to his art.

When they arrived in the passage they found the mighty iron door fallen outward, frame and all. It lay with the time lock and the letter attachment still in their places, leaving a black cavernous opening, into which the light of the bull's-eye lanterns refused to penetrate.

The foreman stooped as he came up.

'It's not a pennypiece the worse,' he said, examining the fallen door with professional solicitude.

But the doctor pushed him aside and entered. As he shed the light of his lantern around he gasped in that horrid atmosphere like a man in extremity, for surely a stranger or a more terrible sight human eyes had never looked upon.

Two dark forms, those of a man and a woman, lay upon the floor, the man prone on his face with his hands stretched out before him, the woman crouched far back in the corner with her mouth wide open and her eyes starting from her head with absolute and ghastly terror. Yet both eyes and mouth were obviously those of a corpse. In the centre of the room were three coffins laid upon narrow tables, the same that Cleg had so often seen. But now they were all three open, and in each reclined a figure arrayed in white, with the head raised on a level with the coffin-lid.

In the coffin in the centre lay General Theophilus Ruff, with an expression of absolute triumph on his face. He appeared to lean forward a little towards the woman in the corner, and his dead, wide-open eyes were fixed upon her. An empty opium box was by his side. A revolver lay across his knees, evidently fallen from his right hand, which hung stiffly over the coffin edge. His Oriental pipe stood on the floor, and the amber mouthpiece was still between his lips.

But the other two coffins contained the strangest part of the contents of this room of horrors. To the right of the General lay the perfectly preserved body of a woman, whose regular features and delicate skin had only been slightly marred at the nostrils by the process of embalming. She was dressed in white, and her hands were crossed upon her bosom. A man, young and noble-looking, lay in the same position in the other coffin upon the General's left.

But the most wonderful circumstance was, that the necks of both the man and the woman were bound about with a red cord drawn very tight, midway between the chin and the shoulder. Upon the breast of the man on the left were written in red the words:

> 'FALSE FRIEND.'

And on the breast of the fair woman upon the right the words:

> 'FALSE LOVE.'

A row of tall candlesticks stood round the coffins, six on either side. The great ceremonial candles which they had once contained, had burned down to the sockets and guttered over the tops. The floor was strewn with the contents of drawers and papers, and with dainty articles of female attire. A small glove of dainty French make lay at the doctor's feet.

He lifted it and put it into his pocket mechanically before turning his attention to the bodies in this iron charnel-house. They were, of course, all long since dead. The weasel-faced man on the floor had a bullet through the centre of his forehead. The woman in the corner, on the other hand, was wholly untouched by any wound. But from the expression on her face, she must have died in the most instant and mortal terror.

When the first wild astonishment of the searchers had abated a little, the lawyers ordered the men from Messrs. Cox and Roskell's to open the various receptacles in the strong room. Strangely enough, nothing whatever was found in them, excepting some articles of jewellery and a packet of letters in a woman's hand, which the lawyers took possession of. The three confidential artificers from London remained in charge till measures could be taken to clear out the strong room.

The doctor examined Cleg with care and tact, for it was to him that the lawyers looked for the explanation of the mystery. But first they provided the mechanicians with very substantial reasons for secrecy, if they would give their services to prevent a scandal in these very remarkable family circumstances. The men, accustomed to secrecy, and recognising the future and personal application of the lawyer's logic, readily promised.

So far as the doctor could make out, this was what had happened. Cleg told the truth fully, but he made no discovery of the relationship in which he stood to the man who had so murderously attacked him. Nor yet did he say anything of his knowledge of Sal Kavannah's identity. After a little study and piecing of evidence, however, the process of events seemed fairly clear.

When Cleg first sent his warning cry through the house, the General had doubtless been engaged in arranging for his expected departure out of the life which had brought him so little happiness. For, like an Oriental, he knew, or supposed that he knew, the exact moment of his death—though, as we now know, his first impression had proved erroneous.

For some unknown purpose he had left the strong room and hastened through the passages till he had been stopped by the hideous uproar in the kitchen. Whereupon he had promptly retreated to the strong room, in all probability to get his revolver. While there a mad idea had crossed his mind to receive his visitors in his coffin. At any rate, upon entering he left the red door open behind him. A few moments later Tim Kelly came rushing in hot upon the trail, followed by the woman Kavannah. His hands were wet and red with his son's blood. His heart was ripe for murder. And this was the sight which met him—a room with open coffins in a row and three dead folk laid upon them, six great candles burning upon either side—all the horrors of a tomb in the place where he had counted to lay his hand upon uncounted treasure.

Then, while Timothy Kelly and Sal Kavannah stood a moment looking with fearful eyes on the tall ceremonial candles, which must have been specially ghastly to them on account of their race, the strong door swung noiselessly to upon its hinges. For the water balance had filled up, and they found themselves trapped.

What happened after this was not so clear. Probably the robber was proceeding in his desperation to rifle the open depositories of the letters and gear, which the searchers found strewed up and down the floor, when Theophilus Ruff sat up suddenly in the centre coffin, with his revolver in his hand, just as Cleg had seen him the first time he entered the chamber of death. Whether the ruffian had first attacked the madman, or whether he had simply been shot down where he stood, will never be known. But certain it is that he died instantly, and that the horror of the sight killed Sal Kavannah where she sat crouched low in the corner, as if trying to get as far as possible from the grisly horrors of the three coffins.

Then, having done his work, Theophilus Ruff calmly swallowed all that remained of his drugs, and slept himself into the land where vengeance is not— dying with the mouthpiece of his pipe in his mouth and his revolver upon his knees.

The heads of the embalmed bodies were turned so that they looked towards Theophilus Ruff as he sat in his coffin. For twenty years it is probable that he had gone to sleep every night with those dead faces looking at him. For the Indian servant who had helped him to carry out his mad vengeance had done his work well.

The coffins were buried as privately as possible, the two embalmed bodies being laid within the private mausoleum at the foot of the garden. For in noble families a private burying-place is a great convenience in such emergencies. Here also Tim Kelly and Sal Kavannah took their places with nobler sinners, and no doubt they lie there still, mixing their vulgar earth with finer clay, and so will remain until the final resurrection of good and evil.

Doctor Sidey certified truthfully that the death of General Theophilus Ruff was due to an overdose of opium. And as there is no coroner's inquest in Scotland (another convenience), matters were easily arranged with the Procurator-Fiscal of the county—who was, in fact, a close friend of the distinguished and discreet firm of Hewitson and Graham at Drumnith.

ADVENTURE LIX

THE BEECH HEDGE

'And the queer thing o' it a' is,' said Cleg, 'that there's no as muckle as a brass farthin's worth o' lyin' siller to be found.'

'Ye tak' it brave and cool, my man,' said Mistress Fraser. 'My certes, gin I had been left thirty thoosand pound, and then could find nane o't, I wad be fair oot o' my mind wi' envy and spite. Save us a', man. Ye hae nae spunk in ye ava.'

'And what a wonderfu' thing it is,' said Mirren Douglas, 'that Maister Iverach, the young lad frae Edinburgh, gets a' the land and the hooses, but no a penny forbye!'

They were sitting—a large company for so small a place—in the little ben room of Sandyknowes, with the roses again looking in the window. For another spring had come, and a new year was already stretching itself, and getting ready to waken from its winter swaddling-bands.

'What was it that the lawyer man read from the will aboot your bequest?' asked Mistress Fraser.

'"But a' my lying money in the house o' Barnbogle and about the precincts thereof, to be the property of Cleg Kelly, my present body-servant, in regard of his faithful tendance and unselfishness during the past four years,"' quoted Cleg, leaning his head back with the air of a languid prince. He was sitting on the great chest in which Mirren kept all the best of her napery and household linen.

'My certes, ye tak' it braw and canny,' repeated Mistress Fraser. 'What says Vara to a' this?'

Vara came out from the little inner room where she had been dressing for the afternoon.

'What says Vara?' said Mistress Fraser, looking a little curiously at the girl as she entered. Half a year of absolute freedom from care and anxiety in the clear air of Sandyknowes had brought the fire to her eye and the rose to her cheek.

'I think,' she said, soberly, 'that Cleg will find the siller yet. Or, if he doesn't, he will be able to do withoot it.'

'It will make an awfu' difference to his plenishing when he comes to set up a hoose,' said the mother of eleven; 'there's naebody in the world kens what it tak's to furnish a hoose, but them that has begun wi' naething and leeved through it!'

'Mr. Iverach is comin' frae Edinburgh the day,' said Cleg, 'to see aboot knockin' doon the auld hoose o' Barnbogle!'

'He's no willing to bide in it,' said Mirren Douglas. 'Lod, I dinna wonder. Wha could bide in a place wi' siccan a chamber o' horrors doon the cellar stairs as that was!'

Which showed that some one must have been telling tales.

'I'm to gang and meet him,' said Cleg. 'Vara, will ye come? Ye may chance to foregather wi' a friend that ye ken.'

Vara Kavannah nodded brightly, and glanced at the widow Douglas.

'If Mirren will gie a look to the bairns,' she said.

At that moment there was a noisy rush past the window, and certain ferocious yells came in at the door.

'Preserve me,' said Mistress Fraser, 'thae bairns are never back frae the schule already. Faith, I maun awa' hame, or my evil loons and limmers will no leave a bite o' bread uneaten, or a dish o' last year's jam unsupped in a' my hoose!'

But as she rose to go her husband's form darkened the doorway.

'Tam Fraser,' she cried, 'what are ye doing there? Are ye no awa' at Auld Graham's funeral? A lawyer deid! The deil will dee next.'

'I hae nae blacks guid enough to gang in,' said Tam Fraser; 'ye spend a' my leevin' on thae bairns o' yours.'

'Hoot, man,' retorted his wife, 'gang as ye are, an' tak' your character on your back, and ye'll be black eneuch for ony funeral.'

Tam Fraser stood a moment prospecting in his mind for a suitable reply.

'Meg,' he said at last, 'dinna learn to be ill-tongued. It doesna become ye. D'ye ken I was juist thinking as I cam' in that ye grow younger every year. Ye are looking fell bonny the day!'

'Faith,' said his wife sharply, 'I am vexed I canna return the compliment, Tam. Ye are looking juist like a crawbogle, and that's a Guid's truth.'

'Aweel, guidwife,' said Tam, seeing a chance now to get in his counter, 'if ye had only been ceevil eneuch, ye micht e'en hae telled a lee as weel as mysel'!'

And with this he betook himself over the dyke, leaving his wife for once without a shot in her locker.

THE BEECH HEDGE

Vara had gone quietly out at Cleg's bidding and put on her hat. This demurely sober lass had quite enough of beauty to make the country lads hang a foot, and look after her with desire to speak as she passed by on her way to kirk and market.

Vara and Cleg walked quietly along down the avenue, t/king the shortest road to the house of Barnbogle.

'Vara,' said Cleg, 'I think we will do very well this year with the flooers and the bees—forbye the milk.'

'I am glad to hear it, for Mirren's sake,' answered Vara, without, however, letting her eyes rest on the lad.

'I selled baith my barrels o' milk and the ten pund o' butter forbye this morning, a' in the inside o' an hour,' said Cleg.

For during the last half-year Cleg had been farming the produce of Mirren's little holding with notable success.

'Vara,' said Cleg, in a shy, hesitating manner, 'in a year or twa I micht be able to tak' a lease of the Springfield as weel. Do ye think that ye could'—(Cleg paused for a word dry enough to express his meaning) —'come ower by and help me to tak' care o't ? I hae aye likit ye, Vara, ye ken.'

'I dinna ken, I'm sure, Cleg,' said Vara soberly ; 'there's the bairns, ye ken, Hugh and Gavin.'

'Bring them too, of course,' said Cleg. 'I never thocht o' onything else.'

'But then there's Mirren, and she wad fair break her heart,' protested Vara.

'Bring her too !' said Cleg practically.

He had thought the whole subject over. They

were now coming near the old house of Barnbogle, which its new owner had doomed to destruction. Cleg glanced up at the tall grey mass of it.

'I'm some dootfu' that we will never touch that siller o' the General's,' he said.

'Then,' said Vara firmly, 'we can work for mair. If we dinna get it, it's a sign that we are better wantin' it.'

She glanced at the youth by her side as she spoke.

'Vara,' said Cleg quickly, 'ye are awsome bonny when ye speak like that.'

Perhaps he remembered Tam Fraser, for he said no more.

Vara walked on with her eyes still demurely on the ground. They were just where the high path looks down on the corner of the ancient orchard.

'Vara,' said Cleg, 'what's your hurry for a meenit? There's—there's a terrible bonny view frae hereaboots.'

Cleg, the uninstructed, was plunging into deep waters. Vara looked over the wall into the garden beneath at his word. There were three people to be seen in it. First there was a young woman in a bright summer dress, with a young man who walked very close beside her. Behind a thick wall of beech, which went half across the orchard, an older man was standing meditatively with his hands clasped behind his back. He was apparently engaged in trying how much tobacco-smoke he could put upon the market in a given time, for he was almost completely lost from sight in a blue haze.

The young people walked up and down, now in view of their meditative elder and now hidden from him by the hedge. And as Cleg and Vara watched, they noticed a wonderful circumstance. As often as the young man and his companion were out of sight behind the young beech hedge, his arm stole round the waist of the summer dress. But so soon as they emerged upon the gravel path, lo! they were again walking demurely at least a yard apart.

The strangest thing about it all was, that the young woman appeared to be entirely unconscious of the circumstance.

'That's an awesome nice view,' said Cleg, when the pair beneath had done this four or five times. And such is the fatal force of example, that he put his own arm about Vara's waist each time the young man in the orchard below showed him how. And yet, stranger than all, Vara also appeared to be entirely unconscious of the fact.

This went on till the pair beneath were at the end of their tenth promenade—the elderly man over the beech hedge was still studying intently an overgrown bed of rhubarb—when, at the innermost corner, the young lady in the summer dress paused to pluck a spray of honeysuckle. The youth's arm was about her waist at the moment. Perhaps it was that she had become conscious of it for the first time, or perhaps because it cinctured the summer dress a little more tightly than the circumstances absolutely demanded. However this may be, certain it is that the girl turned her head a little back over her shoulder, perhaps to reproach the young man, or to request him to remove his property, and in the future to keep it from trespassing on his neighbour's premises. Cleg and Vara could not tell from the distance. But, at any rate, the young man and the young woman stood thus a long moment, she looking up with her head turned a little back and he looking intently down into her eyes. Then their lips drew together, and, softly as if they sighed, rested a moment upon each other.

'It's an *awesome* nice view,' said Cleg, with conviction and emphasis. And forthwith did likewise.

The old man with his hands behind his back had a little while before ceased his meditations upon the rhubarb leaves, and had walked quietly all unperceived to the corner of the beech hedge. Here he stood looking down towards the corner of the orchard where the summer dress was plainly in view. Then he raised his eyes to the road above, where stood Vara and Cleg Kelly, similarly entranced. His pipe fell from his mouth with astonishment, but he did not stop to pick it up. He turned and stole hastily away on tiptoe.

Then he too sighed, and that more than once, as soon as he had got himself out of the orchard into the garden.

'It's just thirty years since—last July,' he said.

And Mr. Robert Greg Tennant remained longer in meditation than ever, this time upon a spindling rose which was drooping for want of water.

ADVENTURE LX

CLEG'S TREASURE-TROVE COMES TO HIM

PRESENTLY Cleg and Vara walked down, and when they came into the garden they found Miss Celie Tennant in animated conversation with her father. She was clinging very close to his arm, as though she never could be induced upon any pretext to leave it even for a moment. The old man was smiling somewhat grimly. And Vara thought what a little hypocrite Celie was. The Junior Partner was much interested in a curious pattern of coloured stones, which the General had arranged with his own hand about a toy fountain. Five more innocent and unconcerned people it would have been impossible to meet with in broad Scotland.

But when Cleg Kelly was introduced to Mr. Robert Greg Tennant, he was astonished to notice an unmistakable air of knowledge in that gentleman's face. Indeed, something that was not far from a wink wrinkled his cheek. The original Cleg instantly rose triumphant—and he winked back.

Then Mr. Greg Tennant put his hands into his pockets, and strolled off whistling a refrain which was popular at that remote date—

> I saw Esau kissing Kate,
> And he saw I saw Esau!

Cleg went away with the Junior Partner to take another look at the house, which was now wholly dismantled and about to be pulled down to the foundations. The Junior Partner, who was henceforward to be a sleeping partner only, intended to build a mansion on another part of the property, so that all memory of the horrors which had been contained within the Red Door was to be blotted out.

'And the sooner the better, sir,' said Mr. Tennant, grimly. He had just joined them.

'When I have money enough!' stammered the Junior Partner, not sure of his meaning.

He looked about him. Cleg was still exploring far ahead in a ruined tower, from the windows of which the frames and bars had already been removed.

'I have been going to speak to you about Miss Tennant, sir,' said the Junior Partner, 'but the fact is, sir, that till to-day I have had no permission and no right.'

The elder man clapped the younger upon the back.

'All right,' he said heartily, 'I have been behind beech hedges myself in my time. But I must say,' he went on, 'that I generally kept a better watch upon the old man!'

The Junior Partner blushed red as a rose—a peony rose.

'And if that is your meaning,' continued Mr. Tennant, 'why, get the house built. I daresay there's tocher enough to go with my little lass to pay for the stone and lime.'

At this moment a whirlwind of primrose-coloured summer lawn, twinkling black stockings, and silver-buckled shoes fell tumultuously upon the two of them, and reduced the Junior Partner to a state of smiling, vacuous inanity.

'Come, come quick!' Celie Tennant cried, with the most charming impetuosity, seizing them by a hand apiece, and dragging them forward towards the brick kitchen. 'We have found it—at least Vara has! There's millions of gold—all new sovereigns and things. And I'm to be bridesmaid!'

What the Junior Partner made out of this no one can tell. For at the time he was certainly not in the full possession of his senses. But Mr. Tennant was well used to his impetuous daughter's stormy moods, and understood that something which had been lost was at last found.

Celie imperiously swept them along with her into the little brick building.

'Not so fast, you small pocket hurricane!' cried her father, breathlessly. 'At my time of life I really cannot rush along like an American trotter!'

They entered the kitchen. Vara was standing at the table at which Cleg used to cut the bacon for the General's breakfast and his own. She was calmly opening tin after tin of Chicago corned beef, cans of which stood in rows round the walls. Each was full to the brim of bright newly-minted sovereigns.

'It is Cleg's money,' cried Celie wildly, 'and I found it all myself—or, at least, Vara did, which is the same thing. There were just two tins, one at each end, full of real, common, nasty beef for eating—and the rest are all sovereigns. And I'm to be bridesmaid!'

And though a Sunday-school teacher of long standing and infinite gravity, the little lady danced a certain reckless breakdown which she had learned in the Knuckledusters' Club from Cleaver's Boy.

'Well, Miss Quicksilver, you had better go and tell him!' said her father; 'he is in the tower yonder.'

Mr. Donald Iverach was starting out of the door to do it himself. But Celie seized him tragically. 'Father—Donald—how can you?' she cried, more in sorrow than in anger at their stupidity and ignorance. 'Of course, let *her* go!'

And Vara went out of the door to seek for Cleg.

'Oh, I wish it was me!' Celie said wistfully and ungrammatically, stamping her foot. 'It's so splendidly romantic! Donald, why didn't you make it turn out so that I could have come and said to you, "I have a secret. Hush! you are heir to a hidden treasure!" You never do anything really nice for me!'

'Why, because the old man didn't leave the money to me,' said the Junior Partner.

'And a good job for you, too, you great goose,' cried Celie, daringly; 'for if he had I should certainly have made love to Cleg, and we would have set up a market garden together. I am sure I should have liked the cherries very much.'

And at that time Vara was telling Cleg in the tower that his treasure had come to him at last.

And Cleg was sure of it.

LETTER ENCLOSED

(*Being a fragment from the postscript of a note, dated some years later, from Mrs. Donald Iverach to the Girl over the Wall—who has been her dearest friend ever since her engagement was announced.*)

'And the funny thing is that, after all, they *have* a market garden! I've just been to see them, and they live in the loveliest little house down near the sea.

And Cleg says that he is going to make their little Donald (called after my Incumbrance, the old Dear) a market gardener too—" Fruits in their Seasons," and that kind of thing, you know. And I think it's so nice and sensible of them. For, of course, they could never have gone into society, though she is certainly most charmingly behaved. But Cleg likes to go barefoot about the garden still, and you know that is not quite usual. Gavin is at the Academy and is dux of his class. He is what is called a " gyte," which is a title of honour there.

'And what do you think? Cleaver's Boy is married, and they have got a baby also—not so lovely as its father was, but the sweetest thing! He is foreman now, and Janet never even thinks of telling a fib, even to afternoon callers. Don't you think that's rather too much? Oh, I forgot! Her uncle came in while I was there, and said to Mirren Douglas—that's the little widow, you know, who lives with Cleg and Vara—" I saw Hugh Kavannah walking to-day on Princes Street with little Miss Briggs!" But I don't think there can be anything in it, do you? For, after all, she's a lady, and he is only a student. Of course, I know, when we were girls—but then that was so different.

'Kit Kennedy has just been matriculated or rusticated or something, at the university. Everybody is very pleased. He is going in for agriculture, and tells Cleg when to sow his strawberry seed.

'And the man who used to be Netherby carrier has come to help them to take their stuff to market—so nice of him. And their baby is the prettiest you ever saw. But you should see mine. *He* is a darling, if you like. He has four teeth, and I am quite sure he tries to say Papa!—though Donald laughs, and says it is only wind in his little—— That was Donald who came just then and joggled my elbow. He is a HORROR!

'And just think, Cleg Kelly has built, and my Donald has furnished, the most wonderful Club in the South Back of the Canongate. It was opened last week. Bailie Holden—who is now Lord Provost, and a very good one—opened it. But Cleg made the best speech. " Mind, you chaps," he said—and they were all as quiet as mice when he was speaking—" mind, you chaps, if I hear o' ony yin o' ye making a disturbance, or as muckle as spittin' on the floor—weel, ye ken Cleg Kelly!"'

SMITH, ELDER, & CO.'S PUBLICATIONS.

THE WHITE COMPANY. By A. CONAN DOYLE, Author of 'Micah Clarke' &c. Fifteenth Edition. Crown 8vo. 6s.

THE SOWERS. By HENRY SETON MERRIMAN, Author of 'With Edged Tools' &c. Second Edition. Crown 8vo. 6s.

DISTURBING ELEMENTS. By MABEL C. BIRCHENOUGH. Crown 8vo. 6s.

IN SEARCH OF QUIET: a Country Journal. By WALTER FRITH. Crown 8vo. 6s.

KINCAID'S WIDOW. By SARAH TYTLER, Author of 'Citoyenne Jacqueline' &c. Crown 8vo. 6s.

THE SIGNORA: a Tale. By PERCY ANDREAE, Author of 'The Mask and the Man' &c. Crown 8vo. 6s.

GERALD EVERSLEY'S FRIENDSHIP: a Study in Real Life. By the Rev. J. E. C. WELLDON, Head Master of Harrow School. Fourth Edition. Crown 8vo. 6s.

THE MARTYRED FOOL. By D. CHRISTIE MURRAY, Author of 'Rainbow Gold,' 'Aunt Rachel,' 'Joseph's Coat,' &c. Crown 8vo. 6s.

A FATAL RESERVATION. By R. O. PROWSE, Author of 'The Poison of Asps' &c. Crown 8vo. 6s.

THE MASK AND THE MAN. By PERCY ANDREAE, Author of 'Stanhope of Chester.' Crown 8vo. 6s.

THE VAGABONDS. By MARGARET L. WOODS, Author of 'A Village Tragedy' &c. Crown 8vo. limp red cloth, 2s. 6d.

GRANIA: the Story of an Island. By the Hon. EMILY LAWLESS. Crown 8vo. 3s. 6d.

ROBERT ELSMERE. By Mrs. HUMPHRY WARD, Author of 'Marcella,' 'The History of David Grieve,' &c. Popular Edition, crown 8vo. 6s.; CHEAP EDITION, crown 8vo. limp cloth, 2s. 6d.; Cabinet Edition, 2 vols. small 8vo. 12s.

By the same Author.

THE HISTORY OF DAVID GRIEVE. Popular Edition. Crown 8vo. 6s. Cheap Edition. Crown 8vo. limp cloth, 2s. 6d.

MARCELLA. Popular Edition. Crown 8vo. 6s.

A BRIDE FROM THE BUSH. By E. W. HORNUNG. Crown 8vo. limp red cloth, 2s. 6d.

JESS. By H. RIDER HAGGARD, Author of 'King Solomon's Mines,' &c. Crown 8vo. limp red cloth, 2s. 6d.

VICE VERSÂ; or, a Lesson to Fathers. By F. ANSTEY. Crown 8vo. limp red cloth, 2s. 6d.

By the same Author.

A FALLEN IDOL. Crown 8vo. 6s. Cheap Edition, crown 8vo. limp red cloth, 2s. 6d.

THE PARIAH. Crown 8vo. 6s. Cheap Edition, crown 8vo. limp red cloth, 2s. 6d.

THE GIANT'S ROBE. Crown 8vo. 6s. Cheap Edition, crown 8vo. limp red cloth, 2s. 6d.

THE TALKING HORSE, and other Tales. Crown 8vo. 6s. Cheap Edition, cr. 8vo. limp red cloth, 2s. 6d.

London: SMITH, ELDER, & CO., 15 Waterloo Place.

SMITH, ELDER, & CO.'S PUBLICATIONS.

OFF THE MILL. By the Right Rev. G. F. BROWNE, D.C.L., Bishop of Stepney. With 2 Illustrations. Crown 8vo. 6s.

FIFTY YEARS; or, Dead Leaves and Living Seeds. By the Rev. HARRY JONES, Prebendary of St. Paul's Author of 'Holiday Papers,' 'East and West London,' &c. Second Edition. Crown 8vo. 4s.

RECOLLECTIONS OF A MILITARY LIFE. By General Sir JOHN ADYE, G.C.B., R.A., late Governor of Gibraltar. With Illustrations by the Author. Demy 8vo. 14s. net.

HISTORY OF THE UNITED STATES. By E. BENJAMIN ANDREWS, D.D., LL.D., President of the Brown University. 2 vols., crown 8vo. with Maps, 16s.

IN STEVENSON'S SAMOA. By MARIE FRASER. Second Edition. With Frontispiece. Crown 8vo. 2s. 6d.

THE HAWARDEN HORACE. By CHARLES L. GRAVES, Author of 'The Blarney Ballads,' 'The Green above the Red,' &c. Third Edition. Small post 8vo. 3s. 6d.

OUR SQUARE AND CIRCLE; or, The Annals of a Little London House. By 'JACK EASEL,' sometime *Punch's* Roving Correspondent. With a Frontispiece. Crown 8vo. 5s.

THE GAMEKEEPER AT HOME; or, Sketches of Natural History, Poaching, and Rural Life. By RICHARD JEFFERIES. With Illustrations. Crown 8vo. 5s.

A PAIR OF LOVERS; and other Tales. 'The Short and Simple Annals of the Poor.' By IDA LEMON. Crown 8vo. 4s. 6d.

WHAT OUR DAUGHTERS CAN DO FOR THEMSELVES: a Handbook of Women's Employments. By Mrs. H. COLEMAN DAVIDSON, Author of 'Dainties: English and Foreign,' 'Eggs,' &c. Crown 8vo. 3s. 6d.

GLEAMS OF MEMORY; with some Reflections. By JAMES PAYN. Second Edition. Crown 8vo. 3s. 6d.

AN ARTIST'S REMINISCENCES. By RUDOLF LEHMANN. With Portrait. Demy 8vo. 12s. 6d. net.

A SHORT HISTORY OF THE RENAISSANCE IN ITALY. Taken from the work of JOHN ADDINGTON SYMONDS. By Lieut.-Col. ALFRED PEARSON. With a Steel Engraving of a recent Portrait of Mr. Symonds. Demy 8vo. 12s. 6d.

VOLTAIRE'S VISIT TO ENGLAND, 1726-1729. By ARCHIBALD BALLANTYNE. Crown 8vo. 8s. 6d.

THE JOCKEY CLUB AND ITS FOUNDERS. By ROBERT BLACK, M.A., Author of 'Horse Racing in France,' &c. Crown 8vo. 10s. 6d.

THE LIFE AND LETTERS OF ROBERT BROWNING. By Mrs. SUTHERLAND ORR. With Portrait, and Steel Engraving of Mr. Browning's Study in De Vere Gardens. Second Edition. Crown 8vo. 12s. 6d.

MORE T LEAVES; a Collection of Pieces for Public Reading. By EDWARD F. TURNER, Author of 'T Leaves' &c. Second Edition. Cr. 8vo. 4s. 6d.

By the same Author.

T LEAVES; a Collection of Pieces for Public Reading. Seventh Edition. Crown 8vo. 3s. 6d.

TANTLER'S SISTER; AND OTHER UNTRUTHFUL STORIES: being a Collection of Pieces written for Public Reading. Third Edition. Crown 8vo. 3s. 6d.

London: SMITH, ELDER, & CO., 15 Waterloo Place.

www.ingramcontent.com/pod-product-compliance
Lightning Source LLC
Chambersburg PA
CBHW022134300426
44115CB00006B/178